Lecture Notes in Business Information Processing 95

Remco Dijkman
Jörg Hofstetter
Jana Koehler (Eds.)

Business Process Model and Notation

Third International Workshop, BPMN 2011
Lucerne, Switzerland, November 21-22, 2011
Proceedings

Springer

Volume Editors

Remco Dijkman
Eindhoven University of Technology
School of Industrial Engineering
P.O. Box 513
5600 MB Eindhoven
The Netherlands
E-mail: r.m.dijkman@tue.nl

Jörg Hofstetter
Lucerne University of Applied Sciences and Arts
Engineering & Architecture
Technikumstrasse 21
6048 Horw
Switzerland
E-mail: joerg.hofstetter@hslu.ch

Jana Koehler
Lucerne University of Applied Sciences and Arts
Engineering & Architecture
Technikumstrasse 21
6048 Horw
Switzerland
E-mail: jana.koehler@hslu.ch

ISSN 1865-1348 e-ISSN 1865-1356
ISBN 978-3-642-25159-7 e-ISBN 978-3-642-25160-3
DOI 10.1007/978-3-642-25160-3
Springer Heidelberg Dordrecht London New York

Library of Congress Control Number: 2011939858

ACM Computing Classification (1998): J.1, H.3.5, H.4, D.2

Typesetting: Camera-ready by author, data conversion by Scientific Publishing Services, Chennai, India

Printed on acid-free paper

Springer is part of Springer Science+Business Media (www.springer.com)

Preface

The Business Process Model and Notation (BPMN) has seen a huge uptake in both academia and industry over the past years. It is seen by many as the de facto standard for business process modeling and has become very popular with business analysts, tool vendors and end users. As of version 2.0, the BPMN contains a comprehensive set of concepts and notational elements, as well as an execution semantics, an interchange format and a mapping to the Business Process Execution Language (BPEL). This enables it to be used for many different purposes, such as business process modeling and the development of tools for workflow enactment or simulation.

The BPMN 2011 workshop was the third workshop in the BPMN workshop series and was held in Lucerne, Switzerland, at the University of Applied Sciences and Arts. The workshop lasted two days and consisted of both a scientific and a practitioner event. These proceedings contain the papers that were presented at the workshop. They contain eight full research papers that were selected from 20 submissions. In addition, the proceedings contain ten short papers; five of these were submitted as short papers and five were submitted as full papers and accepted as short papers after reviewing. The workshop had a thorough reviewing process, during which each paper was reviewed by three Program Committee members.

We would like to use this opportunity to thank everyone involved in making the workshop a success. We would like to thank the authors who submitted their valuable work to the workshop. Clearly, the workshop would not have been possible without them. We would also like to thank the developers of EasyChair, whose system was a great help in the preparation of the proceedings. Finally, we would like to thank the people who were involved in the organization of the workshop: the Program Committee members, the additional reviewers and the local Organizing Committee members. We appreciate all your continued involvement and support.

September 2011

Remco Dijkman
Jörg Hofstetter
Jana Koehler

Organization

Program Committee

Thomas Allweyer	FH Kaiserslautern, Germany
Gero Decker	Signavio, Germany
Remco Dijkman	Eindhoven University of Technology, The Netherlands
Marlon Dumas	University of Tartu, Estonia
Philip Effinger	University of Tübingen, Germany
Florian Evéquoz	HES-SO Valais, Switzerland
Dirk Fahland	Eindhoven University of Technology, The Netherlands
Jakob Freund	Camunda Services GmbH, Germany
Andreas Gadatsch	Hochschule Bonn-Rhein-Sieg, Germany
Denis Gagné	Trisotech Inc., Canada
Felix Garcia	University of Castilla-La Mancha, Spain
Luciano García-Bañuelos	University of Tartu, Estonia
Thomas Hettel	Queensland University of Technology, Australia
Knut Hinkelmann	Fachhochschule Nordwestschweiz, Switzerland
Jörg Hofstetter	Hochschule Luzern, Switzerland
Hans-Peter Hutter	Zürcher Hochschule für Angewandte Wissenschaften, Switzerland
Marta Indulska	The University of Queensland, Australia
Oliver Kopp	University of Stuttgart, Germany
Agnes Koschmider	Karlsruher Institute of Technology, Germany
Frank Michael Kraft	AdaPro GmbH, Germany
Jana Köhler	Hochschule Luzern, Switzerland
Ralf Laue	University of Leipzig, Germany
Niels Lohmann	Universität Rostock, Germany
Alexander Luebbe	Hasso Plattner Institute, Germany
Jan Mendling	Humboldt-Universität zu Berlin, Germany
Bela Mutschler	University of Applied Sciences Ravensburg-Weingarten, Germany
Markus Nüttgens	Universität Hamburg, Germany
Andreas Oberweis	Universität Karlsruhe, Germany
Chun Ouyang	Queensland University of Technology, Australia
Susanne Patig	University of Bern, Switzerland
Karsten Ploesser	SAP Research, Australia
Frank Puhlmann	Inubit AG, Germany
Jan Recker	Queensland University of Technology, Australia
Manfred Reichert	University of Ulm, Germany

Hajo A. Reijers	Eindhoven University of Technology, The Netherlands
Stefanie Rinderle-Ma	University of Vienna, Austria
Stefan Stöckler	FH St. Gallen, Switzerland
Lucinéia Heloisa Thom	Federal University of Rio Grande do Sul, Brazil
Barbara Thönssen	Fachhochschule Nordwestschweiz, Switzerland
Hagen Voelzer	IBM Research, Switzerland
Konrad Walser	Berner Fachhochschule, Switzerland
Barbara Weber	University of Innsbruck, Austria
Matthias Weidlich	Hasso Plattner Institute, Germany
Mathias Weske	University of Potsdam, Germany
Stephen White	IBM, USA
Karsten Wolf	Universität Rostock, Germany
Peter Wong	Fredhopper B.V., The Netherlands

Additional Reviewers

Kabicher, Sonja
Kriglstein, Simone
Leopold, Henrik
Müller-Wickop, Niels
Schultz, Martin
Unger, Tobias
Van Lessen, Tammo

Organizing Committee

Florian Evéquoz
Knut Hinkelmann
Hans-Peter Hutter
Sandro Pedrazzini
Stefan Stöckler
Barbara Thönssen
Konrad Walser

Table of Contents

Full Papers

Short Papers

Towards a BPMN 2.0 Ontology

Christine Natschläger

Software Competence Center Hagenberg GmbH, Austria
christine.natschlaeger@scch.at
www.scch.at

Abstract. The Business Process Model and Notation (BPMN) is a widely used standard for business process modelling and maintained by the Object Management Group (OMG). However, the BPMN 2.0 specification is quite comprehensive and spans more than 500 pages. The definition of an element is distributed across different sections and sometimes conflicting. In addition, the structure of the elements and their relationships are described within the metamodel, however, further syntactical rules are defined within the natural text. Therefore, this paper defines an ontology that formally represents the BPMN specification. This ontology is called the BPMN 2.0 Ontology and can be used as a knowledge base. The description of an element is combined within the corresponding class and further explanations are provided in annotations. This allows a much faster understanding of BPMN. In addition, the ontology is used as a syntax checker to validate concrete BPMN models.

Keywords: BPMN, Ontology, Knowledge Base, Syntax Checker.

1 Introduction

The Business Process Model and Notation (BPMN) is a standard maintained by the Object Management Group (OMG) and is aimed at business analysts and technical developers. BPMN provides a graphical notation that is widely used for process modelling; however, the specification is comprehensive and partially conflicting. Therefore, this paper presents an ontology that provides a formal definition of BPMN and can be used as a knowledge base. The ontology is based on the final release of BPMN 2.0 (see [1]), which was published in January 2011.

An ontology is a formal representation of knowledge and consists of statements that define concepts, relationships, and constraints. It is analogous to an object-oriented class diagram and forms an information domain model [2]. According to [3], an ontology allows a shared common understanding, the reuse of domain knowledge and the analysis of domain knowledge. An ontology is, therefore, suited to represent the BPMN metamodel.

The remainder of this paper is structured as follows: Section 2 describes the problems with the BPMN specification and the goals of the *BPMN 2.0 Ontology.* Related work with focus on formal specifications of BPMN and other BPMN ontologies is studied in section 3. In section 4, the *BPMN 2.0 Ontology* is presented in detail and section 5 evaluates the ontology using reasoners and syntax checking. Finally, the conclusion sums up the main results in section 6.

R. Dijkman, J. Hofstetter, and J. Koehler (Eds.): BPMN 2011, LNBIP 95, pp. 1–15, 2011.

Notational Remark: Throughout this paper, all BPMN elements and relationships are named according to the BPMN metamodel and the *BPMN 2.0 Ontology* (e.g., *SubProcess* instead of *Sub-Process*) and have an italic font.

How to obtain the ontology: The BPMN 2.0 Ontology is available under the creative commons licence (CC BY-NC-SA 3.0) (`http://creativecommons.org/licenses/by-nc-sa/3.0`). To receive the ontology please contact the author.

2 Problems and Goals

The BPMN 2.0 specification is comprehensive and spans more than 500 pages. The definitions of elements are distributed across various sections (e.g., *StartEvents* are described several times within the overview, in chapters *Process*, *Choreography* and *BPMN Execution Semantics* as well as in sections describing other elements that can include *StartEvents*). Furthermore, the BPMN metamodel describes the structure of the elements and their relationships, however, further syntactical rules are defined within the natural text of the BPMN specification, for example:

> "A Start Event MUST NOT be a target for Sequence Flows; it MUST NOT have incoming Sequence Flows." [1, p. 245]

In addition, the BPMN specification is sometimes contradictory and confusing. For example, in the metamodel the *Transaction* element specifies two attributes *protocol* and *method* both of type string [1, p. 176], but in the corresponding description only *method* is mentioned and defined to be of type *TransactionMethod* [1, p. 180].

All these issues not only make the understanding of BPMN difficult and time-consuming, but also hamper the development of syntax checkers. The main goals of the *BPMN 2.0 Ontology* are, therefore, as follows:

- Knowledge Base: The primary goal of the ontology is to provide a knowledge base that can be used to familiarize oneself with BPMN. The syntactical rules are combined within the corresponding element and every restriction provides the full text of the BPMN specification in an annotation.
- Syntax Checker: The ontology can be used as a syntax checker to validate concrete BPMN models as described in section 5.2.
- Contradiction Identification: When defining the ontology, several contradictions, for example between the BPMN class diagram and the XML schema, were identified. Up to now, more than 30 issues were reported to the OMG.

3 Related Work

The following two subsections present formal specifications of BPMN as well as other BPMN ontologies.

3.1 Formal Specifications of BPMN

First of all, the BPMN 2.0 specification [1] provides a metamodel for BPMN elements as a UML class diagram and in the form of an XML schema. BPMN 2.0 is the first release to provide such a formal definition.

According to [4], the static analysis of BPMN models is complicated by the complexity of the language. The lack of formal semantics of BPMN hinders the development of tool support for checking the correctness of BPMN models from a semantic perspective. Therefore, this publication provides a formal semantics of BPMN defined in terms of a mapping to Petri Nets.

According to [5], the specification of BPMN does not include formal semantics. Hence, this paper describes the abstract syntax for a subset of BPMN using Z schemas and the behavioural semantics in CSP. Such semantics allow developers to formally analyse and compare BPMN diagrams.

In addition, an approach that defines the syntax of a visual language by a graph grammar has been applied to business process models by [7].

A further approach defines the dynamic semantics of the core process modelling concepts of BPMN in terms of Abstract State Machines (ASMs) [6]. This model can be used to test reference implementations.

3.2 BPMN Ontologies

Two other BPMN ontologies have been published and are described below.

The first BPMN ontology is called the sBPMN ontology and specifies a semantically enhanced BPMN [8]. The ontology is developed within the SUPER project[1] and based on the final release of BPMN 1.0. The classes correspond to the elements of BPMN and are divided in categories like Flow Objects, Connecting Objects, Swimlanes, Artifacts and Processes. The whole ontology consists of 95 classes and about 50 axioms.

The second BPMN ontology is based on BPMN 1.1 and presented in [9]. Again, the specification is based on the BPMN elements resulting in 95 classes, 108 object properties, 70 data properties and 439 class axioms. The elements are divided into two categories representing Supporting Elements and Graphical Elements, the latter category is further refined in Flow Object, Connecting Object, Swimlane and Artifact. In subsequent publications, for example [10], this ontology is called BPMNO. According to [9], the ontology does not contain a description of all properties documented in the BPMN specification, since some describe the execution behaviour of the process and others cannot be defined based on the well-known limitations in the expressiveness of OWL (e.g., default values). BPMNO is also not intended to model the dynamic behaviour of diagrams (how the flow proceeds within a process) [10]. These limitations also apply to the *BPMN 2.0 Ontology* provided in this paper. BPMNO has been adapted to BPMN 1.2 by Michael zur Muehlen et al. as described in [11].

Both ontologies, sBPMN and BPMNO, are based on former releases of BPMN and classes are mainly defined for concrete BPMN elements. The *BPMN 2.0*

[1] SUPER project: www.ip-super.org

Ontology, however, is based on the BPMN metamodel leading to a different and more extensive structure which better reflects the BPMN specification.

4 BPMN 2.0 Ontology

This section presents the *BPMN 2.0 Ontology*, which is based on the BPMN 2.0 specification (final release in January 2011) and developed using the Web Ontology Language (OWL) and the open source ontology editor Protégé (see [13]). The *BPMN 2.0 Ontology* is divided in two sub-ontologies; the first is called *bpmn20base* and presented in section 4.1. This ontology only contains the specifications taken from the BPMN metamodel including all class diagrams, the tables specifying the attributes and model associations as well as the XML schemas. The second sub-ontology is called *bpmn20* and presented in section 4.2. This ontology is derived from the first ontology and provides an extension. The *bpmn20* ontology contains almost all further syntactical requirements taken from the natural text of the BPMN specification. It may refine inherited restrictions but does not change them. Furthermore, it contains some new classes (e.g., subclasses of *SubProcess*), which are justified in section 4.2. Together, the two ontologies build the *BPMN 2.0 Ontology*, which is presented in section 4.3. Finally, some remarks are provided in section 4.4.

4.1 BPMN 2.0 Base Ontology (bpmn20base)

The *bpmn20base* ontology is based on the specification of the BPMN metamodel including all class diagrams, the tables specifying the attributes and model associations as well as the XML schemas. Every BPMN element is inserted as a class; the full hierarchy is shown in Fig. 5. Some elements are shown twice, since multiple-inheritance is used in the BPMN metamodel and, therefore, also in the ontology (e.g., *SubProcess* is derived from *Activity* and *FlowElementsContainer* (cf. [1, p. 176])). The definition of the hierarchy has been complicated, since some inheritances are not explicitly described in the BPMN class diagram. The superclasses are sometimes only mentioned in the natural text of the specification, within the XML schema or in the case of *InteractionNode* the superclass is not described at all (assumed to be derived from *BaseElement*). Nevertheless, a hierarchy that corresponds to the BPMN metamodel could have been defined.

Different subclasses are specified to be disjoint to avoid that individuals can be an instance of several classes (e.g., *ExclusiveGateway* is disjoint from *EventBasedGateway*, *ComplexGateway*, *InclusiveGateway* and *ParallelGateway*). Furthermore, the BPMN metamodel specifies the package of a class. However, this

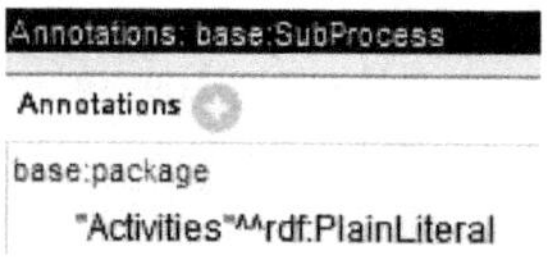

Fig. 1. Annotations of Class *SubProcess*

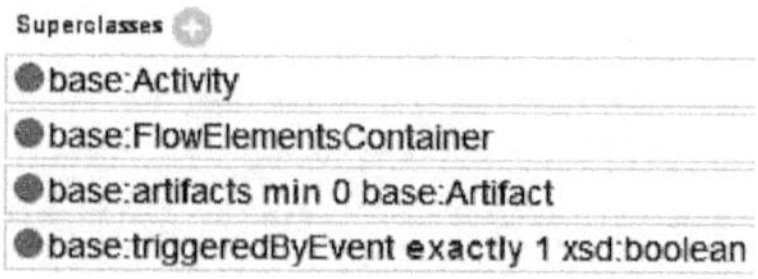

Fig. 2. Properties of Class *SubProcess*

information is not inherited and subclasses may be contained in a different package. Therefore, this information cannot be stored within a restriction; instead an annotation is used as shown in Fig. 1.

After describing classes in general, relationships are defined to restrict the classes and specify the details. An ontology supports two types of relationships:

1. Object Property (see Fig. 6): Describes the relationship between two individuals.
2. Data Property (see Fig. 7): Describes the relationship between individuals and data values.

The properties of the class *SubProcess* are shown in Fig. 2. The object property *artifacts* defines a relationship between individuals of the class *SubProcess* and individuals of the class *Artifact*. In addition, the data property *triggeredByEvent* defines a relationship between individuals of the class *SubProcess* with boolean data values (cf. [1, p. 176]).

Every restriction further defines the cardinality of allowed relationships. In the *bpmn20base* ontology the following cardinalities are used:

– Exactly x: Exactly the value x
– Min x: Cardinality $[x..n]$
– Max x: Cardinality $[0..x]$

In several cases the cardinality is strengthened in subclasses (e.g., the minimum boundary is increased or the maximum boundary is decreased). A cardinality of type [x..y] is not used within the *bpmn20base* ontology, but would require two restrictions.

The BPMN specification further defines instance attributes for some BPMN elements (e.g., *Process* has an instance attribute *state* (cf. [1, p. 149])). In an ontology it is difficult to distinguish attributes and instance attributes since the same object and data properties are used to define the relationship. Therefore, an annotation property named *instanceAttribute* has been created and is set to *yes* for every instance attribute as shown in Fig. 3.

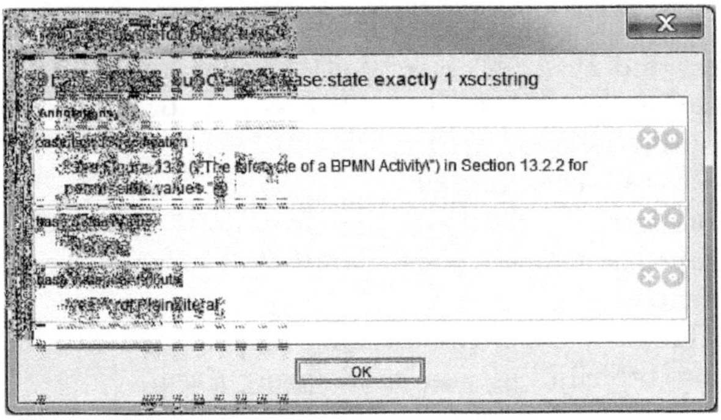

Fig. 3. Annotations of Instance Attribute *state*

The BPMN specification also provides for default values (e.g., the instance attribute *state* has the default value *None*). These default values are not definable within a monotonic OWL. Therefore, in the *bpmn20base* ontology default values are specified by an annotation property *defaultValue* as shown in Fig. 3. An alternative approach for non-monotonic reasoning based on Reiter's default logic is provided in [12] and supports default property values as well as an unspecified version of the closed world assumption.

The fourth and last annotation property is called *bpmnSpecification* and includes for every attribute and relationship the corresponding definition from the BPMN specification (see Fig. 3). In the *bpmn20base* ontology the text is taken from the description/usage column of the corresponding attributes and model associations table. In the *bpmn20* ontology further syntactical requirements are specified and the text for the annotation is taken from the natural text of the BPMN specification. In both cases, this annotation property is very important since it supports the usage of the *BPMN 2.0 Ontology* as a knowledge base. While the descriptions of a BPMN element are spread across the BPMN specification, the descriptions in the ontology are combined within one class and further explanations are provided in the annotation. This allows for a much faster understanding of the BPMM element.

4.2 Extended BPMN 2.0 Ontology (bpmn20)

The *bpmn20* ontology is derived from the *bpmn20base* ontology and provides an extension to it. It contains further syntactical requirements taken from the natural text of the BPMN specification. Therefore, the *bpmn20* ontology adds new or refines existing classes and restrictions but does not alter or remove them. The overall goal is that the *BPMN 2.0 Ontology* serves as a knowledge base for almost all syntactical rules of the BPMN specification.

Additional Classes: The following additional classes have been inserted in the *bpmn20* ontology based on the natural text of the BPMN specification:

- Collapsed/Expanded classes (detailed description follows),
- Subclasses of *SequenceFlow*: *SequenceFlowConditional*, *SequenceFlowDefault* and *SequenceFlowNormal*,
- *PublicProcess* and *PrivateProcess* (with further subclasses),
- *EmbeddedSubProcess* and *EventSubProcess* as subclasses of *SubProcess* (detailed description follows),
- *AbstractTask* as subclass of *Task*,
- Subclasses of *Gateway* specifying the direction,
- *ExclusiveEventBasedGateway* and *ParallelEventBasedGateway* as subclasses of *EventBasedGateway*,
- Several subclasses of *Event* representing the markers with further subclasses for expressing interrupting/non-interrupting *Events*,

- Subclasses of *StartEvent*: *StartEventEventSubProcess* (StartEvent of an EventSubProcess) and *StartEventNotEventSubProcess* (StartEvent not of an EventSubProcess),
- *EventMarkerEnumeration*, *TransactionResultEnumeration* and *MarkerEnumeration* as further enumerations.

Collapsed/Expanded Classes: Three BPMN elements can be collapsed or expanded, namely *SubProcess*, *SubChoreography* and *SubConversation*. The collapsed view shows a *CollapsedMarker*, whereas the expanded view shows the details but no *CollapsedMarker*. The two subclasses are defined to be disjoint from each other, but are not disjoint from any further subclasses (e.g., a concrete *SubProcess* can be simultaneously collapsed and a *Transaction*).

For example, the class *CollapsedSubProcess* has two necessary conditions:

```
base:SubProcess
hasMarker exactly 1 CollapsedMarker
```

The first restriction defines that the class *CollapsedSubProcess* is a subclass of *SubProcess*. The second restriction specifies that it must have exactly one *CollapsedMarker*. This restriction differs from that of an expanded class, since expanded classes have no *CollapsedMarker*. The two restrictions together are defined to be sufficient. Since both classes specify necessary and sufficient conditions, they are called *Defined Classes*.

Further classes (*CallActivity*, *CallChoreography* and *CallConversation*) are sometimes also shown with a *CollapsedMarker*. However, these classes call other elements and only display the markers of the called element. If they call, for example, a *GlobalTask*, then collapsing or expanding is not possible at all.

SubProcess: Considering the subclasses of *SubProcess*, the BPMN metamodel only refers to two subclasses (*AdHocSubProcess* and *Transaction*) (cf. [1, p. 176]), whereas the natural text mentions five different types (*EmbeddedSubProcess*, *CallActivity*, *EventSubProcess*, *Transaction* and *AdHocSubProcess*) (cf. [1, 173-183]). The *CallActivity* corresponds to the *Reusable SubProcess* in BPMN 1.2 and is now derived from *Activity* and, therefore, a sibling of *SubProcess*. However, the question remains, why *EmbeddedSubProcess* and *EventSubProcess* have not been defined as subclasses in the BPMN metamodel and whether they should be or not.

First of all, class *SubProcess* defines the following restriction (cf. [1, p. 176]):

```
base:triggeredByEvent exactly 1 xsd:boolean
```

The data property *triggeredByEvent* serves as a flag. If set to true, the *SubProcess* is an *EventSubProcess* else it is a "normal" *SubProcess* (*EmbeddedSubProcess*).

The data property *triggeredByEvent* of *SubProcess* is inherited by the subclasses *Transactions* and *AdHocSubProcesses*; however, no restriction specifies that it must be false within a subclass. Therefore, the following combinations are possible:

1. *AdHocSubProcess* and *EmbeddedSubProcess* (*triggeredByEvent*: false)
2. *Transaction* and *EmbeddedSubProcess* (*triggeredByEvent*: false)

3. *AdHocSubProcess* and *EventSubProcess* (*triggeredByEvent*: true)
4. *Transaction* and *EventSubProcess* (*triggeredByEvent*: true)

Since the *EmbeddedSubProcess* represents the "normal" *SubProcess*, the first two cases can be reduced to *AdHocSubProcess* and *Transaction*. However, the last two cases are problematic. A combination of *AdHocSubProcess* and *EventSubProcess* conflicts with the BPMN specification, since an *AdHocSubProcess* may be part of the normal flow (cf. [1, p. 153]) whereas an *EventSubProcess* is not allowed to have incoming and outgoing *SequenceFlows* (cf. [1, p. 176f]). Moreover, an *AdHocSubProcess* is not allowed to have a *StartEvent* (cf. [1, p. 182]), whereas every *EventSubProcess* must have exactly one *StartEvent* (cf. [1, p. 177]). Therefore, the combination *AdHocSubProcess* and *EventSubProcess* should be forbidden. In addition, the combination of *Transaction* and *EventSubProcess* is contradictory as well. Again the integration in the normal flow and the number of *StartEvents* are conflicting. Furthermore, only a *Transaction* is allowed to have a *BoundaryEvent* with a *Cancel* marker (cf. [1, p. 255]).

Therefore, the author suggests that *triggeredByEvent* must be false for *Transactions* and *AdHocSubProcesses*. In addition, the question remains whether *EmbeddedSubProcess* and *EventSubProcess* should be subclasses of *SubProcess*. Several reasons militate in favour of this suggestion:

- Explicit/Implicit Classes: In the BPMN metamodel only two classes are explicit whereas the others are implicit. However, the natural text of the BPMN specification explicitly describes all *SubProcess* types on the same level and as distinct elements. Therefore, all classes should be explicit.
- Disjoint: The four classes can be defined to be disjoint. This explicitly forbids combinations of different types.
- Inherited Restrictions: Since restrictions are inherited, only *Transaction* and *AdHocSubProcess* (but not *EmbeddedSubProcess* or *EventSubProcess*) can refine a restriction. According to the BPMN specification, only a *Transaction* is allowed to have a *BoundaryEvent* with a *Cancel* marker (cf. [1, p. 255]). The structure of the metamodel allows to specify that an *AdHocSubProcess* must not have a *BoundaryEvent* with a *Cancel* marker, whereas a *Transaction* is allowed to have such a *BoundaryEvent*. However, it is not possible to specify that an *EmbeddedSubProcess* or an *EventSubProcess* must not have such a *BoundaryEvent*, since both classes are described within the class *SubProcess*. If *Cancel* markers are forbidden in the superclass, then *Transaction* inherits this restriction and cannot have a *Cancel* marker itself.
- Further Restrictions: If explicit subclasses are used, further restrictions that only apply to *EventSubProcess* or *EmbeddedSubProcess* can be easily specified. For example, an *EmbeddedSubProcess* is only allowed to have *StartEvents* with marker *None* (cf. [1, p. 241f]), whereas an *EventSubProcess* must not have a *None* marker (cf. [1, p. 177]). If the two elements are expressed within one class and only distinguished by a data property, then the restrictions require implications and are more complex.

Based on these arguments, the author defines *EventSubProcess* and *EmbeddedSubProcess* as subclasses of *SubProcess* and suggests an adaptation of the BPMN metamodel.

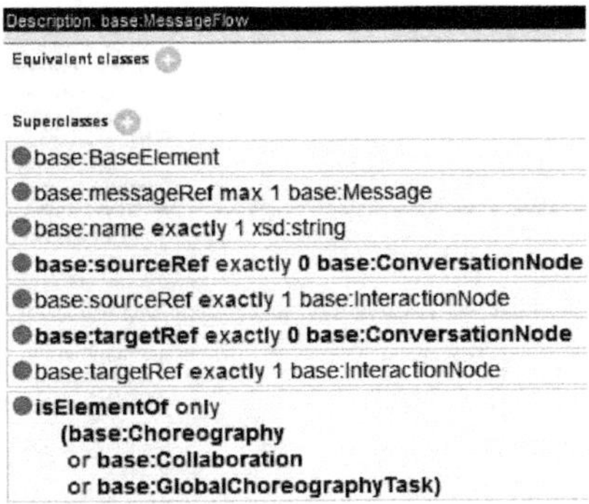

Fig. 4. *MessageFlow* Restrictions

Additional Restrictions: Besides the additional classes, more than 300 further restrictions have been specified for existing classes in the *bpmn20* ontology according to the natural text of the BPMN specification. The restrictions of the class *MessageFlow* are shown in Fig. 4. Note that the restrictions defined in the *bpmn20* ontology have a bold font.

4.3 BPMN 2.0 Ontology (*bpmn20base* and *bpmn20*)

Together, the *bpmn20base* and *bpmn20* ontologies form the *BPMN 2.0 Ontology*. The hierarchy of the *BPMN 2.0 Ontology* with about 260 classes is divided into two columns and shown in Fig. 5. Some classes are not expanded due to space limitations. Note that the classes and properties defined in the *bpmn20base* ontology are shown with the "base:" prefix, whereas those defined in the *bpmn20* ontology have no prefix. Classes that have been created or extended in the *bpmn20* ontology have a bold font.

Furthermore, Fig. 6 shows an extract of the 178 object properties and Fig. 7 an extract of the 59 data properties. In addition to the predefined annotation properties, four further properties (*bpmnSpecification*, *defaultValue*, *instanceAttribute* and *package*) are defined in the *bpmn20base* ontology and shown in Fig. 8.

4.4 Further Remarks

After introducing the ontologies, some remarks are presented in this section.

Distinct Names and Keywords: In the BPMN metamodel relationships with the same name are used several times between different classes. However, the names of object and data properties in an ontology must be distinct. Therefore, object and data properties with the same name are reused in different restrictions and the domain and range of the property is extended to cover all classes. Also reused in different enumerations are classes representing values like *None* and *Both*. In addition, the class and property names "Import", "value" and "language" are keywords in the ontology and the Pellet reasoner (see section 5.1) defines

Fig. 5. Class Hierarchy of *BPMN 2.0 Ontology*

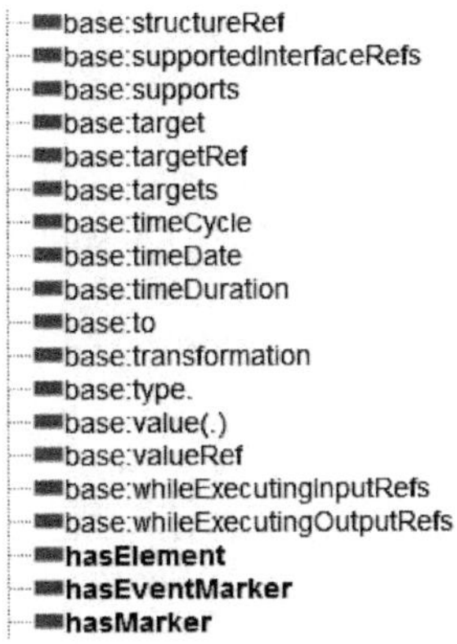

Fig. 6. Object Properties

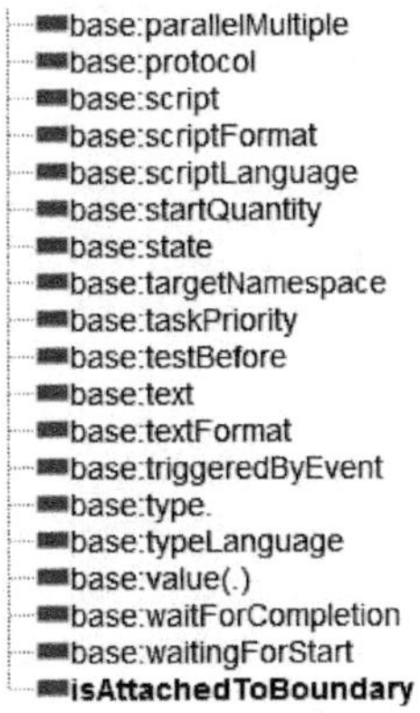

Fig. 7. Data Properties

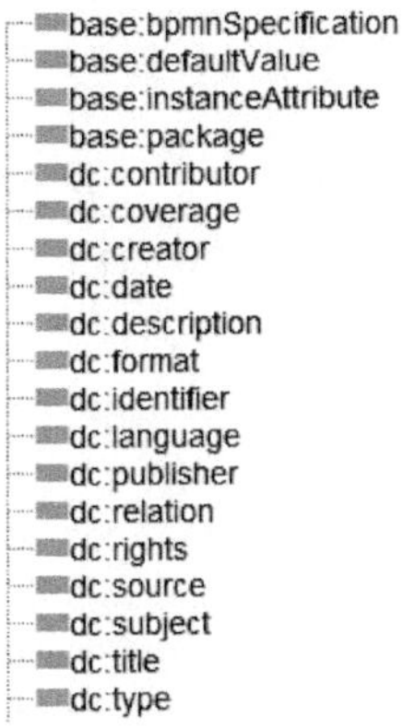

Fig. 8. Annotation Properties

some further keywords. To distinguish these names from the keywords, a dot is appended (e.g., "Import.").

Association and Composition: The BPMN metamodel distinguishes between different types of relationships: associations and compositions. This distinction is not expressed in the ontology, although in most cases the different types also affect the cardinality (e.g., compositions tend to have a cardinality of 1 or 0..1 on the source side while associations often have a cardinality of * on both sides). An approach to express part-of relations in ontologies is provided in [14].

Implication: Some syntactical requirements include an implication (e.g., if a *SequenceFlow* originates from a *StartEvent*, then the *conditionExpression* must be set to *None* [1, p. 245]). OWL only provides constructs for intersection (and), union (or) and complement (not), however, an implication (A $\rightarrow$ B) can be expressed with union and complement: $\neg$A $\vee$ B. This alternative representation is used several times within the ontology.

Open Syntactical Restrictions: Almost all syntactical rules are specified in the ontology. The only exceptions are syntactical rules with open questions or rules that depend on other elements in a complex way. For example, for the requirement "The Initiator of a Choreography Activity MUST have been involved ... in the previous Choreography Activity." [1, p. 336] it is not sufficient to determine the source of the incoming *SequenceFlow*, since *Gateways* and *Events* can be defined in between. Instead a new object property *previousChoreographyActivity* can be defined; however, the value of the property cannot be determined automatically. Nevertheless, most rules that depend on other elements can be specified as, e.g., the rule "Target elements in an Event Gateway configuration MUST NOT have any additional incoming Sequence Flows ..." [1, p. 298]. This rule can be expressed with the following restriction for an *EventBasedGateway*:

```
base:outgoing only (base:targetRef only
(base:incoming exactly 1 base:SequenceFlow)))
```

Contradictions in the BPMN Specification: During the definition of the *BPMN 2.0 Ontology* several contradictions in the BPMN specification were identified. Up to now, more than 30 issues were reported to the OMG. Some examples are given below:

- According to the class diagram, *InteractionNode* has four subclasses: *Participant*, *ConversationNode*, *Task* and *Event* (cf. [1, p. 122]). However, the natural text mentions the subclass *Activity* instead of *Task* (cf. [1, p. 123]) and the connection rules of *MessageFlow* allow to connect to a *SubProcess* (cf. [1, p. 44]) (a subclass of *Activity*).
- According to the class diagram, *StandardLoopCharacteristics* defines a relationship to *Expression* called *loopMaximum* (cf. [1, p. 189]). However, in the corresponding attribute description, *loopMaximum* is defined to be an attribut of type integer (cf. [1, p. 191]).
- According to the class diagram, *Collaboration* references exactly 1 *ConversationAssociation*, but in the corresponding description of the model associations, the relationship is defined to have a cardinality of [0..n] (cf. [1, p. 109f]).

5 Evaluation

The consistency and correctness of the ontologies is evaluated based on two different methods. First, several different reasoners have been used to validate the *bpmn20base* and the *bpmn20* ontologies and are described in section 5.1. In addition, concrete BPMN models are checked against the ontology and presented in section 5.2. Considering the open questions and contradictions, proving the completeness of the ontologies is currently not possible. However, the author has revised the whole BPMN specification several times to ensure an almost complete *BPMN 2.0 Ontology*.

5.1 Reasoner

A reasoner is also known as a classifier and used for consistency checking as well as to compute the inferred class hierarchy. A class in an ontology is classified as consistent if it can have instances, otherwise it is inconsistent. The following three reasoners have been used to classify the *BPMN 2.0 Ontology*:

- *FaCT++* is an OWL-DL reasoner that is available under the GNU Public License (GPL) and implemented using C++ [15].
- *Pellet* is an open source OWL 2 reasoner that is based on Java [16]. Pellet also supports some forms of closed world reasoning, which is required for one of the examples described in section 5.2.

- *HermiT 1.2.4* is an OWL 2 reasoner that is compatible with Java. HermiT is released under the GNU Lesser General Public License (LGPL) and pre-installed in Protégé [17].

The ontology is classified to be correct by all three reasoners.

5.2 Syntax Checking

In addition to validation through reasoners, the *BPMN 2.0 Ontology* is used as a syntax checker and concrete BPMN models are checked against the ontology. Therefore, new ontologies are created for every example and derived from the *bpmn20* ontology. The three examples show a correct, incorrect and incomplete model. More complex examples are checked similarly, but the definition of the model requires more effort. Thus, the syntax checker will be extended with a graphical tool as described in section 6. A major advantage of the ontology is the possibility to draw conclusions as shown in the first example. If it can be concluded that an element of type *A* must in fact be an element of subtype *B*, then this conclusion allows to check whether the element fulfills the restrictions defined by the subtype.

Example 1: The first example consists of one *StartEvent*, one *EndEvent*, two *SequenceFlows* and one *Task* as shown in Fig. 9. Instances of the same class (e.g., the *SequenceFlows*) are defined to represent different individuals. For all elements the data property *id* is defined, the *Activities* further specify a *name* and the *isInterrupting* property of the *Events* is set to true. Considering object properties, all *SequenceFlows* specify the *sourceRef* and *targetRef*, and the *Activities* define the *incoming* and *outgoing SequenceFlows*. The model is then classified to be correct. Note that based on the open world assumption it is not necessary to specify all mandatory properties (e.g., the class *Activity* defines some further mandatory properties like *isForCompensation* or *startQuantity* that have not been defined for this example).

Afterwards the example is adapted and the data property *isInterrupting* of *StartEvent* is set to false. Since only *EventSubProcesses* are allowed to have non-interrupting *StartEvents* (cf. [1, p. 242ff]), the reasoner automatically concludes that the *StartEvent* must be of type *StartEventEventSubProcess* as shown in Fig. 12. However, if we specify that the *StartEvent* is of type *StartEvent-NotEventSubProcess*, then an inconsistency is reported by all reasoners.

Example 2: The second example comprises an *EventSubProcess* as shown in Fig. 10. The *EventSubProcess* specifies the data properties *id*, *name* and *triggeredByEvent* with the last property set to true. In addition, the *incoming* and

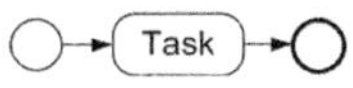

Fig. 9. Example 1

Fig. 10. Example 2

Fig. 11. Example 3

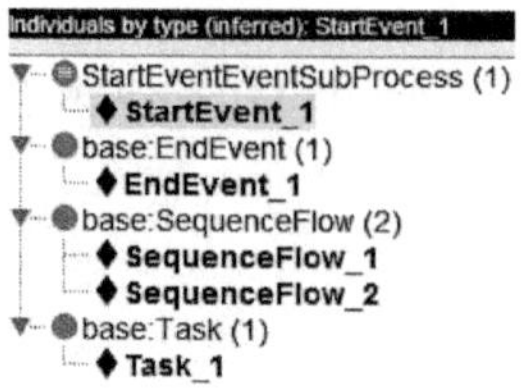

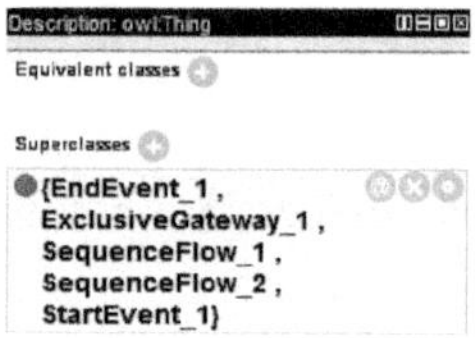

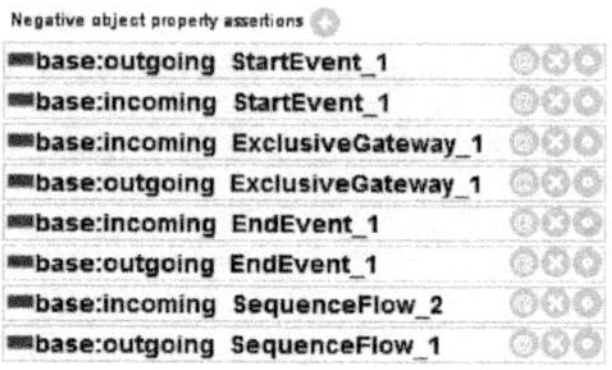

Fig. 12. Inferred Individuals **Fig. 13.** Class *owl:Thing* **Fig. 14.** Negative Assertions

outgoing SequenceFlows are specified. The BPMN model is incorrect, since an *EventSubProcess* is not allowed to have *incoming* or *outgoing SequenceFlows* (cf. [1, p. 176f]). The ontology is classified to be inconsistent by all reasoners.

Example 3: In the third example, a *Gateway* is inserted between the two *SequenceFlows* as shown in Fig. 11. This model is incomplete, since the *Gateway* has only one *incoming* and one *outgoing SequenceFlow*, but is required to have at least two *incoming* or at least two *outgoing SequenceFlows* (cf. [1, p. 290]):

```
(base:incoming min 2 base:SequenceFlow)
or (base:outgoing min 2 base:SequenceFlow)
```

In a first step, the inconsistency cannot be detected based on the open world assumption, since the *Gateway* might have further unspecified *incoming* or *outgoing SequenceFlows*. This problem is solvable by closed world reasoning as described for the Pellet reasoner in [16]. The class *owl:Thing* must be equivalent to the enumeration of all known individuals as shown in Fig. 13 and it is necessary to define negative assertions for things that are definitely not true as shown in Fig. 14. Afterwards, the ontology is classified to be inconsistent by all reasoners.

6 Conclusion

This paper described the development of two ontologies that formally represent the BPMN 2.0 specification. The *bpmn20base* ontology is based on the BPMN metamodel and the *bpmn20* ontology contains further syntactical requirements taken from the natural text of the BPMN specification. Together, the two ontologies form the *BPMN 2.0 Ontology*. This ontology can be used as a knowledge base, since the descriptions are combined within the corresponding class and further explanations are provided in annotations. This allows a much faster understanding of BPMN. In addition, the ontology can be used as a syntax checker. Finally, three different reasoners prove the consistency of the ontology.

Further Issues: The next goal is to automatically generate the basic structure of the *bpmn20base* ontology from the XML schema of the BPMN specification once the XML schema corresponds with the UML class diagram. In addition, syntax checking currently requires the manual definition of concrete models, so only simple models have been defined up to now. Thus, another goal is to extend the syntax checker with a graphical tool (e.g., BPMN Modeler for Eclipse [18]), and to automatically check the model against the ontology. For this purpose, the Jena Semantic Web framework can be used as suggested in [2].

Acknowledgement. The project *Vertical Model Integration* is supported within the program "Regionale Wettbewerbsfähigkeit OÖ 2007-2013" by the European Fund for Regional Development as well as the State of Upper Austria.

References

1. Business Process Model and Notation (BPMN) 2.0, www.omg.org/spec/BPMN/2.0
2. Hebeler, J., Fisher, M., Blace, R., Perez-Lopez, A.: Semantic Web Programming. Wiley Publishing (2009)
3. Noy, N., McGuinness, D.: Ontology Development 101: A Guide to Creating Your First Ontology. Stanford Knowledge Systems Laboratory Technical Report KSL-01-05 and Stanford Medical Informatics Technical Report SMI-2001-0880 (2001)
4. Dijkman, R., Dumas, M., Ouyang, C.: Formal semantics and automated analysis of BPMN process models. Technical Report (2007)
5. Wong, P.Y.H., Gibbons, J.: A Process Semantics for BPMN. In: Liu, S., Araki, K. (eds.) ICFEM 2008. LNCS, vol. 5256, pp. 355–374. Springer, Heidelberg (2008)
6. Börger, E., Sörensen, O.: BPMN Core Modeling Concepts: Inheritance-Based Execution Semantics. In: Handbook of Conceptual Modelling. Springer, Heidelberg (2010)
7. Mazanek, S., Minas, M.: Business Process Models as a Showcase for Syntax-Based Assistance in Diagram Editors. In: Schürr, A., Selic, B. (eds.) MODELS 2009. LNCS, vol. 5795, pp. 322–336. Springer, Heidelberg (2009)
8. Abramowicz, W., Filipowska, A., Kaczmarek, M., Kaczmarek, T.: Semantically enhanced Business Process Modelling Notation. In: Work. on Semantic Business Process and Product Lifecycle Management, SBPM (2007)
9. Ghidini, C., Rospocher, M., Serafini, L.: A formalisation of BPMN in Description Logics. Published as: Technical Report TR 2008-06-004, FBK-irst (2008), https://dkm.fbk.eu/images/3/35/-3631-_BPMNOntology.pdf
10. Di Francescomarino, C., Ghidini, C., Rospocher, M., Serafini, L., Tonella, P.: Reasoning on Semantically Annotated Processes. In: Bouguettaya, A., Krueger, I., Margaria, T. (eds.) ICSOC 2008. LNCS, vol. 5364, pp. 132–146. Springer, Heidelberg (2008)
11. Zur Muehlen, M., et al.: BPM Research Forums - Process Modeling, www.bpm-research.com/forum/index.php?showtopic=502 (visited February 2011)
12. Kolovski, V., Parsia, B., Katz, Y.: Implementing OWL Defaults. In: Workshop on OWL: Experiences and Directions (2006)
13. Protégé, http://protege.stanford.edu (visited February 2011)
14. Aitken, J.S., Webber, B.L., Bard, J.B.L.: Part-of Relations in Anatomy Ontologies: A Proposal for RDFS and OWL Formalisations. In: Pacific Symposium on Biocomputing (2004)
15. FaCT++, http://owl.man.ac.uk/factplusplus (visited February 2011)
16. Pellet, http://clarkparsia.com/pellet (visited February 2011)
17. HermiT 1.2.4, http://hermit-reasoner.com (visited February 2011)
18. BPMN Modeler, www.eclipse.org/bpmn (visited February 2011)

On the Expressiveness of BPMN for Modeling Wireless Sensor Networks Applications

Alexandru Caracaş and Thorsten Kramp

IBM Zurich Research Laboratory
(xan,thk)@zurich.ibm.com

Abstract. Business processes describe the transformations which add economic value to products and services. Wireless sensor networks (WSN) are a pervasive means for business processes to interact in real time with the environment. In this paper, we analyze the business process model and notation (BPMN) standard with respect to its expressiveness for capturing the reactive, communication, and heterogeneous aspects of such WSN applications. Our analysis is based on a representative set of WSN applications for which we found the BPMN language adequate in capturing high-level specifications.

Keywords: modeling style, reactive patterns, embedded business processes, wireless sensor networks.

1 Introduction

Business processes add economic value to both companies and their respective customers in a dynamic and global economy. Such processes specify the sequence of activities, events, and interactions between humans, information technology systems and the physical environment in order to fulfill a specific business goal. Over the last two decades, several languages have evolved which allow to describe business processes using graphical models. The business process model and notation (BPMN)[1] is emerging as the de-facto standard with an ever increasing number of practitioners.

In parallel to the developments in the business process space, the performance of information technology system increased following Moore's law. As such, embedded devices are continuously miniaturized to the point where they become ubiquitous. Consequently, the technology offered by wireless sensor networks (WSN) allows business processes to be embedded even deeper into the physical environment. Examples include safety processes for storing hazardous materials [2], securing shipping and handling of containers to comply with government regulations [3], parcel delivery of perishable goods [4], automating hospital processes [5], precision farming [6], as well as irrigation [7] and water management [8]. In this way, business processes can better monitor and interact in real-time with the entities they control, thus decreasing operational costs and improving responsiveness.

R. Dijkman, J. Hofstetter, and J. Koehler (Eds.): BPMN 2011, LNBIP 95, pp. 16–30, 2011.

To reduce investments costs and energy consumption [9], WSNs rely on the low end spectrum of embedded devices. In previous work [10] we have shown that executable WSN applications can be automatically generated from a refined business processes model specification. Business domain experts provide the relevant business logic which is aligned to the corresponding implementation. Reusable building blocks which efficiently implement low-level functionality are provided by application developers. Thus, organizations can use WSN technology to adapt faster to a dynamic competition and can meet quicker the demands of a diverse customer base. The business-relevant behavior of remote sensors and actuators becomes visible in models and is fully aligned with the corresponding implementation. Furthermore, graphical models foster communication among the different business participants and technology implementers using the same lingua franca.

In this paper, we focus on a modeling style using the BPMN language to capture the different aspects of WSN applications with sufficient details to allow code generation. To reach a larger audience and adhere to the standard specification, we explicitly avoid changing the syntax or execution semantics of the BPMN language.

This paper is organized as follows. In Chapter 2, we discuss several approaches which aim to align business process with WSN applications. Next, we describe the characteristics of WSN applications in Chapter 3. Subsequently, in Chapter 4, we describe a pattern-based modeling style which captures the behavioral aspects of typical WSN applications. In Chapter 5, we discuss the usage of BPMN symbols and particular aspects of models in our application domain. The analysis is based on a set of representative models for WSN applications.

2 Related Work

Integrating and aligning WSN with business processes in enterprise applications is not an entirely new idea. Existing approaches [11,12,13] focus on the SOA paradigm and advocate exposing WSN devices as a Web Service natively or through gateways. The Web Services 4 Devices Profile (WS4DP) aims to provide and efficient implementation for all aspects of the Web Services standard including communication based on XML and SOAP and support for service discovery. In general, Web Services still imposes a significant overhead for resource-constrained devices. Consequently, [14] addresses the resource constraints of WSN by compressing the verbose SOAP/XML format used by Web Services and introducing a lean transport protocol (LTP).

In [14], BPEL is used to graphically specify the execution of a process controlled on the server side which invokes the exposed Web Service provided by the WSN devices. The same approach is taken by the GWELS [15] environment which uses BPEL running on back-end servers to orchestrate the execution of workflows distributed in a WSN. Other approaches borrow the SOA concepts and introduce an object-oriented programming of WSN applications which allows dynamic service discovery and composition as well as using external

Web Services through custom gateways to augment the capabilities of a WSN. The Web Services standard and respective approaches are fully complementary to our work which does not impose a restriction on communication.

Even though the existing approaches allow WSN devices to natively expose their functionality as a standard Web Service, the implementation behind the service is not fully aligned with the business process models. Changes in business requirements imply changes to the implementation of the corresponding service provided by the device. Business process models do not execute directly in the network but on back-end servers.

All presented approaches are not concerned with energy consumption nor execution efficiency. These aspects are critical for WSN application which have to rely on a limited set of batteries for long periods of operation. In addition, the existing approaches lack the support of an open-industry standard graphical notation which hinders the interchange and reuse of business process models.

3 Characteristics of WSN Applications

Wireless sensor and actuator networks are a particular instance of distributed applications. Such applications are *reactive* by nature and require *real-time* synchronization using a shared medium for *wireless communication*. Moreover, applications potentially consist of a large number of *heterogeneous* nodes, commonly referred as *motes* [16,17,23].

3.1 Reactive Behavior

Wireless sensor applications follow a reactive paradigm and for an efficient execution they rely on event-based run-time environments such as TinyOS[16] or the IBM Mote Runner[17]. This behavior stems from the fact that wireless communication and sensor operations take a considerable amount of time. Consequently, actively polling for the result of actions is not efficient because energy is spent while the system is blocked from executing further operations. In such cases, a more efficient implementation uses operations with an *asynchronous interface* which will first trigger the action to be performed. If the system has no further actions to execute, a scheduler then decides to turn off certain parts of the system to save power, including the micro-controller (MCU) which is put into an appropriate sleep mode. When the action completes, the system is asynchronously notified about the result using an event which is placed into an *event queue*. The scheduler monitors this event queue and passes the top event to the application for processing. In this way, multiple operations, such as radio communication and sensing, execute virtually in parallel and the run-time system can efficiently manage the scarce computational and energy resources.

In general, an operation with an asynchronous interface can signal three distinct states. The common scenario is the *normal completion* of the operation, preferably with one or more return values. In addition, applications have to be prepared to deal with exception cases which deviate from the normal execution path. Such cases represent an *exception completion* of operations, preferably with the reason for the failure so that the application can react accordingly. For example, in WSNs, a hardware malfunction can occur while reading a sensor because the respective sensor board was detached. Consequently, the sampling operation fails, which means the respective activity is terminated with an exception. Lastly, a *significant state* may occur while the asynchronous operation continues execution. As an example consider an application which continuously tracks beacon messages in a TDMA[1] communication protocol. In this case an event notifies the application that a beacon was received, which represents a significant point for time synchronization. In contrast to the previous cases, the operation which tracks beacons remains active and can send further notifications to the application.

3.2 Heterogeneous

The hardware capabilities define the role a mote can take in a WSN. In terms of hardware, there is a large choice available for MCUs, radio chips, power supplies, and highly specialized sensors and actuators. For example, a constantly powered gateway node can serve as the entry point into the WSN, forwarding and possibly translating messages to backend servers from the WSN and vice-versa. Other motes which are equipped with a more powerful MCU and a larger battery supply can serve as relay points for network traffic. Finally the cheaper and resource-constrained devices operating on batteries represent the leaf nodes in the WSN which sample, process and forward sensor information to the gateway.

Programmers typically use a *platform API* to develop WSN applications. This API represents the interface between applications and the operating system (OS) as well as additional utility libraries which are part of the portfolio of a particular development environment. Whether certain interfaces are available for a platform API depends on the particular hardware. For example, in terms of wireless communication the radio chip defines what physical layer protocols are available. Moreover, the platform API may add common abstractions and, where needed, even the functionality which is not implemented directly in hardware.[2]

3.3 Communication

In general, communication has two main aspects: i) the protocol used to exchange messages using a certain format, and the ii) unique addresses which distinguish between different entities such that messages are delivered to the required destination. Furthermore, the physical topology of a WSN defines how the motes are distributed in the environment. The topology can be fixed or can change dynamically based on environmental and mobility conditions of sensor nodes.

[1] Time Division Multiple Access (TDMA) is a channel access method for shared medium networks.

[2] The slotted Carrier Sense Multiple Access (CSMA) for the IEEE 802.15.4 MAC protocol, for example, is not implemented in hardware by most modern radio chips.

The literature provides a vast collection of custom WSN communication protocols [18] as well as different standards concerned with the different communication layers of the OSI reference architecture in a WSN. Standard examples include IEEE 802.15.4 [19] for the physical and data link layers, 6LoWPAN [20] for the network layer, and various application profiles for ZigBee [21].

For address resolution, communication participants must have unique addresses. Typically, in a WSN, each mote has a globally unique 64-bit address or extended unique identifier (EUI) encoded in the hardware at manufacturing. This EUI is akin to the MAC address used by network interface cards in standard IP networks.

3.4 Real-Time

Communication protocols and sensing in a WSN must be minutely scheduled for efficiency reasons and to meet the sampling requirements of the application. Thus, the notion of an accurate real-time is essential for the correct and efficient functionality of such a network. For example, when using a TDMA protocol for communication all devices must wake-up and receive a beacon in a synchronized manner, then perform useful work in their allocated time slot, and forward their local results towards the gateway nodes, possibly via peer or relay nodes.

Each mote in a network can have two views over the passing of time: a global view and a local view. Global time is based on the universal time, e.g. UTC from GPS and linked to different calendars. Local time starts when the mote is powered up and can in general be derived from the global time. However, for typical WSN applications, it suffices for individual sensor nodes to keep track of an accurate local time and occasionally synchronize with a peer which has an accurate view of the global time. In this case, motes require a common understanding of time intervals.

4 BPMN Modeling Style for WSN

In this section, we focus on how the previously described aspects of WSN applications can be modeled using the existing set of features provided by the BPMN language. Because BPMN allows to express the same behavior in different ways, a certain modeling style is required to describe precise models. Such refined and precise models are necessary and ease the task of generating executable and efficient code [10] for WSN applications.

4.1 Reactive-Behavior

We first consider the events which signal the *normal completion* of an asynchronous operation. The BPMN language per-se does not distinguish between asynchronous and synchronous activities. As such, there is no special annotation which can be used for the asynchronous tasks which are common in the WSN domain. However, the BPMN language allows the definition of additional

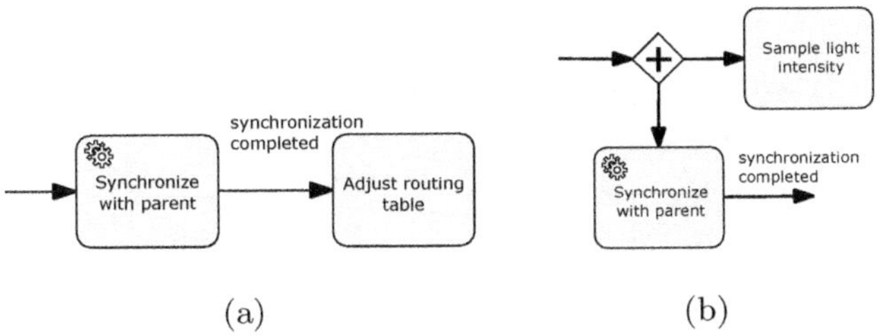

Fig. 1. (a) Normal completion of an asynchronous operation. (b) Starting an asynchronous operation in parallel to allow for immediate execution of further tasks. As an example of visual distinction the asynchronous activities are marked with the `cog-wheels` annotation.

task annotations. Such an extension would help the visual distinction between synchronous and asynchronous tasks.

Because the normal completion of an asynchronous operation is unique, we model this implicitly using sequence flows as shown in Figure 1(a). A typical case in WSN applications is to start a new operation as soon as an asynchronous activity was triggered. In this case, a parallel split gateway is required which is shown in Figure 1(b). If the gateway is omitted the model remains valid but the `Sample light intensity` activity will only be executed after the asynchronous operation completes.

The *exception completion* of an asyncchronous operation can be captured using interrupting border events as shown in Figure 2(a). For conditions which occur internal to the operation, the BPMN escalation event type is appropriate as it can only be thrown from within the respective task. Other types of events which notify about exception condition are timeouts, messages, signals, and cancellations. The main difference is that the latter are triggered by factors external to the task. For critical exceptions which are triggered by the execution of the operation, we employ the BPMN error event symbol.

Some exception completions can affect the entire system, thus they not only signal the interruption of a particular task but of the entire enclosing process. A typical example is a system critical error such as a memory access violation. These exceptions can be modeled using event sub-processes with a start event with an interrupting semantic as shown in Figure 2(b). If this situation occurs, then the handler catches the event and the enclosing process is terminated.

For describing the occurrence of a *significant state* during the execution of the process, the BPMN language provides several possibilities using non-interrupting events. The first approach, shown in Figure 3(a), explicitly uses the task `Track beacon messages` to mark the start of an asynchronous operation. At a later point the operation will throw an event `beacon received` which is handled by the event sub-process `handle beacons` which toggles an LED for visual feedback. The event does not terminate the enclosing process because the application should continue tracking beacons. This type of modeling is the closest to a typical event-based program. However, such a modeling style might be hard

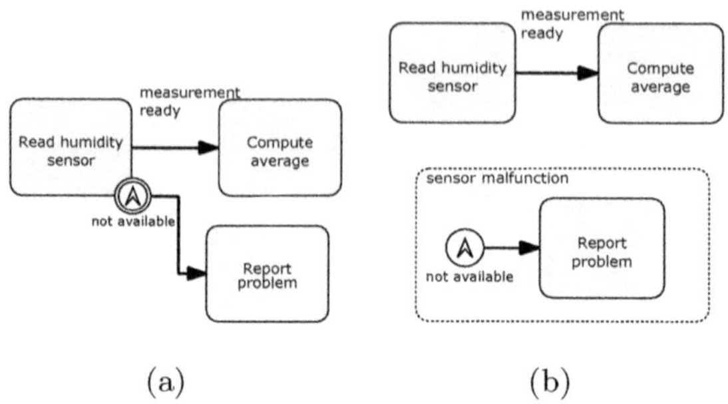

Fig. 2. Different ways of handling the exception completion of a task with an asynchronous interface

to manage and understand without a visual aid as it grows in complexity with the number of events. As an aid, the model editor could highlight possible throw events when corresponding catch events are selected and vice-versa.

Another approach of modeling the occurrence significant states is by using non-interrupting border events attached to tasks. Figure 3(b) is semantically equivalent with the previous example. In contrast to the border events in Figure 2(a), the event `beacon received` is non-interrupting. The advantage of using this style is that tasks with an asynchronous interface and corresponding events are visually linked and the start and end of such activities is explicit. As long as the `Track beacon messages` task is active it can potentially generate multiple events which are processed potentially in parallel. As there can be potentially multiple tokens arriving to the `Toggle yellow LED` task, this case can be considered a *lack of synchronization* in the model [22]. However, for WSN applications such a model represents a valid behavior. Synchronous tasks are implicitly serialized as there is only one execution unit, whereas for asynchronous tasks multiple instances will be instantiated according to the standard.

A modeling variation which uses several implicit assumptions is shown in Figure 3(c). This model assumes that tracking of beacons should be started automatically as soon as the enclosing task is active. The second assumption is that the events `tracking completed` and `beacon received` can only be triggered by this activity. The main difference to the previous two variants is that in this case the events can occur as soon as the enclosing process in active, whereas in the previous variants, the corresponding events can only occur once task `Track beacon messages` is active. The advantage of this approach is that it provides a good visual separation for event handlers. Moreover, if the tracking beacons activity never completes the top event handler can be omitted, which results in a visually compact representation. The disadvantage is that this modeling style uses implicit assumptions which must be understood by the modeler. Moreover, the control flow inside the event handlers cannot be merged with control flow outside the respective event sub-processes. For frequently used and common WSN activities such as watchdog timers this solution is well suited. When control flow clarity is more important than visual compactness, the two previous styles represent more general solutions.

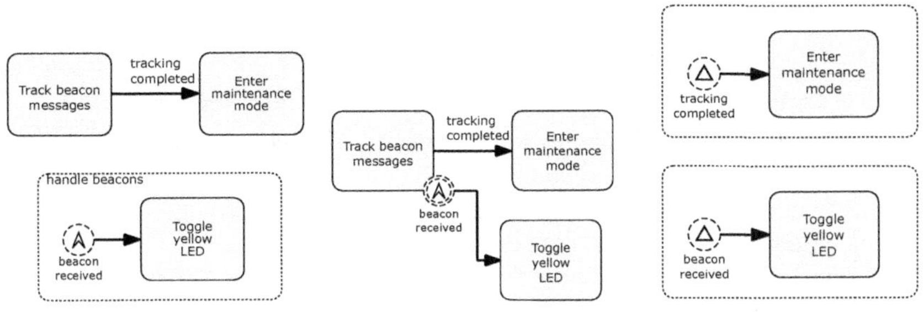

(a) (b) (c)

Fig. 3. Different ways of modeling significant states for an asynchronous interface

In practice, the semantic of events generated by an asynchronous operations is defined in the documentation for the respective platform API. Alone from the corresponding function signature or even provided with the source code, it is not possible to infer whether an event signals normal or exceptional completion of an activity. Moreover, it is not possible to distinguish whether the event simply notifies about a significant state while the operation continues its activity. In absence of source-code annotations for the asynchronous operations provided by the platform, translating an API to BPMN symbols is thus semi-automatic. With appropriate API annotations, this translation can be fully automated, and for each API function the corresponding BPMN task with the appropriate border events can be generated. These annotations can be provided by developers at the same time as writing the documentation.

4.2 Communication

A network configuration describes how many sensor nodes are part of the network and what is their behavior type. Whereas, the network topology describes the logical connectivity. We describe both aspects in a single BPMN *conversation diagram* by representing groups of nodes using the parallel multi-instance pools. In this case, the groups of nodes are defined based on common behavior.

Figure 4 shows a network configuration with three types of entities in a static star topology. There is a only one instance for both the entities `Truck` and `Gateway`, whereas there are multiple instances of type `Parcel` running in parallel. The latter form a group with logical connections only to the `Truck` entity. The cardinality for a certain entity type can be set using the BPMN `participantMultiplicity` property for the respective pools. If the network topology is dynamic the same notation can be used. In this case, the diagram will represent a snapshot of the network configuration and topology at a specific point in time.

In a simulation environment, the network configuration might also include parameters which characterize a real environment such as packet error rate, sensor noise, clock drift, the physical position in a given coordinate system, or

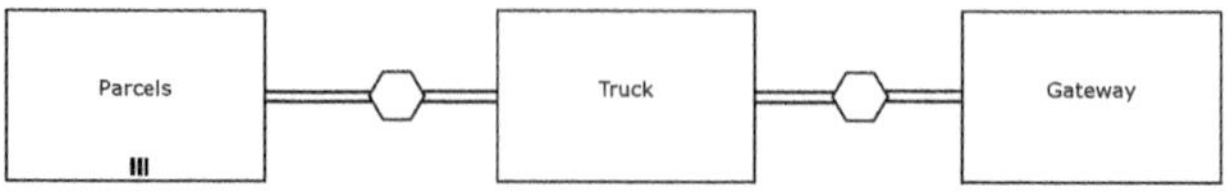

Fig. 4. Network configuration overview and fixed star topology

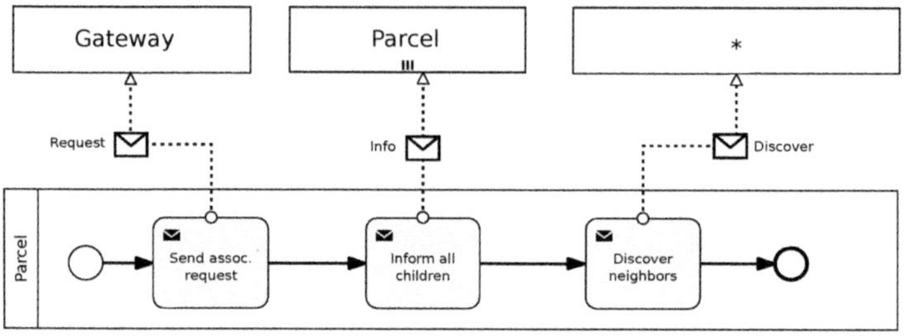

Fig. 5. Addressing a unique mote, groups of motes, or broadcast

the node failure probability. These parameters can be specified by using the extension mechanisms provided by BPMN. In our case, these extensions do not modify the execution semantics nor syntax of the BPMN language, they are simply aids in defining a detailed network configuration.

In a BPMN process, communication is modeled explicitly with sender and receiver bound to the start and end of message flows, respectively. Thus, as a general address resolution principle, entities are identified by their name. In Figure 5, we distinguish between the different cases for addressing a single node and a group of nodes.

In the case where the entity name describes a single instance entity the mapping to an EUI address is straight forward as shown by the `Request` message addressed to the `Gateway`. In case the entity represents multiple instances, the message is delivered to all entities in the respective group.[3] This case is modeled by the `Info` message which is addressed to all instances of type `Parcel`.

Furthermore, WSN applications heavily use broadcast messages which are received by all direct neighbors of the sender with access to the physical medium. For this purpose, we define a special pool name for which we use the `*` wild card symbol. Thus the message `Discover` is addressed to all one-hop physical neighbors, irrespective of their type. Depending on their physical location, both the `Gateway` and possibly all nodes of type `Parcel` will receive the message.

Often WSN protocols require addressing a particular node in a group. Such a selection can be specified in several ways. For example using the group name and an index (`Parcel[1]`) or by using the unique address of a mote.[4] Often for protocol specifications the address for the communication partner is not known and can change dynamically according to changes in the network topology during

[3] This functionality must be provided by the corresponding communication protocol.

[4] A unique 64-bit address (e.g., 02-00-00-00-A1-B2-C3-D4) or the short 16-bit address according to the IEEE 802.15.4 specification.

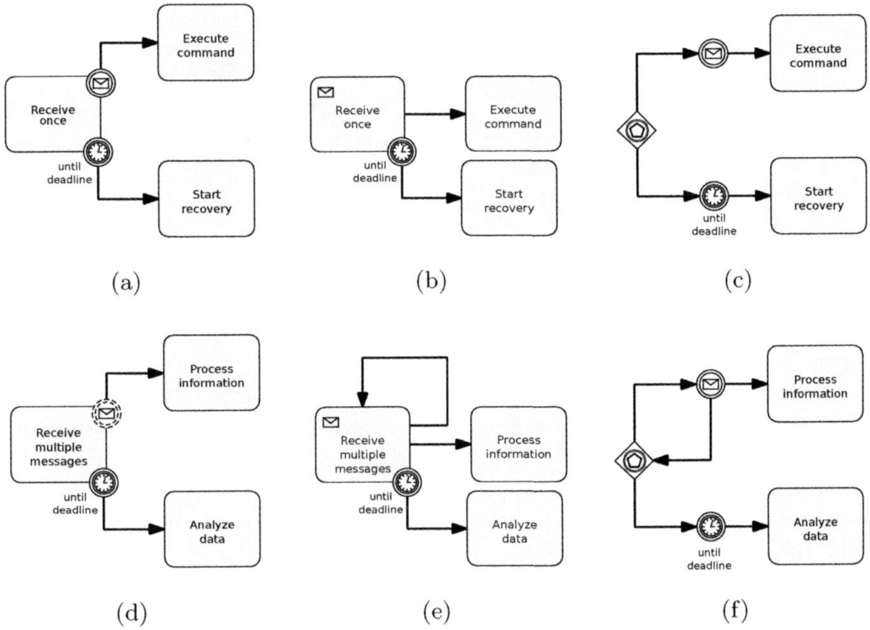

Fig. 6. Different possibilities of modeling the reception of a single message (a,b,c) or possibly multiple messages (e,f,g) with a timeout deadline. The `Receive once` and `Receive multiple` building blocks are provided by the respective platform API.

the process execution. To enable such dynamic specifications, the value of a BPMN data item can be used to specify all of the above addressing modes.

The communication protocol can be specified using the `category` property of the BPMN message envelope. This property can refer to an existing standard WSN protocol such as ZigBee or 6LoWPAN, or a well established communication protocol such as UDP, TCP/IP for wired communication or simply the raw frame format of the IEEE 802.15.4 wireless links. The choice of protocols is limited by the available implementations for the specified platform API as defined in the enclosing pool. The building blocks for sending and receiving messages using a specific communication protocols will thus appear as send and receive tasks when refining the respective pool. To visually distinguish such communication tasks from other activities in the model, we use the corresponding messaging annotations as depicted in Figure 6.

The communication protocol specified in the message envelope must match the end points which are bound to both the sender and the receiver pools or respective tasks. The model is inconsistent in case of a mismatch. As a default case, that is, when no protocol is specified by the message envelope nor the respective send and receive tasks or events, communication is mapped to the physical layer protocol. For of a typical WSN network, messages without a specified protocol are implicitly mapped to the raw IEEE 802.15.4 frame format. Furthermore, the header of the message is automatically initialized based on

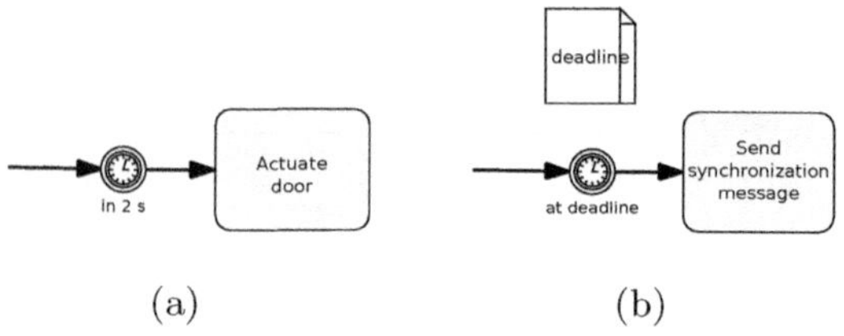

Fig. 7. Example time specifications which give an overview over real-time behavior

the address resolution scheme described above and according to the specified protocol.[5]

Modeling communication is thus flexible and exchanging the communication protocol only involves adapting the message envelopes and exchanging the respective communication tasks. As this approach is not dependent on a particular communication protocol, other standards can be easily supported (e.g., Web Services) provided a corresponding and sufficiently efficient implementation exists for the respective execution platform.

The second function of a BPMN message envelope is a container for the data payload which is transferred between entities. The data structure for the payload can be specified directly in the BPMN model or by using a reference to an existing, typically more complex, model from an object repository. The data models in the repository can be defined using other modeling tools such as the UML class diagrams. For faster prototyping of applications, the data structure can be directly defined in the BPMN model itself by using the *ItemDefinition* property which allows to specify the name, data type, and optionally a value.

To transfer the payload the corresponding data structure must be serialized by the sending activity and de-serialized by the corresponding receive activity. Using association flows on the sender side data objects are pushed into the send activity. On the receiver side the data objects are extracted from the corresponding receive activity. We use the name of the data objects for binding to the correct items in the payload.

4.3 Real-Time

The behavior of WSN application is often tightly synchronized. Consequently, a modeling languages must have the ability to specify time, both global and local. In BPMN this is possible using timer events. For this purpose the mutually exclusive properties `timeDate`, `timeCycle`, `timeDuration` allow to specify the values for timer events from the perspective of a global time. The ISO-8601 representation format is used for both recurring and non-recurring time-intervals.

[5] When using the raw IEEE 802.15.4 format, we define for each group of sensors a personal area network identifier (PANID) based on the hash of the group name. Messages which are addressed to all nodes in a group will use the `BEACON` frame type, the PANID of the group, and a broadcast short destination address `0xFFFF`.

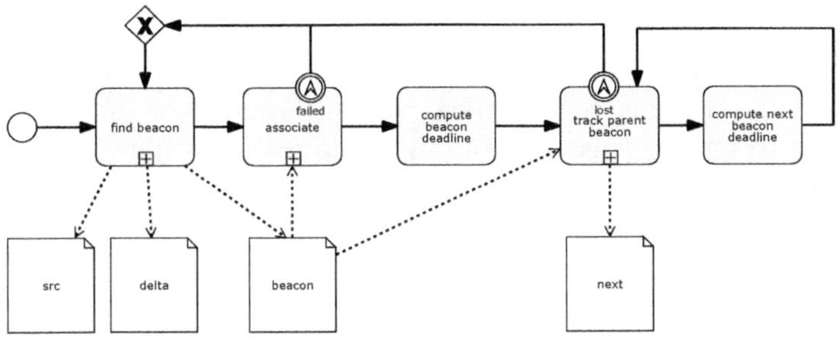

Fig. 8. The top-level process describing the behavior of a child node in a TDMA protocol which continuously tracks beacons from its respective parent

For WSNs, we focus on the local time as viewed by a sensor node as this perspective is sufficient to specify a mote's behavior. We assume that the platform API provides means to query the current local time. The translations to and from a global time or calendar dates can be provided as utility functions by the platform API.

To make timers descriptive, we suggest using the name of the timer events to specify time predicates using the syntax `PREPOSITION TIME [UNIT]`. In the frame reference of the mote, we allow both relative and absolute time specifications. The preposition `at` is used for precise moments in time, whereas the preposition `in` defines time spans starting from the moment a sequence flow token reaches the timer event. The time value can be either a constant number or the name of a data item as shown in Figure 7. The time units match the intervals relevant for a mote's behavior, namely s, ms, and μs.

4.4 Heterogeneous

To bind a certain entity in a model to a particular WSN platform the properties of BPMN pool can be used, in particular the *processCategory*. Based on this selection the corresponding model editor can display only the BPMN tasks which are available for the corresponding platform API. An alternative is to specify the platform API only when models are compiled to executable applications.

However, for portable business process models which allow migration to improved hardware platforms this approach should be avoided. Instead, the execution platform should be generic and flexible enough to allow for execution of the same application model independent of the actual hardware platform. This criterion is fulfilled for example by using a portable virtual machine [17] which abstracts from the underlying hardware and implements a core platform API.

5 Evaluation

To evaluate our BPMN-based model-driven methodology, we integrated the required compiler and debugging tools into the widely used Oryx model editor [10].

We evaluated the expressiveness of the approach by modeling several WSN application archetypes [23] including different communication protocols. Figure 8 shows a model which deals with the communication aspect of the applications we modeled. In addition we quantified the performance of the code generation with respect to energy consumption and resource usage for such applications. Our transformation generates Java and C# code which executes on the Mote Runner [17] WSN platform. Our evaluation results on several case studies show that the generated code is only 1% less energy efficient than hand-written equivalents. However, overall memory usage is strongly affected by optimizations. On average generated code requires 10% more RAM and 44% more flash when using compiler optimizations. Without optimizations, the RAM overhead is 50%, whereas the flash space is three fold. Nevertheless, we could show that the generated applications fit on standard motes.

One interesting aspect for the BPMN models in our application domain is that there is no end event on the top most process level. This is because a WSN application is a long-running, continuous process. For our application set we found no scenario where the compensation event was required. Moreover, our models do not use the BPMN signal event type as this represents an out of band communication mechanism[6] which bypasses wireless links.

With respect to the different gateways provided by BPMN, we used all types[7] for control flow and synchronization. In particular the event-based, exclusive, and parallel gateways are used frequently, whereas the OR gateway is used rarely. In general, our models use parallel gateways to allow synchronous activities to execute while asynchronous operation are being started. For our scenarios, the number of gateways decreases for models with a higher abstraction level.

Due to the reactive nature of our models, we make extensive use of the different types of events provided by BPMN. In particular the escalation, timer, and message events are the most frequent components in our models. In addition we used the error event for critical failures.

Our applications typically maintain different states such as sensor values and intermediate results. Hence, we employ a considerable number of data items for volatile variables, and data stores for persistent variables. For passing data inputs and output to and from sub-process, messages, and events, we mainly use data associations. However, when models increase in complexity the data associations may clutter the diagram. Thus for trivial parameters we use the data input and output sets for the corresponding task.

An important BPMN feature which helped us model functionality which could be reused across different WSN application is the encapsulation mechanism provided by sub-processes. For our application domain the same encapsulation of pools would prove a useful mechanism for building a group hierarchy.

However, there are also limitations to the modeling approach described in this paper with respect to conventional programming languages. One such limitation is that it is not possible to change the binding between an event and an

[6] The signal event propagates both across sub-process hierarchies and pool boundaries.
[7] We exclude the complex gateway which has no execution semantic.

asynchronous operation once the latter has been started. Even though this is possible with conventional programming languages, such a style is prone to errors which might be difficult to trace. Moreover, from our practical experiences, computationally intensive tasks such as averaging and filtering are created faster using conventional methods. These tasks should then be encapsulated and provided as building blocks which can be reused in models. Another aspect which is better controlled by conventional programming methods are low-level operations and optimizations for an efficient and compact implementation. However, we argue that the benefit of modeling and the graphical overview of the application structure out weights such limitations for certain application scenarios.

6 Conclusion

In this paper, we report on our experiences of using BPMN as a modeling language for the WSN domain. We describe a modeling style which captures the reactive behavior of WSN applications. Consequently, the most frequent BPMN symbols in our models are events and corresponding event sub-processes. Moreover, we describe patterns for specifying precise communication as well as the real-time behavior of such applications. Subsequently, such models are used for generating efficient executable code.

For our set of WSN archetype applications we deem the BPMN language expressive enough to specify behavior at both higher and lower levels of abstraction. However, for lower level tasks, which require efficient and compact implementations, traditional software development methods are superior. This low level functionality can be encapsulated in tasks which are provided as reusable building blocks for modeling.

References

1. OMG: Business Process Model and Notation (BPMN) 2.0, `bpmn.org`
2. Spieß, P., et al.: Integrating sensor networks with business processes. In: Real-World Sensor Networks Workshop at ACM MobiSys. ACM (2006)
3. Schäfer, S.: Secure trade lane: A sensor network solution for more predictable and more secure container shipments. In: Companion to the Sym. on Object-Oriented Programming Systems, Languages, and Applications, pp. 839–845. ACM (2006)
4. Ilic, A., et al.: Using sensor information to reduce the carbon footprint of perishable goods. IEEE Pervasive Computing 8, 22–29 (2009)
5. Krishnamurthy, S., et al.: Distributed interactions with wireless sensors using TinySIP for hospital automation. In: Proc. of the Int. Conf. on Pervasive Computing and Communications, pp. 269–275. IEEE (2008)
6. Bencini, L., et al.: Agricultural monitoring based on wireless sensor network technology: Real long life deployments for physiology and pathogens control. In: Proc. of the Int. Conf. on Sensor Technologies and Applications, pp. 372–377. IEEE (2009)
7. McCulloch, J., et al.: Wireless sensor network deployment for water use efficiency in irrigation. In: Proc. of Real-world Wireless Sensor Networks, pp. 46–50. ACM (2008)

8. O'Flynn, B., et al.: Smartcoast: A wireless sensor network for water quality monitoring. In: Proc. of the Conf. on Local Computer Networks, pp. 815–816. IEEE (2007)
9. Reinhardt, A., Steinmetz, R.: Exploiting platform heterogeneity in wireless sensor networks for cooperative data processing. In: Proc. of the GI/ITG KuVS Fachgespräch "Drahtlose Sensornetze" (August 2009)
10. Caracaş, A., et al.: Compiling business process models for sensor networks. In: Int. Conf. on Distributed Computing in Sensor Systems. IEEE (2011)
11. Karnouskos, S., et al.: Towards the real-time enterprise: Service-based integration of heterogeneous SOA-ready industrial devices with enterprise applications. In: Proc. of the Sym. on Information Control Problems in Manufacturing (2009)
12. Spieß, P., et al.: SOA-based integration of the internet of things in enterprise services. In: Proc. of the Int. Conf. on Web Services, pp. 968–975. IEEE (2009)
13. Marin-Perianu, M., et al.: Implementing business rules on sensor nodes. In: Emerging Technologies and Factory Automation, pp. 292–299. IEEE (2006)
14. Glombitza, N., et al.: Integrating wireless sensor networks into web service-based business processes. In: Proc. of the Int. Workshop on Middleware Tools, Services and Run-Time Support for Sensor Networks, pp. 25–30. ACM (2009)
15. Glombitza, N., et al.: Using graphical process modeling for realizing SOA programming paradigms in sensor networks. In: Proc. of the Int. Conf. on Wireless On-Demand Network Systems and Services, pp. 57–64. IEEE (2009)
16. Hill, J., et al.: System architecture directions for networked sensors. ACM SIGPLAN Not. 35(11), 93–104 (2000)
17. Caracaş, A., et al.: Mote Runner: A multi-language virtual machine for small embedded devices. In: Proc. of the Int. Conf. on Sensor Technologies and Applications, pp. 117–125. IEEE (2009)
18. Bachir, A., et al.: MAC essentials for wireless sensor networks. IEEE Communications Surveys and Tutorials 12(2) (2010)
19. IEEE: Wireless medium access control (MAC) and physical layer (PHY) specifications for low rate wireless personal area networks (LR-WPANs) (2006)
20. Shelby, Z., Carsten, B.: 6LoWPAN: The Wireless Embedded Internet. Wiley (2009)
21. ZigBee: Standards Overview, `zigbee.org`
22. Favre, C., Völzer, H.: Symbolic Execution of Acyclic Workflow Graphs. In: Hull, R., Mendling, J., Tai, S. (eds.) BPM 2010. LNCS, vol. 6336, pp. 260–275. Springer, Heidelberg (2010)
23. Bai, L.S., et al.: Archetype-based design: Sensor network programming for application experts, not just programming experts. In: Proc. of the Int. Conf. on Information Processing in Sensor Networks, pp. 85–96. IEEE (2009)

Faster Or-Join Enactment for BPMN 2.0

Beat Gfeller[1], Hagen Völzer[1], and Gunnar Wilmsmann[2]

[1] IBM Research – Zurich, Switzerland
[2] IBM Software Group, Böblingen, Germany

Abstract. We propose an efficient algorithm that enacts the control-flow of BPMN, in particular the inclusive Or-join gateway. The original algorithm for enacting Or-joins in BPMN 2.0 needs, upon each token move in the diagram, linear time in the number of edges of the diagram to find out whether a given Or-join is enabled, whereas our proposal essentially needs only constant time to do so.

1 Introduction

To enact BPMN diagrams, one needs to implement an algorithm that determines, for each execution state of the diagram, the set of *flow nodes*, e.g. tasks, gateways and events, that are enabled in the given state. This is straightforward for flow nodes with a *local* semantics, i.e., if the enabledness of the flow node depends only on the state of its adjacent edges.

However, the converging inclusive gateway, also known as *Or-join*, has a non-local semantics and its enabledness may depend on the state of the edges of the entire diagram. A simple algorithm [8] for enacting the standardized semantics of the Or-join [4] searches the entire diagram for tokens upon each state change and therefore needs linear time to update the enabledness of an Or-join upon each state change. No faster algorithm was published so far.

In this paper, we propose an algorithm that essentially needs only constant time to decide whether an Or-join is enabled in a given state. More precisely, it needs constant time to update this information for *most* state changes and it can take up to linear time for *some special* state changes. This can be captured more precisely by analyzing the effort for a so-called execution *round* with respect to an Or-join. For such a round, the total effort reduces from quadratic time to linear time.

The new algorithm achieves the speedup by keeping track, in a dedicated data structure, of the token that may still reach the Or-join in the future and therefore may influence its enabledness.

The paper is structured as follows: In Section 2, we formally define the problem of enacting Or-joins, and describe the known approach to solve it. In Section 3, we describe our new approach to solve the problem more efficiently. Section 4 contains further optimizations which can be used to enhance our algorithm for typical instances. In Section 5, we give a detailed analysis of our approach and show its advantages over the straightforward one, before concluding the paper in Section 6.

R. Dijkman, J. Hofstetter, and J. Koehler (Eds.): BPMN 2011, LNBIP 95, pp. 31–43, 2011.

2 Problem Definition

In this section, we describe and formalize the problem of Or-join enactment. We start with the preliminary definitions of workflow graphs and their semantics, including the Or-join semantics from BPMN 2.0 [4,8].

Workflow graphs. A workflow graph is a directed graph that describes the basic control flow of a BPMN diagram. For the purposes of this paper, it suffices to consider only gateways and tasks as control flow elements.

A *workflow graph* $G = (V, E, \ell)$ consists of a set V of *nodes*, a set $E \subseteq V \times V$ of directed *edges*, and a partial mapping $\ell : V \to \{\text{And}, \text{Xor}, \text{Or}\}$ such that

1. $\ell(x)$ is defined if and only if x has more than one incoming edge or more than one outgoing edge,
2. there is exactly one source and at least one sink,
3. the source has exactly one outgoing edge and each sink has exactly one incoming edge, and
4. every node is on some path from the source to some sink.

The source is also called the *start node*, a sink is called an *end node*, and $\ell(x)$ is called the *logic* of x. If the logic is And, Or or Xor, we call x a *gateway*; if x has no logic and x is no start or end node, we call x a *task*. We use BPMN to depict workflow graphs, i.e., gateways are drawn as diamonds, where the symbol "+" inside stands for And, a circle stands for Or, whereas no decoration stands for Xor. Tasks are drawn as rectangles, start and end nodes as circles. A gateway that has more than one incoming edge and only one outgoing edge is also called a *join*, a gateway with more than one outgoing but only one incoming edge is also called a *split*. We may assume for simplicity of the presentation that every gateway is either a split or a join. Moreover, we may omit the depiction of tasks in example graphs, except for the start and end nodes. The reader may imagine task on each edge that is shown. We say that an edge e is *incident* to a node v if e is incoming to v or outgoing from v.

The semantics of a workflow graph is, similarly to Petri nets, defined as a token game. The state of a workflow graph is represented by tokens on the edges of the graph. Let $G = (V, E, \ell)$ be a workflow graph. A *state* of G is a mapping $s : E \to \mathbb{N}$, which assigns a natural number to each edge. When $s(e) = k$, we say that edge e carries k *tokens* in state s. The *initial state* of G is the state where there is no token present on any edge of the workflow graph. The initial state must be followed by a state where there is exactly one token on the unique outgoing edge of the start node and no token anywhere else. We write $s \xrightarrow{v} s'$ when s changes to s' by executing node v. When a token reaches a sink, it may be consumed in the next state transition. The execution of a workflow graph is *terminated* when no edge carries any tokens anymore.

The state of a workflow graph changes by executing an *enabled* gateway, where the enabledness of a gateway is defined as follows: An And-join is enabled if (and only if) there is a token on each of its incoming edges. An Xor-gateway (join or split) is enabled iff there is a token on at least one of its inputs. An Or-split is enabled iff there is a token on its input edge.

The rest semantics of the various nodes is also defined in the standard way, as follows. An And-gateway removes one token from each of its ingoing edges and adds one token to each of its outgoing edges. An Xor-gateway nondeterministically chooses one of its incoming edges on which there is at least one token, removes one token from that edge, then nondeterministically chooses one of its outgoing edges, and adds one token to that outgoing edge. As usual, we abstract from the data that controls the flow in Xor-gateways, hence the nondeterministic choice.

Figure 1 shows a workflow graph which we will use as a running example throughout the paper.

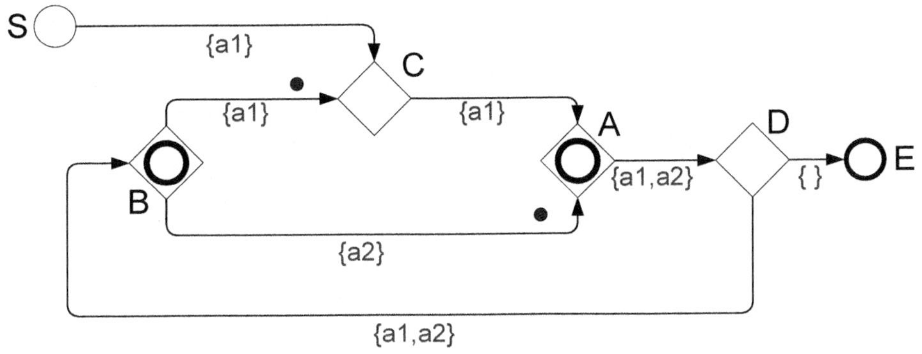

Fig. 1. An example workflow graph

Or-join semantics. Note that for both And-gateways, Xor-gateways and Or-splits, it is easy to determine whether they are enabled in a given state. In contrast, the enabledness of an Inclusive Or-Join, called simply *Or-join* in the following, is more complex. It is defined in BPMN 2.0 [4] as follows (cf. also [8]):

Definition 1. *An Or-join A is* enabled *in state s if*

1. *there is an incoming edge e of A such that* $s(e) \geq 1$ *and*
2. *for each edge e′ of the graph with* $s(e') \geq 1$*, we have: If there is a path from e′ to some incoming edge e of A with* $s(e) = 0$ *that does not visit A, then there is a path from e′ to some incoming edge e of A with* $s(e) > 0$ *that does not visit A.*

Let *A* be an Or-join. An *inhibiting path* to *A* is a path from a token to an empty incoming edge of *A* such that the path does not visit *A*. Furthermore, an *anti-inhibiting path* to *A* is a path from a token to a non-empty incoming edge of *A* such that the path does not visit *A*. An Or-join *A* has to wait only for those tokens that have an inhibiting path but no anti-inhibiting path to *A*. Therefore, an Or-join *A* is enabled iff it has at least one token on an incoming edge, and there is no token which has an inhibiting path leading to *A* but no anti-inhibiting path leading to *A*. Or-join *A* in Fig. 1 is not enabled in the state shown as it has to wait for the token on the edge from *B* to *C*. Once that token has moved to the edge from *C* to *A*, *A* is enabled.

When an Or-gateway executes, it consumes a token from each incoming edge that carries a token and produces a token for each edge of a nonempty subset of its outgoing edges. That subset is chosen nondeterministically, again abstracting from data-based decisions. For a detailed motivation of this Or-join semantics we refer the reader to [8].

Or-join enactment. The problem of Or-join enactment is to compute the enabledness of a given Or-join in a given state. A simple algorithm to enact Or-joins is described in [8], from which the following description is taken.

If an Or-join A has at least one token on an incoming edge, we have to determine whether there are any inhibiting and anti-inhibiting paths to A. The algorithm consists of two parts. First we mark all edges of the graph that contribute to anti-inhibiting paths. Those can be determined by backward reachability search starting from the non-empty[1] incoming edges of A. We mark all those edges in red. We stop exploration when we reach A itself in order not to mark the empty incoming edges of A. The second part of the algorithm marks all edges in green that are not red already and that are backward-reachable from any empty incoming edge of A. Again, we stop exploration when we reach A itself in order not to mark any non-empty incoming edge of A. This part computes the inhibiting paths. The Or-join A is then enabled if and only if there is no token on some green edge. The Pseudo-code in Algorithm 1 describes this algorithm in more detail.

IsEnabled(Workflow graph G, State s, Or-join A)
Red := $\{e \mid e$ is an incoming edge of A such that $s(e) > 0\}$
while *there exist edges* $e = (v_1, v_2) \in \mathtt{Red}$ *and* $e' = (v_3, v_4) \notin \mathtt{Red}$ *such that* $v_4 = v_1 \neq A$ **do**
    Red := Red $\cup\{e'\}$
Green := $\{e \mid e$ is an incoming edge of A such that $s(e) = 0\}$
while *there exist an edge* $e = (v_1, v_2) \in \mathtt{Green}$ *and* $e' = (v_3, v_4) \notin (\mathtt{Green} \cup \mathtt{Red})$ *such that* $v_4 = v_1 \neq A$ **do**
    Green := Green $\cup\{e'\}$
return $\mathtt{Green} \cap \{e \mid s(e) > 0\} = \emptyset$.

Algorithm 1. Returns *true* iff Or-join A is enabled in state s

It is not difficult to see that this algorithm can be implemented to run in linear time in the size of the workflow graph, i.e., in $O(m + n)$ time in the worst case. For a small example such as the one in Figure 1, this effort might be acceptable. However, for larger examples, a linear cost per token movement might be too much, since the total execution time for a process might become quadratic: See for example the workflow graph shown in Figure 2, which is discussed in Section 5.

To facilitate a faster Or-join enactment, we can implement a data structure that keeps track of certain aspects of the evolving state in an execution to provide a more explicit representation of Or-join enabledness. Note that any process execution engine needs to track each individual token in the workflow graph. Therefore, we assume that the algorithm for computing the enabledness of an Or-join obtains all token movements as its input. More precisely, we formalize the problem as follows.

Definition 2. *Any data structure which solves the* enactment problem *for a given Or-join gateway A provides the following operations:*

- Init(G,A): *Given a workflow graph G and an Or-join A, initialize the data structure to represent the initial state of the workflow graph.*

[1] An edge is *non-empty* if it contains at least one token.

- Update(L): *Given some change of the currently represented state which result from a node's execution, update the data structure to represent the new state. The change is specified as a set* $L = \{(e,d),(e',d'),\ldots\}$ *of updates for the number of tokens on some edges, where each update* (e,d) *is a pair consisting of an edge* e *and the increase (resp. decrease)* d *in the number of tokens it carries (*d *may be negative to represent a decrease).*
- Query(): *Answers whether the Or-join A is enabled in the represented state.*

Note that we define the Update(L) method somewhat more general than required, since the execution of any gateway only changes the tokens on its incident edges. The solution we will introduce later works also for the more general updates we defined here.

3 Faster Or-Join Enactment

In this section, we describe a technique to check Or-join enabledness in a faster way than with the known technique described above.

The basic idea behind our approach of computing the enabledness of an Or-join A is to use various counters to keep track of all the relevant tokens that are present in the current state. Each counter keeps track of the number of tokens present in certain parts of the process. The counters are defined by labels on the edges, which are defined as follows.

Consider an Or-join A, with input edges $a_1, a_2, \ldots, a_k$. We label each edge of the graph by the set of input edges (*inputs* for short) of A that can be reached from this edge without first going through A. We keep a counter for every distinct label that appears on some edge e. Note that several edges may have the same label: in this case, they all refer to one common counter. We call this counter the *associated counter* of the edge e.

In our example in Figure 1, the enumeration of the inputs of Or-join A is given implicitly by their labels. The associated counter of the edge (S,C) has the label $\{a_1\}$ because $a1$ is the only input of A that can be reached without visiting A before.

Each counter C_S, representing a subset S of A's inputs, stores the number of tokens in the current state for which for *each* of the inputs in S, there is a path to an input of A which does not contain A. In the situation shown in Figure 1, the value of the counter associated with edge (S,C) is 1, since there is a token on the edge (B,C) which has the same label.

Note that the number of counters required for an Or-join is bounded by the number of edges in the process model.

In addition, each counter can be marked as *ignored* (details follow below). Moreover, to quickly decide whether the Or-join is enabled, we keep a variable q which stores the number of counters that are currently non-zero and non-ignored.

In the following, we describe how this counter-based data structure is used to efficiently perform the operations Init(G), Update(L) and Query(). In addition, our approach requires a preprocessing step, in which the edges of the workflow graph are labelled as described above. Since this step only needs to be performed once for each workflow graph, we separate it from the Init(G) operation, and describe it as an operation named Preprocess(G). The operations are described in words as well as in pseudocode. We use our running example, shown in Figure 1, to illustrate the method.

Preprocess(G). As a preprocessing step, we need to compute the label of each edge of the workflow graph G. This is done with a simple process: For each input edge a_i of Or-join A, we mark all edges that can be reached by going backwards starting from a_i. In the example, from input edge a_1 (which is the edge (C, A) from gateway C to Or-join A), we can reach the edges (S, C), (B, C), (D, B) and (A, D). From input edge $a_2 = (B, A)$, we can reach the edges (D, B) and (A, D). After performing this process for each input edge of A, we have obtained the labels of all edges of the workflow graph.

Init(G). By going once through all edges, we obtain the set of counters that will be needed (we need a counter for each label that actually occurs in the workflow graph)[2]. In our example, the sets that occur are $\{a_1\}, \{a_2\}$, and $\{a_1, a_2\}$, hence it requires three different counters for the Or-join A. All counters are initialized to 0. Initially, no counter is marked as ignored, and $q = 0$.

Input: Workflow graph $G = (V, E, \ell)$, an Or-join A of G, i.e., $A \in V$ and $\ell(A) = Or$.

Output: A label for each edge of G.

```
for edge e ∈ E do
 | e.label = ""
for input edge a_i of Or-join A do
 | for edge e ∈ E reachable from a_i by going backwards do
 | | Add a_i to e.label.
```

Algorithm 2. Preprocess(G)

Update(L). To update the counters, we simply go through each of the entries (e_i, d_i) in the list $L = (e, d), (e', d'), \ldots$, and update the counter associated with e_i (increasing it by d_i). In addition, if a token arrives at an input of the Or-join A, all counters which contain this input (in their representative set) are marked to be ignored, until the Or-join executes. If some of these newly ignored counters are non-zero, we update the value of q correspondingly.

Note: If the Update describes a state change in which the Or-join A itself is executed, all counters become non-ignored again, and the value of q must be updated correspondingly.

Query(). By definition, an Or-join is enabled if a token has arrived at one or more of its inputs, and there is no other token for which it must wait. The latter condition can be checked by looking at the counters: A counter C_S, representing a subset S of A's inputs, can be ignored if one of the inputs in S is already active (because they represent tokens for which the join must not wait). The Or-join is enabled as soon as all of its non-ignored counters are 0.

Hence, the answer of Query() follows directly from the value of q: The Or-join is enabled if $q = 0$ and if there is a token at (at least) one of its input edges.

[2] We assume that the operation *counters.find(e.label)*, which finds the associated counter of a given label, can be implemented in constant time, for example using hashing.

```
Input: Workflow graph G = (V, E, ℓ), an Or-join A of G, i.e., A ∈ V and ℓ(A) = Or.

Output: The (initialized) data structure DS.

if Preprocess(G) has not been run yet then
|  Preprocess(G)
counters := {}
for edge e ∈ E do
    counter = counters.find(e.label)
    if counter = null then
        c = newCounter()
        c.value := 0
        c.label := e.label
        c.ignored := false
        counters.add(c)
        e.label.counter := c
    else
        e.label.counter := counter
DS.Orjoin := A
DS.nonignoredCounters := counters
DS.ignoredCounters := {}
DS.q := 0
DS.someTokenArrived := false
return DS
```

Algorithm 3. Init(G)

In our running example (Figure 1), we see that three different counters are used for A: $\{a_1\}$ and $\{a_2\}$ and $\{a_1, a_2\}$. In the state shown in the figure, (with two present tokens), the counter for $\{a_1\}$ is 1, the counter for $\{a_2\}$ is also 1, and the counter for $\{a_1, a_2\}$ is 0.

The Or-join A is not yet enabled in this state, because the counter for $\{a_1\}$ is not zero. Once the token before gateway C moves past the gateway, the counter $\{a_1\}$ becomes ignored (because now input a_1 has a token), and the Or-join A is enabled.

Pseudocode of the presented algorithms are given in Algorithms 2–5.

3.1 Correctness of Our New Approach

To argue that our algorithms correctly computes the enabledness of the monitored Or-join, we already presented the intuition behind the counters and their relationship with inhibiting and anti-inhibiting paths. We add here one final correctness argument, which is the following invariant:

Invariant 1. *After executing Init(G) or Update(L), the value of DS.q is equal to the number of non-ignored counters whose value is non-zero.*

Proof. After executing Init(G), the invariant clearly holds because there is only one token in the process, and all counters are non-ignored. The value of q needs to change in the following cases:

Input: Workflow graph $G = (V, E, \ell)$, the data structure DS
Output: None.
for (e, d) *in* L **do**
    if $e.label.counter.value = 0$ *and* $d > 0$ *and not* $e.label.counter.ignored$ **then**
        $DS.q := DS.q + 1$
    $e.label.counter.value := e.label.counter.value + d$
    if $d = +1$ *and* $e = (u, DS.Orjoin)$ **then**
        $DS.someTokenArrived := true$
        for c *in* $DS.nonignoredCounters$ **do**
            if $c.label.contains(e)$ **then**
                $c.ignored := true$
                Move c from $DS.nonignoredCounters$ to $DS.ignoredCounters$.
                if $c.value > 0$ **then**
                    $DS.q := DS.q - 1$
    if $d = +1$ *and* $e = (DS.Orjoin, v)$ **then**
        $DS.someTokenArrived := false$
        for c *in* $DS.ignoredCounters$ **do**
            if $c.value > 0$ **then**
                $DS.q := DS.q + 1$
                $c.ignored := false$
                Move c from $DS.ignoredCounters$ to $DS.nonignoredCounters$.

Algorithm 4. Update(L)

Input: the data structure DS
Output: *true* if the Or-join $DS.q$ is enabled, *false* otherwise.
return $DS.q = 0$ *and* $DS.someTokenArrived$

Algorithm 5. Query()

- a non-ignored counter becomes zero
- a non-ignored counter becomes non-zero
- an ignored non-zero counter becomes non-ignored
- a non-ignored non-zero counter becomes ignored

It is easy to verify that Update(L) changes the value of q correctly in each of these cases. □

Due to the invariant, the value $DS.q$ will, at any given time, correctly indicate whether the Or-join is enabled or not, because its value is updated correctly after each state update with Update(L).

3.2 Analysis

In this section, we briefly state the asymptotic running time of each of the operations in our approach, in terms of the following parameters:

- n: the number of nodes in the workflow graph.
- m: the number of edges in the workflow graph.
- Δ: the in-degree of Or-join A.

The running times are as follows (immediately clear from the previous description/pseudocode):

- *Preprocess(G):* $O(m \cdot \Delta)$.
- *Init(G):* $O(m)$.
- *Update(L):* $O(|L| + \Delta + m)$.
- *Query():* $O(1)$.

The above running times are worst case for an individual execution of a graph node. However, these are rather pessimistic, in the sense that the actual execution cost of a typical state change would be much lower. Therefore, in Section 5 we analyze the cost per token move amortized over a so-called *round*, which is defined as the sequence of states from one execution of the monitored Or-join A to its next execution. This analysis is more precise and allows us to more clearly state the advantages of our approach in comparison with the previous approach.

4 Optimizations

In this section, we suggest and discuss a few optimizations for our proposed algorithm. While these do not decrease the worst case cost of our approach, we expect them to reduce costs in instances typically occurring in practice.

4.1 Delayed Token Monitoring

Since a process can have many possible execution traces, the Or-join A which is being monitored for enabledness may not be executed at all in some of these traces. For this scenario, the following optimization is useful: Instead of labelling the workflow graph initially and then updating the counters for A after every token move, no action is taken until some token arrives at an input of A. When this happens, we run a generalized initialization routine, which is given in pseudocode in Algorithm 6.

From then on, Update(L) is executed after every state change. Since the invariant for q holds after executing this initialization routine, this optimized approach still correctly maintains the value of q.

4.2 Fragment-Based Optimization

In this section, we describe an optimization based on the notion of a process *fragment*. A process fragment is a subgraph of the workflow graph that has a single entry and a single exit. We assume here that entry and exit are edges (cf. [7]), but the approach can be generalized to entry and exit being nodes (cf. [6,5]). A decomposition of a workflow graph into fragments can be computed with well-known parsing techniques [7,6,5].

This optimization requires that the workflow graph does not have a *lack of synchronization*, which is defined as follows. A state exhibits a *lack of synchronization* if there is an edge that carries more than one token in s.

For any fragment in the workflow graph which has exactly one incoming edge and one outgoing edge, and which does not contain the Or-join A, the counters for A need

Input: Workflow graph $G = (V, E, \ell)$, an Or-join A of G, i.e., $A \in V$ and $\ell(A) = Or$.

Output: The (initialized) data structure DS.

```
if Preprocess(G) has not been run yet then
| Preprocess(G)
counters := {}
for edge e ∈ E do
    counter = counters.find(e.label)
    if counter = null then
        c = newCounter()
        c.value := 0
        c.label := e.label
        c.ignored := false
        counters.add(c)
        e.label.counter := c
    else
        e.label.counter := counter
    e.label.counter.value := e.label.counter.value+ number of tokens on edge e
DS.Orjoin := A
DS.nonignoredCounters := counters
DS.ignoredCounters := {}
DS.someTokenArrived := false
for input edge a_i of Or-join A which has at least one token do
    DS.someTokenArrived := true
for edge e ∈ E reachable from a_i by going backwards from one input edge a_i of Or-join A
having at least one token do
    e.label.counter.ignored := true
DS.q := 0
for edge e ∈ E do
    if (not e.label.counter.ignored) and e.label.counter.value > 0 then
        DS.q := DS.q + 1
return DS
```

Algorithm 6. OptimizedInit(G)

not be updated for token movements within this fragment. This works because in a sound process, any token which enters such a fragment will eventually result in exactly one token which exits the fragment (even if within the fragment, the token flow is split and later merged again). Therefore, the incoming edge and the outgoing edge of the fragment, as well as *all* edges within the fragment, have the same label. As a result, if we keep the counter corresponding to this label constant, its value will be correct as soon as the token leaves the fragment, and will never be too high while there are tokens within the fragment (it can be too low, however, if there is concurrency within the fragment).

4.3 Omitting Labels for Full Sets

The counter corresponding to the set of *all* inputs of Or-join *A* can be omitted in the labelling process during Init(G), since it will always either have value 0 or be marked as ignored (because as soon as a token arrives at any of *A*'s inputs, the counter will be ignored). Likewise counters corresponding to the empty set can be omitted as well.

5 Analysis and Comparison with Previous Approach

The previous approach, described in Section 2 and in [8], did not use any counters to aid deciding the enabledness of a given Or-join. As a consequence, for deciding enabledness of an Or-join, it was necessary to traverse the graph to search for tokens for which the Or-join needs to wait. This approach requires $\Omega(n + m)$ time in the worst case.

In the following, we compare our new approach with the previous one and explain its main advantages. To that end, we use a generic example, shown in Figure 2, whose size depends on the parameter x. Note that we focus here on the costs of monitoring one Or-join *A*. If there are several Or-joins in the workflow graph, the costs of our approach (as well as those of the previous one) grow linearly with the number of Or-joins. In the end of this section, we will actually take into account also the costs of monitoring the second Or-join *D* present in the example shown in Figure 2. We assume in the following that our new approach is used with the delayed token monitoring optimization described in Section 4.1. Furthermore, we analyze an execution where neither a deadlock nor a lack of synchronization occurs. In the course of this execution, the Or-join A may be executed either not at all, once, or several times. We analyze the cost per node execution amortized over a so-called *round*, which is defined as the sequence of states from one execution of the monitored Or-join A to its next execution. More formally, the first round of an execution starts when the first token enters the workflow graph. The first round ends when the Or-join A is executed for the first time, or when the process terminates. Whenever the Or-join A is executed (i.e., it fires and produces a token on its outgoing edge), the current round ends, and a new round starts.

The preprocessing step, which is only executed once (before execution of the process is started), takes $O(m\Delta)$ time. The costs of our approach for one round, consisting of a sequence of k state changes, can be bounded as follows:

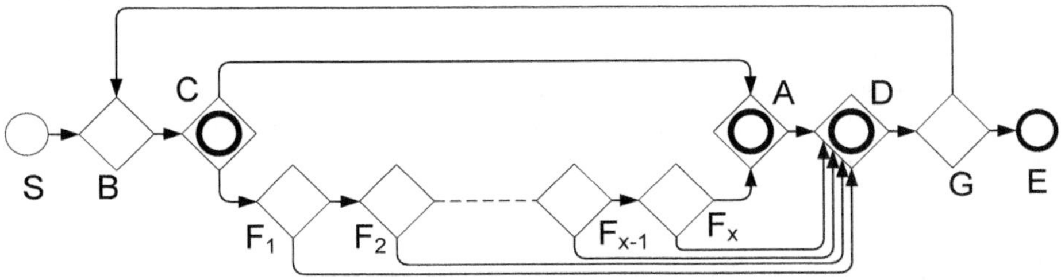

Fig. 2. A second example workflow graph

- OptimizedInit(G): During one round, this is executed at most once. Its run time is $O(m)$.
- Update(L): This operation is executed k times during one round, say, with arguments $L_1, L_2, \ldots, L_k$. Its run time is bounded by $O(\sum_{i=1}^{k} |L_i| + m)$. Note that the total cost of marking counters as ignored during all Update operations of a round is bounded by m (and not $k \cdot m$ as it may seem) because each counter that becomes ignored during a round cannot become non-ignored again in the same round.
- Query(): This operation is executed k times during one round, which costs $O(k)$ time in total.

Hence, the run time of our approach for one round is $O(\sum_{i=1}^{k} |L_i| + m)$. In comparison, the previous approach, described in Section 2, requires $O(\sum_{i=1}^{k} |L_i| + mk)$ time for one round. For rounds with more than a few token movements, our approach is therefore significantly faster. Note that any approach will require at least $\Omega(\sum_{i=1}^{k} |L_i|)$ time, because this is the number of token movements that occur, and any approach clearly needs to keep track of the current position of all tokens. The distinguishing factor of the run time of different approaches is therefore how much additional time beyond this lower bound is required.

We compare the our new approach with the previous one for two different scenarios:

- **An execution with only one round:** In this case, our approach requires $O(\Delta m + \sum_{i=1}^{k} |L_i|)$ time, whereas the previous approach requires $O(mk + \sum_{i=1}^{k} |L_i|)$ time. Our approach is hence better if $k \in \omega(\Delta)$.
- **An execution with l rounds:** Let $\mathcal{L} := \sum_{j=1}^{l} \sum_{i=1}^{k_j} |L_i^j|$ be the sum of all $|L_i^j|$ for all rounds. In this case, our approach requires $O((\Delta + l)m + \mathcal{L})$ time, whereas the previous approach requires $O(lkm + \mathcal{L})$ time.

In a typical workflow graph, we expect the indegree of any Or-join to be essentially constant. Thus, apart from the cost $\mathcal{L}$ which is required to track the tokens (which is necessary in any process execution approach), the cost of our approach per round is essentially linear in the size of the process. The cost of the previous approach is quadratic per round if the length k of a round is similar to the number of m of edges.

To see an example where the improvement can be clearly seen, consider the workflow graph shown in Figure 2, and assume that the execution proceeds as follows: The initial token travels from S through B to C, where one token is created and travels to F_1. From there, it continues to $F_2, F_3, \ldots, F_x$, where it exits through A, D, G, E. Thus, at any time, there is exactly one token present in the workflow graph. Note that this workflow graph has two Or-joins.

In the following, we analyze the costs of both approaches in the given scenario. After each token move, the naive approach will traverse the edges $(F_x, A), (F_{x-1}, F_x)$, $(F_{x-2}, F_{x-1}), \ldots$ until it reaches the edge which currently carries the token. The costs of this approach are thus quadratic in x, since for $\Omega(x)$ many steps, the number of traversed edges is $\Omega(x)$. [3] The total costs are thus $\Omega(x^2)$.

Instead, our new approach has costs $O(m + x) = O(x)$ for each of the two Or-joins, which is still $O(x)$ in total. Thus, in our proposed solution the total effort reduces from quadratic time to linear time.

[3] We ignore the costs for the Or-join D here, which cause even some additional costs.

6 Conclusion

We have presented a new approach for computing the enabledness of an Or-join during the execution of a business process modelled with BPMN 2.0. Since the Or-join semantics are defined in a non-local manner, a naive approach may require quadratic execution costs, as shown in an example given in the paper. In contrast, our new approach requires only linear effort in the size of the workflow graph for the same example. We believe that our solution is essentially optimal for tracking the enabledness of a single Or-join in a process. However, there is still potential for improvement in workflow graphs with several Or-joins: Both the naive and our new approach have costs which grow linearly with the number of Or-joins present. Instead of performing a separate computation for each Or-join, it might be possible to reduce execution costs by having a join computation for all the Or-joins present in the process. We leave the exploration of such further optimizations for future work.

We are not aware of any other proposal to execute the BPMN 2.0 Or-join semantics [4]. However, Christiansen et. al [2] consider the same problem for an older version of the Or-join semantics. They propose two algorithms for enactment, one incremental and one distributed. A complexity analysis is not given. Also Dumas et. al [3] use a dynamically updated data structure to speed up an execution algorithm for an Or-join semantics, from quadratic time to linear time. The Or-join semantics they use is different to the ones mentioned above.

References

1. Bravetti, M., Bultan, T. (eds.): WS-FM 2010. LNCS, vol. 6551. Springer, Heidelberg (2011)
2. Christiansen, D.R., Carbone, M., Hildebrandt, T.: Formal semantics and implementation of bpmn 2.0 inclusive gateways. In: Bravetti, Bultan (eds.) [1], pp. 146–160
3. Dumas, M., Grosskopf, A., Hettel, T., Wynn, M.T.: Semantics of Standard Process Models with OR-Joins. In: Meersman, R., Tari, Z. (eds.) OTM 2007, Part I. LNCS, vol. 4803, pp. 41–58. Springer, Heidelberg (2007)
4. OMG. Business process model and notation (BPMN) version 2.0, OMG document number dtc/2010-05-03. Technical report (2010)
5. Polyvyanyy, A., Vanhatalo, J., Völzer, H.: Simplified computation and generalization of the refined process structure tree. In: Bravetti, Bultan (eds.) [1], pp. 25–41
6. Vanhatalo, J., Völzer, H., Koehler, J.: The refined process structure tree. Data Knowl. Eng. 68(9), 793–818 (2009)
7. Vanhatalo, J., Völzer, H., Leymann, F.: Faster and More Focused Control-Flow Analysis for Business Process Models through SESE Decomposition. In: Krämer, B.J., Lin, K.-J., Narasimhan, P. (eds.) ICSOC 2007. LNCS, vol. 4749, pp. 43–55. Springer, Heidelberg (2007)
8. Völzer, H.: A New Semantics for the Inclusive Converging Gateway in Safe Processes. In: Hull, R., Mendling, J., Tai, S. (eds.) BPM 2010. LNCS, vol. 6336, pp. 294–309. Springer, Heidelberg (2010)

Towards Understanding Process Modeling – The Case of the BPM Academic Initiative

Matthias Kunze, Alexander Luebbe, Matthias Weidlich, and Mathias Weske

Hasso Plattner Institute at the University of Potsdam
Prof.-Dr.-Helmert-Str. 2-3
14482 Potsdam, Germany
{matthias.kunze,alexander.luebbe,
matthias.weidlich,mathias.weske}@hpi.uni-potsdam.de

Abstract. Business process models are typically graphs that communicate knowledge about the work performed in organizations. Collections of these models are gathered to analyze and improve the way an organization operates. From a research perspective, these collections tell about modeling styles, the relevance of modeling constructs, and common formal modeling mistakes.

With this paper, we outline a research agenda for investigating the act of process modeling using models of the BPM Academic Initiative. This collection comprises 1903 models, the majority captured in BPMN. The models were created by students from various universities as part of their process modeling education. As such, the collection is particularly suited to investigate modeling practice since it is probably unique in terms of modeling heterogeneity. As a first step, we characterize EPC and BPMN models of the collection using established process model metrics. Further, we investigate the usage of language constructs for these models. Our findings largely confirm the results obtained in prior, smaller studies on modeling in a professional context.

1 Introduction

Business process modeling is at the heart of modern organizations. Process models capture how work is performed in an organization and how business goals are achieved. Large organizations manage literally thousands of process models in process repositories [25]. These models form a knowledge base that is protected since it can be seen as a competitive advantage of an organization. However, analyzing model collections can yield valuable insights for language development and education. Modeling guidelines [21] and best practices for activity labeling [20] have been proposed based on investigations of process model collections.

For instance, deriving the most common set of constructs used in a process modeling language can help to distinguish important from unimportant concepts for process model education. Understanding different modeling styles, their advantages and pitfalls, can be used to propose best practices for modelers. Common errors found in process model repositories can be used for education or for

R. Dijkman, J. Hofstetter, and J. Koehler (Eds.): BPMN 2011, LNBIP 95, pp. 44–58, 2011.

developing more easily comprehensible process modeling languages. Existing research on process model collections has tried to answer these questions partially. However, findings are often limited because the used collections stem from homogeneous groups of modelers. Conclusions drawn have not been validated for a broader public and more research is needed to confirm or revoke existing findings.

In this paper, we outline a research agenda to evaluate a large collection of process models from the BPM Academic Initiative (BPMAI[1]) [13]—a joint venture of academic and industrial partners that aims at providing a mature process modeling platform for researchers and lecturers free of charge. Besides a comprehensive collection of lecture exercises, Signavio[2], industry partner of the BPMAI, offers a set of tools to design and manage business process models online. The modeling languages offered by the BPMAI include, but are not limited to, BPMN [24], EPCs [10,26], and Petri Nets. The BPMAI is used by more than 4500 people from around 450 universities as part of their curriculum. Our investigations are based on anonymized models of a snapshot of the BPMAI collection from early 2011. It comprises 1903 models created by students, of which a majority of 1210 models was created using a BPMN 2.0 compliant shape set; 135 models are EPCs. Note that, due to the applied anonymization, personal and demographic data such as the level of graduation or the study discipline could not be related to the individual models.

The BPMAI collection is particularly suited to investigate modeling practice. In contrast to process model collections that have been around, e.g., the often cited SAP reference model [2], it shows a high heterogeneity along various dimensions. The models have been created by modelers that originate from universities all over the world. Modelers have different educational backgrounds, e.g., in business administration or computer science, capture processes in different natural and modeling languages, and represent operations from different business domains. Hence, empirical insights that are grounded on the BPMAI collection can be assumed to have a high external validity. Results on modeling styles, the relevance of modeling constructs, and common formal modeling mistakes derived from this collection are likely to be independent of any specific context in which process modeling is conducted. This kind of conclusions can hardly be drawn using homogeneous model collections created within a narrow context.

As a first step of a research agenda for the analysis of modeling practice using the BPMAI collection, this paper focuses on characterizing the collection and investigating the language usage for BPMN and EPC models. First, we derive descriptive statistics for the process models using an established set of process model metrics. This provides us with insights on the characteristics of the BPMAI collection. Second, we take up research on the relevance of modeling constructs. We contribute an analysis of the language usage for BPMN models and EPCs. For BPMN, our findings largely confirm the results of prior studies on professional modeling obtained with rather small sets of process models. Further,

[1] http://bpt.hpi.uni-potsdam.de/BPMAcademicInitiative

[2] http://www.signavio.com

we present a comparison of language usage for BPMN and EPC, an aspect that has not been addressed in prior work.

The remainder of this paper is structured as follows. In Section 2, we review related research on process model collections. Then, we characterize the models of the BPMAI collection with process model metrics in Section 3. Section 4 is devoted to the analysis of language usage. We outline further research questions that relate to the BPMAI collection in Section 5, before we conclude in Section 6.

2 Related Work on Process Model Collections

The SAP reference model [2] is probably the most commonly used model collection in research. Published by SAP in 1997, it contains 604 process diagrams of the reference processes implemented in the SAP R/3 system during the mid nineties. These models have been used, e.g., for formal error analysis [18], for process model metrics development [17], extraction of reusable action patterns [27], and label analysis [16]. Approaches towards meaningful process similarity measures leveraged the reference model in conjunction with human assessment for similarity that has been captured in experiments [5,4,11]. Also data structures and algorithms for efficient search in large process model repositories [9,12,30] needed to resort to this collection, as virtually no other available collection contains as many models.

In short, these models became the reference for empirical research on model collections in the last ten years. But this set is not sufficient for research questions on modeling practice. First and foremost, it is limited to 604 models that represent one community of practice. The models have been created by a rather small group of modelers that have a similar background and capture only the processes of a single system. Moreover, the SAP reference model is based on EPCs [10,26] and cannot provide answers to research questions towards other process modeling languages, in particular the Business Process Model and Notation (BPMN) [24].

Existing research on BPMN as a modeling language is limited. The most comprehensive evaluation was performed on a set of 120 models collected from consultants and the web [22]. The focus of this evaluation was on language usage and findings indicated that only a small subset of the BPMN modeling language is used in practice. At that time, it was a significant contribution to the ongoing OMG discussions on a BPMN Core Set. However, the findings resulted from a small collection that was assembled manually by the researchers. The evaluation is limited to the data given, mainly pictures of process models. The authors themselves note that clustering within the set was not possible due to the limited size. To draw conclusions with a high external validity, therefore, requires a large, heterogeneous model collection. In [8], the authors replicated one metric from [22], the syntax complexity graph, based on 166 BPMN models from an online modeling community[3]. The results indicated a quite similar complexity of syntax in both model collections. Unfortunately, further investigation was not

[3] `http://bpmn-community.org`

presented. In Section 4, we use evaluation mechanisms of [22] to investigate and compare the language usage in the BPMAI collection.

In summary, existing work on modeling practice either relied on a rather homogeneous model collection, e.g., the SAP reference model, or used only a small set of process models. In this paper, we build upon prior work towards language usage and apply it to a set of 1345 BPMN and EPC models from the BPMAI collection.

3 Analysis with Process Model Metrics

In this section, we explore the models of the BPMAI collection with an existing set of process model metrics. As such, we derive descriptive statistics to characterize the collection. We first recall the metrics used in our analysis in Section 3.1. Then, Section 3.2 presents the obtained results.

3.1 A Set of Process Model Metrics

In essence, a process model is a graph that consists of nodes and edges. The former represent activities and the latter are used to encode a temporal and logical order of their execution [29]. Depending on the applied process definition language, nodes may also represent means to define control flow routing that goes beyond simple sequencing of activities, i.e., gateways in BPMN and connectors in EPCs. We refer to these nodes as routing nodes.

Against this background, it is not surprising that there have been various efforts to adapt generic structural metrics that are defined for graphs for the use case of process models, e.g., [15,23,1]. Such efforts are particularly inspired by metrics in software engineering or network analysis. Metrics that have their roots in these domains are conceptually close since they are also applied to graphs that define control flow dependencies. See [19] for a discussion of this relation.

For our analysis, we rely on process model metrics that focus on comprehensibility. The process models of the BPMAI collection have been created by students as part of modeling exercises, so that process documentation and communication can be seen as the primary drivers for model creation. Hence, comprehensibility is the major quality criterion for these models. Although we do not assess comprehensibility explicitly, we leverage single metrics for a descriptive characterization of the collection. To this end, we employ the process model metrics presented by Mendling [19]. They integrate many of the aforementioned metrics and provide a multi-dimensional framework for the analysis of single process models. The metrics have been evaluated, again, using the SAP reference model [2] for their ability to predict EPC modeling errors. Nevertheless, the metrics are more universal because they provide a generic characterization of a process model. We focus on the metrics that cover size, density, routing diversity, cyclicity, and concurrency of a process model. For these metrics, we shortly recall their definitions found in [19]. Note that, albeit commonly referred to as metrics, these measures may not be metrics in the mathematical sense.

Size. First and foremost, size of a process model may be assessed using the number of nodes (*NN*). This metric does not differentiate between types of nodes, i.e., activities or routing nodes. In addition, we compute the diameter (*Diam*), which is the longest path between any pair of nodes of a process model.

Density. Metrics for density relate the number of nodes and the number of edges of a process model to each other. In particular, we compute the number of edges divided by the (theoretical) maximum number of edges that may be observed for the number of given nodes (*Dens*). Closely related is the coefficient of connectivity (*CNC*), which is the ratio of edges and nodes. Focusing on the relation of edges and routing nodes, we determine the average and maximum degree of routing (*AvgDR* and *MaxDR*), which capture the average and maximum number of nodes that a routing node is connected to.

Routing Diversity. To take the diversity of routing nodes into account, we compute the routing heterogeneity (*RH*) as the entropy over the observed types of routing nodes. In BPMN, activity nodes disclose implicit routing semantics, referred to as uncontrolled flow [24]. Therefore, BPMN activities have to be treated as exclusive routing nodes for incoming edges, and as concurrent routing nodes for outgoing edges.

Cyclicity. Since cyclic structures influence the comprehensibility of a process model, we also consider cyclicity. It is measured by the ratio of nodes that are part of a control flow cycle to all nodes of the process model (*CYC*).

Concurrency. Comprehensibility is further influenced by the level of concurrency. It is assessed by the token split (*TS*), which is the sum of the outgoing edges of routing nodes that may create concurrent behavior, i.e., AND or inclusive OR semantics, minus one.

3.2 Evaluation of the BPMAI Collection

Using the metrics introduced in the previous section, we investigated all BPMN and EPC models of the BPMAI collection. We implemented the metrics as part of a Java library that also comprises utility classes to access the models of the BPMAI collection[4]. An overview of the obtained results is presented in Table 1. For each of the metrics, the table depicts the average and the maximal value over all BPMN models or EPCs. To further characterize the obtained values, we also list the median along with the upper and lower quartile. Those indicate which values have been obtained for the 25th percentile (Lower Q), the 50th percentile (Median), or the 75th percentile (Upper Q), respectively. In the following, we discuss the results along the aforementioned dimensions of measurement.

It is worth mentioning that whenever we refer to nodes in the context of a metric, we mean a control flow node, i.e., an activity, event, or routing node. In many process model specifications, edges are captured as a pair of connected nodes.

[4] See `http://code.google.com/p/bpmai/`

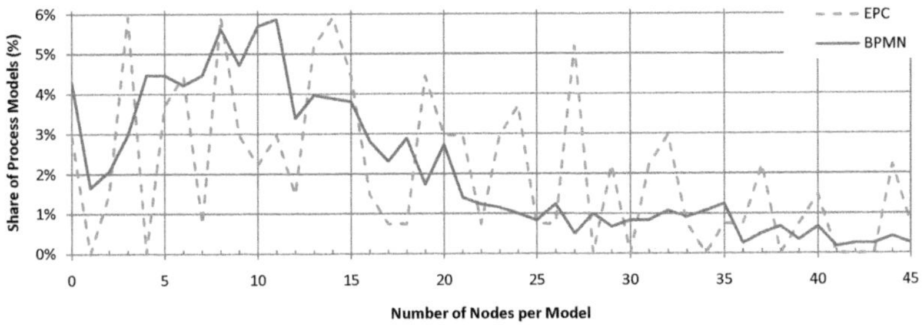

Fig. 1. Share of process models relative to their size, in terms of the number of nodes.

Table 1. Metrics for the BPMN and EPC models of the BPMAI collection

	Size	Density					Rout. Div.	Cyclicity	Concurrency
	NN	*Diam*	*Dens*	*CNC*	*AvgDR*	*MaxDR*	*RH*	*CYC*	*TS*
Results for the BPMN models:									
Avg	15.6	6.52	0.09	0.79	1.15	1.84	0.17	0.03	0.65
Max	156.0	69.0	0.5	1.6	6.0	11.0	0.9	0.75	28.0
Upper Q	19.0	9.0	0.13	1.0	1.4	2.0	0.39	0.0	1.0
Median	11.0	5.0	0.07	0.88	1.23	2.0	0.0	0.0	0.0
Lower Q	7.0	2.0	0.03	0.67	1.0	1.0	0.0	0.0	0.0
Results for the EPC models:									
Avg	19.88	10.84	0.07	0.85	0.9	0.96	0.06	0.03	0.47
Max	123.0	50.0	0.5	1.15	4.0	4.0	1.0	0.57	5.0
Upper Q	27.0	16.25	0.09	1.03	2.0	2.0	0.0	0.0	1.0
Median	15.5	9.0	0.05	0.95	0.0	0.0	0.0	0.0	0.0
Lower Q	8.75	3.0	0.03	0.8	0.0	0.0	0.0	0.0	0.0

However, in the BPMAI modeling tool, cf. Section 1, edges are components of their own and do not need to be connected to nodes. Thus, we only considered those edges that are connecting nodes with both their ends for computing the metrics.

Size. The average size of the models in the BPMAI collection is around 16 nodes (BPMN) and 20 nodes (EPC), respectively. We consider this to be remarkable because we have not applied any filtering to the collection. Our collection includes *all* models created within a certain timeframe, not only those that are intended to be published. Consequently, we assume the collection to include several model stubs that have not been completed by the modeler. Against this background, the observed sizes hint at a considerable complexity of the models with large models comprising more than hundred nodes. Further, the EPCs contain more nodes on average, which may be explained by the bipartite structure of EPC graphs that requires an alternating order of EPC functions and EPC events. This observation is underpinned by the values for the quartiles. 25% of the EPCs have more than 27 nodes compared to 19 nodes for BPMN. The differences in model size between both languages are also illustrated in Fig. 1. It shows that EPCs show a larger variety in their size compared to the BPMN models.

Our assessment of size in terms of the model diameter indicates that we observe longer paths in EPCs compared to BPMN models. For half of the BPMN models, the longest path comprises at most five edges compared to nine edges for EPCs. This difference, nearly twice the value, is larger than what can be expected from the difference in node size between both modeling languages. Finally, the relation between observed node sizes and diameters allows concluding on the complexity of the model structure. A model that is completely sequential shows a diameter that is the number of nodes minus one. As such, our results indicate that the models are not of such a trivial structure.

Density. Since process models are rarely complete graphs (in which each pair of nodes is directly connected), the observed values for the *Dens* metric are rather small. Here, the maximal values of 0.5 are obtained for minimal models that comprise two nodes that are connected by one edge. With the metrics that leverage all nodes and edges, i.e., *Dens* and *CNC*, we obtain similar results for BPMN models and EPCs. Still, there are differences once density is assessed with a focus on routing nodes. The implementation of control flow routing is notably more elaborated for BPMN models compared to EPCs, as more than half of all BPMN models expose a maximum routing degree of greater or equal to 2, whereas this holds only for 25% of EPCs. Note that, values in the *Average* row for *AvgDR* and *MaxDR* of Table 1 result from computing the average over all models, including those that do not comprise any routing at all and thus have a *MaxDR* of 1. Here, the average maximum routing degree of all BPMN models are twice as high as for EPCs. Further, we observe that a routing node in BPMN models is connected to a maximum of 11 nodes, whereas the maximum number of adjacent nodes is four for routing nodes in EPCs. This indicates that the EPCs do not show nodes that fan out a high number of branches, as it can be observed, e.g., in the EPCs of the SAP reference model.

Routing Diversity. A routing heterogeneity of zero indicates that only one type of routing node is used, a value of one means that all types introduced by the language are used in a model. Our results indicate that BPMN models, on average, rely on a larger share of the possible types of routing nodes. This is remarkable since BPMN defines a lot more different types of routing nodes, i.e., types of gateways or tasks with multiple incoming or outgoing control flow edges. Even though there is an EPC that comprises all kinds of routing nodes, at least 75% of the EPCs comprise only a single type of routing node (connector) or no routing nodes at all.

Cyclicity. The models of the BPMAI turn out to be mostly acyclic. There are 178 BPMN models and 18 EPCs that show a control flow cycle. Apparently, this leads to very low values obtained for the cyclicity metric, which assesses the ratio of nodes that are part of a control flow cycle to all nodes. However, there are notable exceptions, such as a BPMN model for which 75% of the nodes are part of a cycle (see Table 1). Note that this metric considers only control flow cycles but neglects high-level constructs, e.g., BPMN loop markers, to express repetitive behavior.

Concurrency. The level of concurrency observed in the model collection is rather low, too. There are 355 BPMN models and 41 EPCs that may show concurrent behavior. Again, we observe models with exceptional behavior. For instance, there is a BPMN model with a token split of 28. Note that such a high token split does not mean that there may be 28 concurrent branches. It may also be caused by several routing nodes, each creating a small number of concurrent branches which are synchronized before further concurrent branches are spawned. Comparing BPMN models and EPCs, we observe that EPCs in the BPMAI collection show less concurrency.

4 Analysis of Language Usage

In their joint paper, zur Muehlen and Recker [22] approached the question "How much language is enough?" and evaluated quantitatively, which of the modeling constructs provided by BPMN [24] are used regularly. We applied their investigations to the BPMAI model collection. In contrast to [22], our evaluation investigates EPCs [10,26] and the more recent version BPMN 2.0 [24]. Again, we implemented the analysis as part of the Java library mentioned in Section 3.2.

4.1 Usage of Process Model Constructs

Process modeling languages usually offer a large set of constructs, each with a unique meaning. While we addressed control flow concepts in Section 3, here we consider the complete spectrum of constructs, BPMN and EPC offer to the modeler, e.g., data, resources, and events. In order to identify, which process model constructs have been used most, we simply counted, for each construct provided by the process modeling language, in how many models it is contained. To further characterize the usage of a modeling language, we also elaborated on the general heterogeneity of process models, i.e., whether process modelers employ the full expressiveness of a language or rather resort to a small share for their models.

In line with [22], we found the BPMN constructs Task, Sequence Flow, Start and End Event to be the most prominent constructs. However, the major share of BPMN models we evaluated also contains Pools, Lanes, and (Databased) Exclusive Gateways, cf. Fig. 2(a). Pools and lanes occur with the same frequency, because, in the BPMAI modeling tool, a pool always contains at least one lane.

A similar usage frequency for corresponding constructs to the above can be observed for EPCs, i.e., Function, Control Flow, and Events occur most frequently, along with the XOR Connector in more than 50% of the models, cf. Fig. 2(b). A Relation is an edge that is supposed to combine a Function or Event with

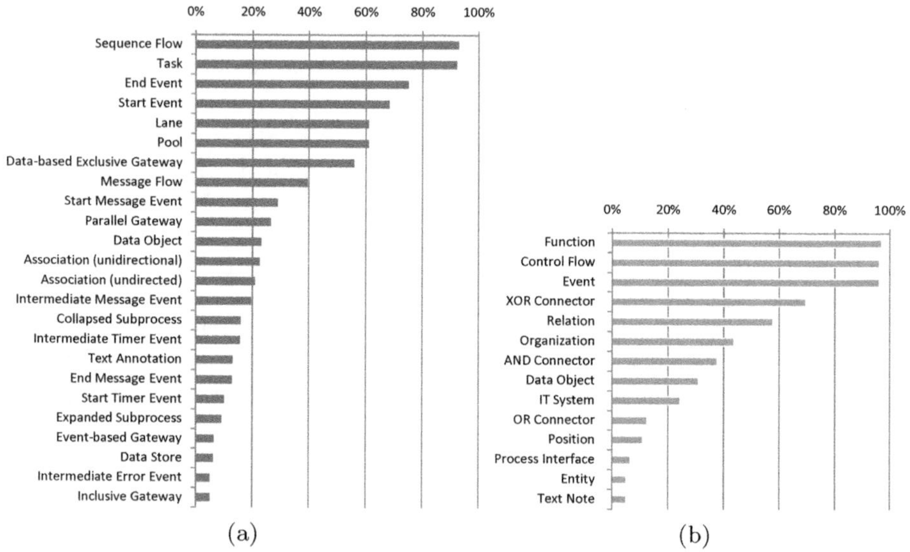

Fig. 2. Usage Frequency of Modeling Constructs from BPMN (a) and EPC (b). (Only constructs with a frequency above 5% are listed.)

an Organization, Position, Data, or System construct. However, as these constructs expose a significantly lower frequency of occurrence, we discovered that the Relation edge has been used falsely in spite of a control flow edge.

The above observation indicates that most process models are very simply, i.e., consist of Tasks and Sequence Flows; EPCs contain almost equally many Events as Functions, as the modeling tool requires Functions and Events to alternate. In practice, we see many of these models that represent business processes in a coarse grain, where tasks describe phases, rather than individual activities. It is also worth noticing that the Parallel Gateway (BPMN) and the AND Connector (EPC) have been used in less than 40% of all models, which suggests that most of the models describe sequential behavior.

In BPMN, we find Message Flow and Message Start Event at high positions, which indicates that modelers actually use the capability of BPMN process diagrams to describe interacting processes of different parties. This concept is not available in EPCs.

To assess the heterogeneity of process models, we examined the number of unique process modeling constructs, i.e., the types of model elements, that have been used in the models of our collection. For BPMN, we differentiate 63 unique modeling constructs, whereas we did not distinguish Interrupting from Non-Interrupting Events, different types of Data Objects, nor different task types, e.g., Human Task, Service Task. For EPC, we distinguished 14 constructs. These numbers are constituted by the modeling tool, cf. Section 1, that has invariably been used to create the models. Fig. 3 shows an overview of the heterogeneity distribution with regard to the number of used modeling constructs.

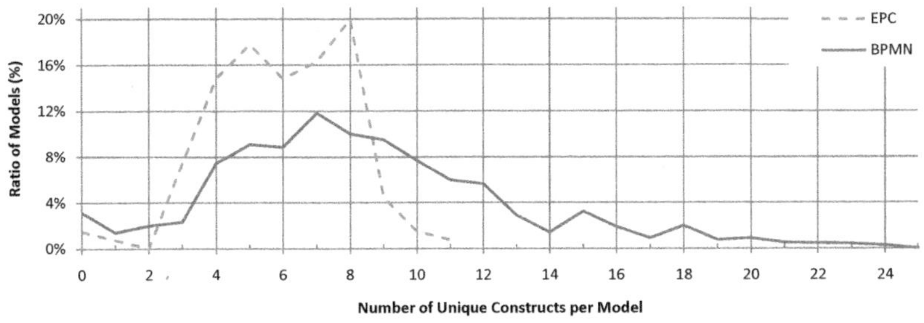

Fig. 3. Frequency of unique constructs per model: BPMN models expose a higher diversity than EPCs

On average, a BPMN model used 8.46 different modeling constructs, compared to 5.97 unique constructs used in EPC models. The most heterogeneous BPMN model used 27 different constructs, compared to 11 in EPCs. For both modeling languages, 75% of all models employed more than 5 distinct constructs. Nevertheless, BPMN models show a considerable higher diversity than EPCs, cf. Fig. 3.

A set of 20 unique constructs of BPMN has been used in less than 10% of all models, but only one has never been used, which is the Event Subprocess. For EPCs there is no single construct that has never been used, and only up to 5 of the 14 unique constructs have been used in less than 10% of all models.

The observations above showed that certain, basic modeling constructs are more prominent than others, which holds true for BPMN and EPC. Also, we discovered that the majority of process models exposes a rather low diversity compared to the expressiveness of the modeling language. This approves the existence of a rather compact vocabulary of modeling constructs used for process modeling.

4.2 Vocabulary of Process Models

In this section, we illustrate subsets of the respective modeling language that are shared among most process models and elaborate on differences of these vocabulary sets between EPC and BPMN.

Thus, we iteratively built sets of the most prominent process model constructs, cf. Fig. 2, and counted those models, which contain the particular set of constructs. Starting from the very core of the constructs used together in the most models, we extended this set stepwise by constructs that would exclude the fewest models. The results are visualized in Fig. 4.

Obviously, the most compact subsets comprise the most prominent modeling constructs. The very core of both modeling languages, BPMN and EPC, is simply made of activities and edges between them, i.e., Tasks and Sequence Flow arcs in BPMN, and Functions, Events, and Control Flow arcs for EPCs, respectively. As mentioned earlier, EPCs require a bipartite structure, which yields the combined usage of Functions and Events.

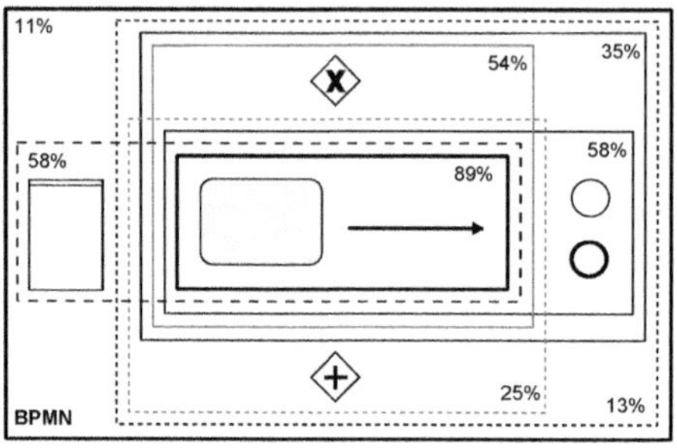

(a)

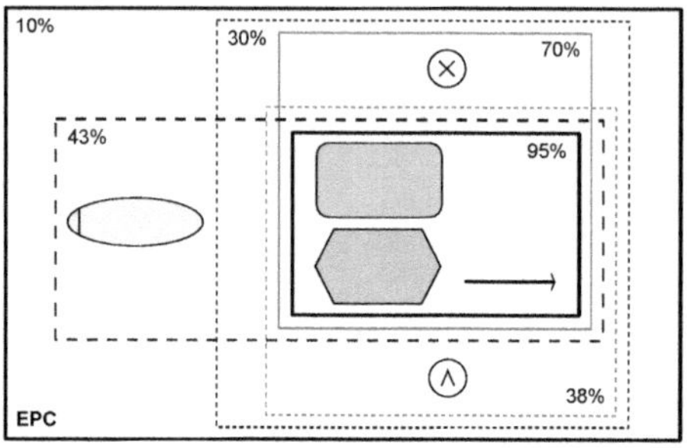

(b)

Fig. 4. Frequency of Used Vocabulary for BPMN (a) and EPC (b) Diagrams

Direct extensions of the core set of BPMN, cf. Fig. 4(a), include Pools and Lanes on the one hand, and Blank Start Events and Blank End Events on the other hand; almost immediately follows the cluster of Tasks, Sequence Flow and Exclusive Gateways—more than half of all models share either of these subsets. Zur Muehlen and Recker [22] recognized the same aspect and attributed it to the two main application areas for BPMN: The usage of Pools and Lanes without advanced control flow constructs is prevalent to express organizational partitioning of a process according to roles and their responsibilities, whereas routing constructs are used separately for a detailed specification of the control flow of a process.

For EPC models, cf. Fig. 4(b), we see a much higher ratio of models that consist of basic control flow and XOR Connectors (70%) than in BPMN, where only 54% of the models share the basic subset with Databased Exclusive Gateways. This is due to the fact that BPMN allows to model choreographies, while EPCs do not.

For both modeling languages, the Parallel Gateway and AND Connector, respectively, follow way behind: Less than half of the models of the above clusters share constructs for parallel routing. The Inclusive Gateway and OR Connector of BPMN and EPC play only a minor role, with 5% in BPMN and 13% in EPCs, respectively.

5 Further Research Agenda

In this paper, we examined aspects of process models and investigated usage of process modeling languages, whereas conclusions and recommendations for practitioners shall be addressed in future work. Accordingly, we plan to direct further research towards communities of practice and model evolution. In this section, we outline a set of research challenges, for which the model collection might be leveraged. The topics are interrelated and can benefit from each other.

Assessing process similarity measures. Many models in the collection have been created based on a limited set of exercises. Thus, we can expect multiple models to represent the same scenario. The BPMAI model collection is unique in this respect and leads to many interesting opportunities. One of them is to review process model similarity measures, cf. [6,4,11], e.g., whether they are able to recover process models sprung from the same scenario.

Identify communities of practice. Based on identification mechanisms, such as similarity measures or the metrics discussed above, we can identify groups of people with similar modeling styles or language sets. A community of practice might result from the education in a university. We might as well be able to identify different communities even within a university. Finally, it might be that a community of practice is established by certain modeling patterns that result from cognitive thinking styles. We can also link that information to people, who have edited the model.

Process model evolution. Based on the versions of each model in the repository, it is possible to trace the process of model creation and get more insights into the act of process modeling. This can also be linked to the number of people that have contributed to the models. On average, models in the BPMAI collection have 4.27 revisions and 20% have 6 or more revisions. One particular BPMN process model even exposed 80 revisions.

Analyze interacting models. The ability to depict processes interacting with other processes is a feature of BPMN but not feasible in EPCs. There exists research on the theoretical aspect of interacting processes, cf. [3]. The BPMAI model collection enables empirical research on the way people use this ability and identify typical mistakes that might result from it. In our snapshot of the BPMAI models, 479 BPMN models contain the Message Flow construct and 458 models consist of more than one Pool, which indicates a reasonably large basis for empirical analysis.

Link modeling errors to process metrics. Analogous to Mendling's [18] evaluation of process model metrics against common EPC modeling errors, this can be done for BPMN and other process modeling languages as well. As a result, one can obtain a weighted set of metrics that predict whether a model might have an error. Comparing this list to the findings by Mendling might result in the identification of a core set of model metrics that are relevant to avoid modeling mistakes. We have to stress, though, that all models where created with a professional tool which excludes many syntactic mistakes by design.

Obtain complex models for understandability tests. Ongoing research on process model understandability [14] and complexity metrics [7] can leverage the models in this sample set. Typically, the models used in those tests have been designed by the researchers because they need to fulfill very specific properties. With the large sample set given and the strong diversity in the collection, it should be possible to identify and reuse models from this collection for empirical research, enabling a higher external validity for the experiments.

Linguistic Analysis. One of the major challenges for recent research topics in BPM, e.g., to compute the similarity of business processes [6,4,11] or to manage consistency between processes [28], is the alignment of process models, i.e., the identification of corresponding nodes in two or more business processes. The main obstacle is the heterogeneity of used terms in process model inscriptions, to which many solutions, based on syntactic, semantic, and linguistic approaches, have been proposed. The BPMAI models show over 25 natural languages, English and German being the most commonly used. This offers a source to train algorithms towards aligning process models, as well as to evaluate other means of process modeling, e.g., the usage of a limited vocabulary for labeling.

This list of research opportunities is not a closed set. We hope to collect more ideas as part of the discussion that is triggered with this paper. We do not claim to tackle all aspects in our future research. Instead we want to inspire researchers to leverage the potential given in such a model collection.

6 Conclusion

In this paper, we laid the foundations for research on modeling practice using a particularly suited model collection, the BPMAI collection. This collection allows for investigating modeling practice in a unique setting. The models show a high heterogeneity with respect to the educational backgrounds of the modelers, the used natural and modeling languages, and the considered business domains. Hence, empirical insights that are derived using the BPMAI collection can be assumed to have a high external validity.

While the process models are well suited for many use cases towards understanding process models, they are limited by few aspects. All models have been created by academics, i.e., mostly by students as part of course assignments. While this leads to a high heterogeneity with regards to modeling practice, usage of process model constructs, and terminology, the models may expose certain characteristics, e.g., modeling style, that is attributed to their lecturers. Also, every model was created with the same tool, the Signavio process model editor, which is aware of syntax rules of modeling language specifications, and thus prevents many modeling mistakes. Consequences of this are, e.g., the bipartite occurrence of Functions and Events in EPCs and the co-occurrence of Pools and Lanes in BPMN.

This paper first presented a characterization of the BPMN models and EPCs of the collection, a set of 1345 models, using several established process model metrics. In this data set, BPMN models expose a higher diversity than EPCs in terms of construct heterogeneity, i.e., the number of unique modeling constructs. This is due to the greater and more detailed expressiveness of the BPMN language compared to EPCs, which is also leveraged in process models. At the same time, the overall heterogeneity of process models is rather low among both modeling languages, which suggests that most models are kept concise.

The investigation of language usage in these models showed results in line with [22]. Most modelers resort to a rather limited set of vocabulary, with simple activity sequences at the very core. Remarkably, the vocabulary subsets of BPMN and EPC are fairly similar. It suggests a true core set of relevant modeling concepts.

We concluded our work with an outline of a research agenda that uses the models of the BPMAI collection. These include more topics towards understanding process modeling, for example, through model evolution, communities of practice, assessing modeling mistakes, but also towards other opportunities that rely on a heterogeneous model collection, e.g., similarity and linguistic analysis of process models.

Acknowledgements. We are grateful to Signavio, in particular Gero Decker, for providing access to a snapshot of anonymized models from the BPM Academic Initiative. We also thank Katrin Honauer and Philipp Berger who supported us in the implementation of the experiments.

References

1. Cardoso, J.: Business Process Control-Flow Complexity: Metric, Evaluation, and Validation. Int. J. Web Service Res. 5(2), 49–76 (2008)
2. Curran, T., Keller, G., Ladd, A.: SAP R/3 Business Blueprint: Understanding the Business Process Reference Model. Prentice-Hall, Inc., Upper Saddle River (1997)
3. Decker, G.: Design and Analysis of Process Choreographies. PhD thesis, Hasso Plattner Institut an der Universität Potsdam (2009)
4. Dijkman, R., Dumas, M., van Dongen, B., Käärik, R., Mendling, J.: Similarity of Business Process Models: Metrics and Evaluation. Information Systems 36(2), 498–516 (2011)
5. Dijkman, R., Dumas, M., García-Bañuelos, L.: Graph Matching Algorithms for Business Process Model Similarity Search. In: Dayal, U., Eder, J., Koehler, J., Reijers, H.A. (eds.) BPM 2009. LNCS, vol. 5701, pp. 48–63. Springer, Heidelberg (2009)
6. Dumas, M., García-Bañuelos, L., Dijkman, R.M.: Similarity Search of Business Process Models. IEEE Data Eng. Bull. 32(3), 23–28 (2009)
7. Figl, K., Laue, R.: Cognitive Complexity in Business Process Modeling. In: Mouratidis, H., Rolland, C. (eds.) CAiSE 2011. LNCS, vol. 6741, pp. 452–466. Springer, Heidelberg (2011)
8. Grosskopf, A., Brunnert, J., Wehrmeyer, S., Weske, M.: BPMNCommunity.org: A Forum for Process Modeling Practitioners – A Data Repository for Empirical BPM Research. In: Rinderle-Ma, S., Sadiq, S., Leymann, F. (eds.) BPM 2009. LNBIP, vol. 43, pp. 525–528. Springer, Heidelberg (2010)
9. Jin, T., Wang, J., Wu, N., La Rosa, M., ter Hofstede, A.H.M.: Efficient and Accurate Retrieval of Business Process Models through Indexing - (Short Paper). In: Meersman, R., Dillon, T.S., Herrero, P. (eds.) OTM 2010. LNCS, vol. 6426, pp. 402–409. Springer, Heidelberg (2010)
10. Keller, G., Nüttgens, M., Scheer, A.-W.: Semantische Prozessmodellierung auf der Grundlage Ereignisgesteuerter Prozessketten (EPK) (1992)

11. Kunze, M., Weidlich, M., Weske, M.: Behavioral Similarity – A Proper Metric. In: Rinderle-Ma, S., Toumani, F., Wolf, K. (eds.) BPM 2011. LNCS, vol. 6896, pp. 166–181. Springer, Heidelberg (2011)
12. Kunze, M., Weske, M.: Metric Trees for Efficient Similarity Search in Large Process Model Repositories. In: zur Muehlen, M., Su, J. (eds.) BPM Workshops. LNBIP, vol. 66, pp. 535–546. Springer, Heidelberg (2011)
13. Kunze, M., Weske, M.: Signavio-Oryx Academic Initiative. In: BPM 2010 Demonstration Track. CEUR, vol. 615 (2010)
14. Laue, R., Gadatsch, A.: Measuring the Understandability of Business Process Models – Are We Asking the Right Questions. In: BPD 2010 (2010)
15. Lee, G.S., Yoon, J.-M.: An Empirical Study on the Complexity Metrics of Petri Nets. Microelectronics and Reliability 32(3), 323–329 (1992)
16. Leopold, H., Mendling, J., Reijers, H.A.: On the Automatic Labeling of Process Models. In: Mouratidis, H., Rolland, C. (eds.) CAiSE 2011. LNCS, vol. 6741, pp. 512–520. Springer, Heidelberg (2011)
17. Mendling, J.: Testing Density as a Complexity Metric for EPCs. In: German EPC Workshop on Density of Process Models (2006)
18. Mendling, J.: Detection and Prediction of Errors in EPC Business Process Models. PhD thesis (2007)
19. Mendling, J.: Metrics for Process Models: Empirical Foundations of Verification, Error Prediction, and Guidelines for Correctness. Springer, Heidelberg (2008)
20. Mendling, J., Reijers, H.A., Recker, J.: Activity Labeling in Process Modeling: Empirical Insights and Recommendations. Inf. Syst. 35(4), 467–482 (2010)
21. Mendling, J., Reijers, H.A., van der Aalst, W.M.P.: Seven Process Modeling Guidelines (7PMG). Information & Software Technology 52(2), 127–136 (2010)
22. zur Muehlen, M., Recker, J.: How Much Language Is Enough? Theoretical and Practical Use of the Business Process Modeling Notation. In: Bellahsène, Z., Léonard, M. (eds.) CAiSE 2008. LNCS, vol. 5074, pp. 465–479. Springer, Heidelberg (2008)
23. Nissen, M.E.: Valuing it Through Virtual Process Measurement. In: ICIS, pp. 309–323 (1994)
24. Object Management Group. Business Process Model and Notation (BPMN) Specification, Version 2.0
25. Rosemann, M.: Potential Pitfalls of Process Modeling: Part A. Business Process Management Journal 12(2), 249–254 (2006)
26. Scheer, A.W., Thomas, O., Adam, O.: Process Modeling Using Event-driven Process Chains (2005)
27. Smirnov, S., Weidlich, M., Mendling, J., Weske, M.: Action Patterns in Business Process Models. In: Baresi, L., Chi, C.-H., Suzuki, J. (eds.) ICSOC-ServiceWave 2009. LNCS, vol. 5900, pp. 115–129. Springer, Heidelberg (2009)
28. Weidlich, M., Mendling, J., Weske, M.: Efficient Consistency Measurement based on Behavioural Profiles of Process Models. IEEE TSE 37(3), 410–429 (2011)
29. Weske, M.: Business Process Management: Concepts, Languages, Architectures. Springer, Heidelberg (2007)
30. Yan, Z., Dijkman, R., Grefen, P.: Fast Business Process Similarity Search with Feature-Based Similarity Estimation. In: Meersman, R., Dillon, T.S., Herrero, P. (eds.) OTM 2010. LNCS, vol. 6426, pp. 60–77. Springer, Heidelberg (2010)

Extending BPMN 2.0: Method and Tool Support

Luis Jesús Ramón Stroppi[1], Omar Chiotti[2], and Pablo David Villarreal[1]

[1] CIDISI, National Technological University Santa Fe Faculty, Lavaise 610, S3004EWB, Santa Fe, Argentina
{lstroppi,pvillarr}@frsf.utn.edu.ar
[2] INGAR-CONICET, Avellaneda 3657, S3002GJC, Santa Fe, Argentina
chiotti@santafe-conicet.gov.ar

Abstract. There are two major pitfalls in the development of extensions to the BPMN 2.0 metamodel. First, there is a lack of methodological guides considering the extensibility approach supported by the extension mechanism of the language. Second, BPMN does not provide any graphical notation for the representation of extensions. This work proposes a method based on Model-Driven Architecture for the development of extensions to the BPMN 2.0 metamodel. It enables the conceptual modeling of extensions by using UML, their graphical representation in terms of the BPMN extension mechanism, and their transformation into XML Schema documents that can be processed by BPMN tools. A tool supporting the proposed method is also presented.

Keywords: BPMN, Extension Mechanism, Method, Model-Driven Architecture.

1 Introduction

Business Process Model and Notation (BPMN) [1] is a broadly accepted language providing a metamodel and a notation to define and visualize business process models. BPMN 2.0 also provides an extension mechanism that allows attaching additional attributes and elements to its original elements.

Extension mechanisms allow representing domain-specific concepts in general purpose modeling languages. They can also be used to add information needed to transform models into platform-specific models or code [2]. A well-known example of these mechanisms is UML Profiles [3,4] that enables the approach of extension by specialization. Unlike this, BPMN enables the approach of extension by addition which consists of attaching new domain-specific elements to the predefined elements of the language [5].

There are two major pitfalls in the development of extensions to the BPMN 2.0 metamodel. First, there is a lack of methodological guides supporting the creation of BPMN extensions considering the extensibility approach provided by the language. Second, the BPMN specification [1] does not provide any graphical notation for the representation of extensions. It includes a sample extension represented with XML Schema. XML Schema allows defining extensions that can be processed by BPMN tools. However, it does not provide an effective way for

R. Dijkman, J. Hofstetter, and J. Koehler (Eds.): BPMN 2011, LNBIP 95, pp. 59–73, 2011.

visualizing the structure of extensions and exposes designers to low level implementation issues [6]. This fact hinders conceptualizing and validating extensions, especially when working with non-technical people like domain experts.

The goal of this work is to propose a method based on Model-Driven Architecture (MDA) for the development of extensions to the BPMN 2.0 metamodel enabling their conceptualization by using UML, their graphical representation in terms of the BPMN extension mechanism, and their transformation into XML Schema documents that can be processed by BPMN tools. This work also presents a tool supporting the proposed method.

This work is structured as follows. Section 2 describes the BPMN extension mechanism. Section 3 presents the proposed method for the development of BPMN extensions. Section 4 presents the tool developed to support the method. Section 5 discusses related work. Finally, section 6 presents the conclusions.

2 The BPMN Extension Mechanism

The BPMN metamodel [1] can be extended by adding new attributes and elements to its predefined elements. This is supported by an extension mechanism consisting of four elements. *ExtensionDefinition* groups new attributes to be added to original BPMN elements under a new concept name. *ExtensionAttributeDefinition* represents an attribute defined for an *ExtensionDefinition* element. *ExtensionAttributeValue* stores the value assigned to an extension attribute of a BPMN element. *Extension* binds/imports an *ExtensionDefinition* element to a BPMN model *Definition.*

The BPMN 2 metamodel [1] was specified using the Meta Object Facility (MOF). Thus, it is possible to position it within the layer architecture of OMG [3] (see Figure 1). The Core package of the UML Infrastructure defines the modeling constructs used to create metamodels. The Profiles package defines mechanisms to customize metamodels defined using the Core package concepts. MOF provides the mechanisms for creating instances of the Core package metaclasses.

Both the BPMN and UML metamodels have been specified using MOF. Notice that a profile could be applied to customize the BPMN metamodel. However, this would force the tools to exchange process models by using XMI while BPMN defines its own extension mechanism and interchange format.

The BPMN extension mechanism is part of the BPMN metamodel. It supports the approach of extension by addition. It allows defining groups of attributes and

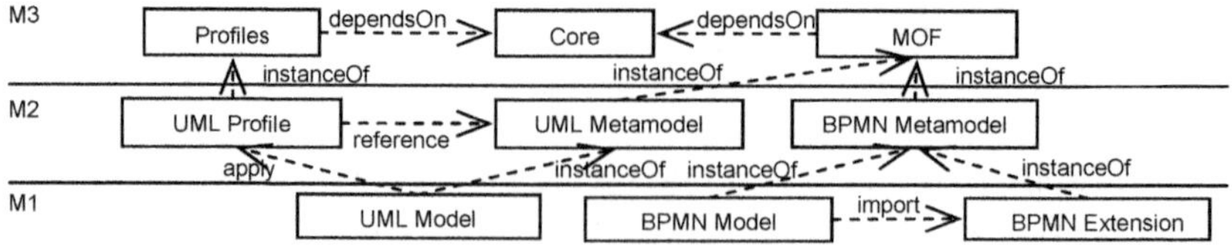

Fig. 1. Position of BPMN within the OMG layer architecture

elements which are attached to the standard BPMN elements. BPMN models using extensions keep interchangeable as the structure of the original elements is not modified. The new attributes specified in a BPMN *ExtensionDefinition* element and bound to a model definition by an *Extension* element can be used by any element within that model being an instance of a subclass of *BaseElement*. This is because the BPMN extension mechanism does not provide any way to specify what element of the language is being extended. That would require defining the extension mechanism at a higher level of abstraction than the BPMN elements to be extended, as it is the case of Profiles.

The BPMN specification provides two representations of its elements. The first one is a MOF metamodel describing the language concepts. The second one is a set of XML Schema documents specifying the interchange format for BPMN models. As MOF has its own interchange format called XML Metadata Interchange (XMI), OMG also provides a set of XSL transformations aimed to convert BPMN models into either the XML Schema or XMI interchange formats. However, in the particular case of the extension mechanism, the MOF and XML Schema representations of BPMN are not equivalent (see Figure 2). Moreover, the aforementioned XSL transformations does not allow converting BPMN extension definitions from one interchange format to the other properly.

The XML Schema representation of BPMN does not include the *ExtensionDefinition*, *ExtensionAttributeDefinition* and *ExtensionAttributeValue* elements defined in the MOF representation. When using the XML Schema representation, the structure of the extensions is represented in separate XML Schema documents which are imported by BPMN model definitions. Figure 3 illustrates the way a BPMN extension is defined using the XML Schema representation and how it is applicated to a BPMN model. The labels link the elements of the documents to the concepts of the MOF representation of BPMN.

Figure 3a shows an XML Schema document defining a BPMN extension. The *ExtensionDefinition* MOF element matches with an <xsd:group> element. The

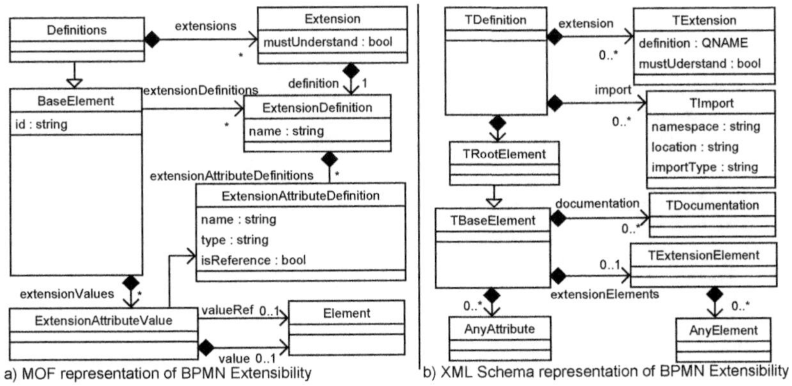

Fig. 2. MOF and XML Schema Representations of the BPMN Extension Mechanism

ExtensionAttributeDefinition element corresponds with <xsd:element> elements nested within the <xsd:group> element. Figure 3b shows an XML document describing a BPMN model applying the defined extension. The *ExtensionAttributeValue* element of the MOF representation of BPMN matches with the elements nested within the <extensionElements> element. The MOF representation of BPMN does not provide any element to define the structure of the types of attribute specified by *ExtensionAttributeDefinition* elements. These types are described in XML Schema by using <xsd:simpleType> or <xsd:complexType> elements. The XML Schema representation of BPMN allows the use of these externally defined types as it specifies that <extensionElements> can contain any element, even defined in other namespace.

```
<?xml version="1.0" encoding="UTF-8"?>
<xsd:schema xmlns:xsd="http://www.w3.org/2001/XMLSchema" xmlns="http://www.cidisi.org/workDistribution"
targetNamespace="http://www.cidisi.org/workDistribution"
xmlns:bpmn="http://www.omg.org/spec/BPMN/20100524/MODEL">
<xsd:import namespace="http://www.omg.org/spec/BPMN/20100524/MODEL" schemaLocation="BPMN20.xsd"/>
<xsd:group name="DistributionStrategy">
  <xsd:sequence>                                   ExtensionAttributeDefinition
    <xsd:element name="distributionAgent" type="tAgentType" minOccurs="1" maxOccurs="1"/>
    <xsd:element name="distributionTrigger" type="xsd:QName" minOccurs="0" maxOccurs="1"/>
    <xsd:element name="taskPrivileges" type="tTaskPrivilege" minOccurs="1" maxOccurs="unbounded"/>
  </xsd:sequence>
</xsd:group>
<xsd:complexType name="tTaskPrivilege" abstract="false">            ExtensionDefinition
    <xsd:attribute name="name" type="xsd:string" />
    <xsd:attribute name="granted" type="xsd:boolean" />
</xsd:complexType>
<xsd:simpleType name="tAgentType">
  <xsd:restriction base="xsd:string">
    <xsd:enumeration value="SYSTEM" />
    <xsd:enumeration value="ADMINISTRATOR" />
  </xsd:restriction>
</xsd:simpleType>
</xsd:schema>                      a) XML Schema Extension Definition Document
```

```
<?xml version="1.0" encoding="UTF-8"?>
<definitions id="ID_1" xmlns="http://www.omg.org/spec/BPMN/20100524/MODEL"
xmlns:xsi="http://www.w3.org/2001/XMLSchema-instance" xmlns:wd="http://www.cidisi.org/workDistribution"
xsi:schemaLocation="http://www.omg.org/spec/BPMN/20100524/MODEL BPMN20.xsd">
    <import location="wd.xsd" namespace="http://www.cidisi.org/workDistribution"
     importType="http://www.w3.org/2001/XMLSchema" />
    <extension mustUnderstand="true" definition="wd:DistributionStrategy" />
    <userTask name="Retrieve Customer Record" id="ID_2">
      <extensionElements>
        <wd:distributionAgent>SYSTEM</wd:distributionAgent>
        <wd:distributionTrigger>ID_3</wd:distributionTrigger>
        <wd:taskPrivileges name="start" granted="true" />
        <wd:taskPrivileges name="complete" granted="true" />
      </extensionElements>          ExtensionAttributeValue
    </userTask>
    <boundaryEvent id="ID_3" attachedTo="ID_2" cancelActivity="false">...</boundaryEvent>
</definitions>                            b) XML BPMN Model Definition Document
```

Fig. 3. An Example of a BPMN Extension and its Application in a BPMN Model

3 MDA-Based Method for the Development of BPMN Extensions

This section presents an MDA-based method for the development of extensions to the BPMN metamodel. It enables defining the conceptual model of an extension, its graphical representation in terms of the BPMN extension mechanism and its transformation into an XML Schema document that can be processed by compliant BPMN tools. The method consists of the steps listed below.

1. Definition of a Conceptual Domain Model of the Extension by using UML.
2. Definition of a BPMN plus Extensions (BPMN+X) model describing an extension in terms of the BPMN extension mechanism.
3. Transformation of the BPMN+X model into an XML Schema Extension Definition Model.
4. Transformation of the XML Schema Extension Definition Model into an XML Schema Extension Definition Document.

This method adopts the approach taken in works providing methodological guides for the development of UML Profiles [5,7,8]. They separate the definition of the conceptual domain model of the extension from its representation through the mechanism provided by the language being extended, as it is specified in the first and second steps of the method.

3.1 Definition of a Conceptual Domain Model of the Extension by Using UML

The first step of the method consists of defining a Conceptual Domain Model of the Extension (CDME) describing the concepts of the domain to be represented in extended BPMN models and their relationships with the concepts of the BPMN metamodel. The CDME is specified in a UML class model, disregarding any restriction imposed by the BPMN Extension Mechanism.

The concepts of a CDME are preliminarily characterized as *BPMN Concepts* or as *Extension Concepts*. The *BPMN Concepts* are those that match with some concept of the BPMN metamodel. The *Extension Concepts* are those defined in the domain of the extension.

As an example, consider an extension to the *UserTask* BPMN element. It is a kind of *Task* representing a step of a process where a human resource perform some work with the aid of a software application. The aim of the extension is to provide a work distribution strategy that is complementary to the ResourceRole assignment provided by BPMN. This strategy enables the specification of more details about the way the work of a task can be distributed to human resources involved in a process. The extension defines three new properties for the *UserTask* element. The first one is *distributionAgent* that indicates whether the work of the task is distributed by the system or by the administrator of the process. The second one is *distributionTrigger* that allows specifying an event causing the start of the work distribution procedure. The last one is *taskPrivileges* that enables the specification of the set of privileges granted to the resources in order to complete the work of the task. Figure 4 shows three alternative CDMEs that can be the result of a first attempt of conceptualizing the above extension. The differences between them and the way they can be represented as a BPMN extension are studied in the following section. In the example, the *BPMN Concepts* (shown in gray) are Task, UserTask and BoundaryEvent; while the *Extension Concepts* (shown in white) are DistributionStrategy, TaskWithDistributionStrategy, AgentType and TaskPrivilege.

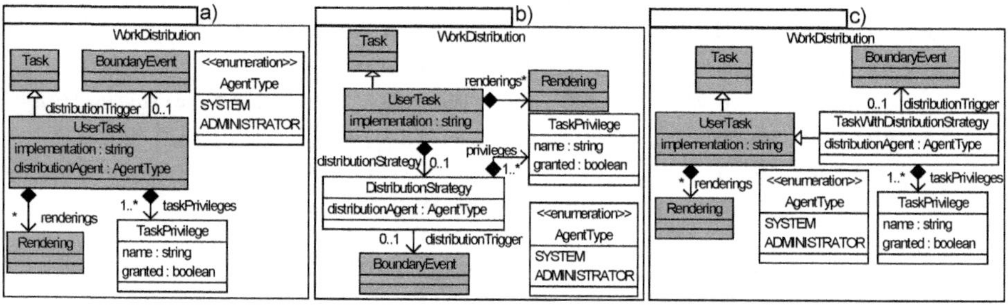

Fig. 4. Alternative Conceptual Domain Models of an Extension

3.2 Definition of a BPMN Plus Extensions Model

The second step is accomplished by developing a BPMN+X model based on the CDME resulting of the first step. BPMN+X is a language developed in this work as a UML profile. Thus, it can be supported by existing UML tools. Another benefit of defining BPMN+X as a profile is that its learning curve will be more effective as UML is a popular modeling language. The semantics and the abstract syntax of the BPMN+X elements are based on the specification of the BPMN extension mechanism [1]. Figure 5 shows the stereotypes of the BPMN+X profile and the UML metaclasses that it specializes.

ExtensionModel is the topmost container of all the elements defining a BPMN extension. *BPMNElement* allows representing an original element of the BPMN metamodel. *BPMNEnum* and *ExtensionEnum* enable representing sets of literals defined in the BPMN metamodel and in the extension model, respectively. *ExtensionElement* allows representing a new element in the extension model

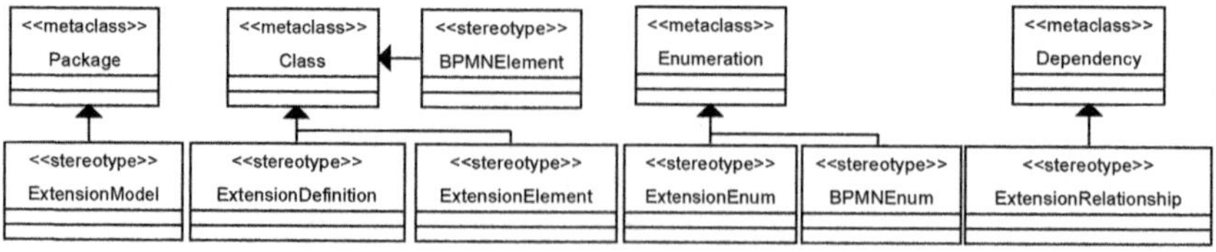

Fig. 5. BPMN+X UML Profile for BPMN extension models

which is not defined in the BPMN metamodel. *ExtensionDefinition* allows specifying a named group of attributes which are jointly added to the original BPMN elements. *ExtensionDefinition* has the same meaning than the ExtensionDefinition element of the BPMN metamodel. The semantics defined by the ExtensionAttributeDefinition element of the BPMN metamodel is captured by the Property metaclass of the UML metamodel. Thus, ExtensionAttributeDefinition is represented in BPMN+X models by UML properties, either owned by the ExtensionDefinition elements or navigable from them through associations. The properties of *ExtensionDefinition* and *ExtensionElement* elements can be typed as a *BPMNElement*, *ExtensionElement*, *BPMNEnum*, *ExtensionEnum* or UML primitive type. Finally, *ExtensionRelationship* specifies a conceptual link between a *BPMNElement* and an *ExtensionDefinition* element aimed to extend it. The BPMN extension mechanism cannot express the BPMN element to be extended by an extension definition. Thus, the definition of an *ExtensionRelationship* does not produce any effect in the resulting BPMN extension. *ExtensionRelationship* is provided to help conceptualizing extensions since extensions are generally defined to customize certain elements of the BPMN metamodel.

Figure 6 shows a set of OCL constraints specified as part of the BPMN+X profile. These constraints ensure that the extensions defined by using BPMN+X are aligned with the BPMN specification. The details about each of the constraints have been omitted for reasons of sapce.

The rest of this section describes a procedure to define a BPMN+X model based on a CDME. It provides a set of rules which help finding a suitable way to represent CDME concepts as BPMN+X elements. The procedure is robust

```
context ExtensionModel
inv define_extensions:self.base_Package.packagedElement->exists(c | not
c.extension_ExtensionDefinition.oclIsUndefined())
inv only_has_stereotyped_classes: self.base_Package.packagedElement-
>forAll(p | p.oclIsTypeOf(uml::Class) implies not (
  p.extension_ExtensionDefinition.oclIsUndefined() and
  p.extension_BPMNElement.oclIsUndefined() and
  p.extension_BPMNElement.oclIsUndefined()))
inv only_has_stereotyped_enumerations: self.base_Package.packagedElement-
>forAll(p | p.oclIsTypeOf(uml::Enumeration) implies not (
  p.extension_ExtensionEnum.oclIsUndefined() and
  p.extension_BPMNEnum.oclIsUndefined()))
inv not_navigable_reference_extension_definition_elements:
self.base_Package.packagedElement->select(o | o.oclIsTypeOf(uml::Association))-
>forAll(a | a.oclAsType(uml::Association).navigableOwnedEnd->forAll(e |
 e.type.extension_ExtensionDefinition.oclIsUndefined()))
inv not_reference_extension_definition_element:
self.base_Package.packagedElement->select(o | o.oclIsTypeOf(uml::Association))-
>forAll(a | a.oclAsType(uml::Association).navigableOwnedEnd->isEmpty() implies
  a.oclAsType(uml::Association).relatedElement->forAll(c |
  c.extension_ExtensionDefinition.oclIsUndefined()))
inv bpmn_elements_only_reference_bpmn_elements:
self.base_Package.packagedElement->select(o | o.oclIsTypeOf(uml::Association))-
>forAll(a | a.oclAsType(uml::Association).relatedElement->exists(c | not
  c.extension_BPMNElement.oclIsUndefined()) implies
  a.oclAsType(uml::Association).navigableOwnedEnd->forAll(e|
   not e.type.extension_BPMNElement.oclIsUndefined()) or
  ( a.oclAsType(uml::Association).navigableOwnedEnd->isEmpty() and
  a.oclAsType(uml::Association).relatedElement->forAll(c | not
   c.extension_BPMNElement.oclIsUndefined())))
```

```
inv only_single_inheritance: self.base_Package.packagedElement-
>forAll(p | p.oclIsTypeOf(uml::Class) implies
  p.oclAsType(uml::Class).generalization->size() <= 1)
inv no_extension_definition_attributes:
self.base_Package.packagedElement->forAll(p | p.oclIsTypeOf(uml::Class)
implies p.oclAsType(uml::Class).attribute->forAll(a |
a.type.extension_ExtensionDefinition.oclIsUndefined()))
context ExtensionDefinition
inv only_inherits_from_extension_definitions: self.base_Class.allParents()-
>forAll(c | not c.extension_ExtensionDefinition.oclIsUndefined())
inv is_abstract: self.base_Class.isAbstract = true
context ExtensionElement:
inv only_inherits_from_extension_elements:self.base_Class.allParents()-
>forAll(c | not c.extension_BPMNElement.oclIsUndefined())
context BPMNElement
inv only_inherits_from_bpmn_elements: self.base_Class.allParents()-
>forAll(c | not c.extension_BPMNElement.oclIsUndefined())
inv only_reference_bpmn_elements:
self.base_Class.ownedAttribute->select(at | at.type.oclIsTypeOf(uml::Class))-
>forAll(a | not a.type.extension_BPMNElement.oclIsUndefined())
context ExtensionRelationship
inv client_must_be_bpmn_element: self.base_Dependency.client->forAll(c |
  not c.extension_BPMNElement.oclIsUndefined())
inv supplier_must_be_extension_definition:
self.base_Dependency.supplier->forAll(s | not
s.extension_ExtensionDefinition.oclIsUndefined())
```

Fig. 6. OCL Constraints of the BPMN+X UML Profile

as it allows producing a unique BPMN+X model from distinct CDMEs representing an extension by applying different rules. This is shown by obtaining the BPMN+X model of Figure 7 from the different CDMEs of Figure 4. The procedure has two stages. The first one consists of creating and populating the BPMN+X model with elements representing the *BPMN Concepts* of the CDME. The second one consists of applying rules to derive BPMN+X elements representing *Extension Concepts*. The rules are based on analysis of the properties and generalization relationships of the CDME classes. The procedure is as follows.

In the first stage, create an ExtensionModel named as the CDME and populate it with one BPMNElement and one BPMNEnum for each class and enumeration of the CDME, respectively characterized as *BPMN Concept*. Then, add an ExtensionEnum for each enumeration characterized as *Extension Concept*.

In the second stage, apply the rules for representing the *Extension Concepts* in the BPMN+X model. Let c be a class of the CDME, and let p be a property of type t that is either an attribute of c or that is navigable from c through an association to t. The representation of c, p, and t in the BPMN+X model depends on whether c is characterized as a *BPMN Concept* or as an *Extension Concept*; whether p is an original or a new property of c; and whether t is a *BPMN Concept*, an *Extension Concept*, or a *Data Type*. A property p of a *BPMN Concept* c is considered as original when there is a property matching p for the class matching c in the BPMN metamodel. Else, p is considered as a new property. Finally, t is a *Data Type* when it is a primitive type or an enumeration. Table 1 summarizes the rules for the representation of a CDME property p in a BPMN+X model, based on these parameters. The representation of c and t is then inferred founded on the representation of p.

Rule 1 applies when p is an original property of a *BPMN Concept*. If t is a Data Type (rule 1a), p is represented as an attribute of the BPMNElement matching c in the BPMN+X model. Else, if t is a BPMN Concept (rule 1b), p is represented as an association navigable from the BPMNElement matching c to the BPMNElement matching t in the BPMN+X model. These situations are illustrated in the BPMN+X model of Figure 7 by the representation of the *implementation* and *renderings* properties defined in the CDMEs of Figure 4.

Rule 2 is valid when p is a new property of a *BPMN Concept*. In this case, p specifies an ExtensionAttributeDefinition that BPMN+X allows defining as a property of an ExtensionDefinition element. Thus, an ExtensionDefinition

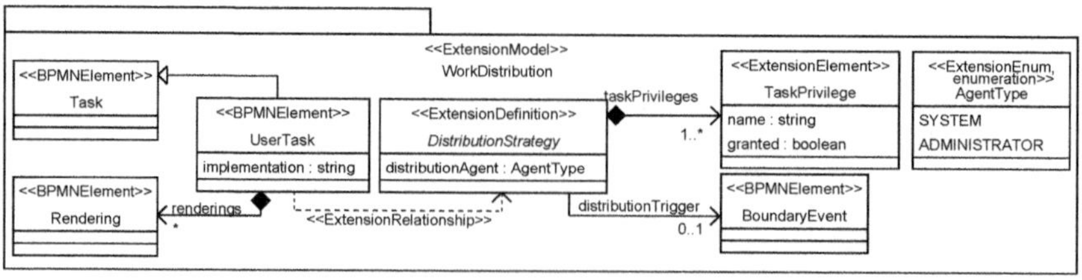

Fig. 7. Example of a BPMN+X model

element related with the BPMNElement matching c by an ExtensionRelationship has first to be created with a meaningful name. After that, if t is a Data Type (rule 2a), p is specified as an attribute of the created ExtensionDefinition element. If t is a *BPMN Concept* (rule 2b), p is specified as an association navigable from the created ExtensionDefinition element to the BPMNElement matching t in the BPMN+X model. Rule 2c is suitable when t is a concrete *Extension Concept* in the sense that t defines a new kind of element to be instantiated in an extended BPMN model. In such case, t is an ExtensionElement and p is an ExtensionAttributeDefinition represented as an association navigable from the created ExtensionDefinition to the ExtensionElement matching t in the BPMN+X model. Rules 2a, 2b and 2c, are illustrated in the BPMN+X model of Figure 7 by the representation of the *distributionAgent*, *distributionTrigger* and *taskPrivileges* properties, respectively defined in the CDME of Figure 4a.

Rule 3 is applicable when p is a new property of a *BPMN Concept* and t is an abstract *Extension Concept* aimed to group a set of properties to be added to c. In such case, t is represented as an ExtensionDefinition element and p is denoted as an ExtensionRelationship from the BPMNElement matching c to the ExtensionDefinition matching t. This is illustrated in the BPMN+X model of Figure 7 by the representation of the *distributionStrategy* property defined in the CDME of Figure 4b.

Rule 4 is applied when p is a property of an *Extension Concept*. A prerequisite for the application of rule 4 is the previous classification of c as an ExtensionDefinition or as an ExtensionElement. This is done by applying rules 2c, 3 or 4c to the properties typed as c, and by applying rules 7 or 8 to generalization relationships involving c. If t is a Data Type (rule 4a), p is specified as an attribute of the element matching c. Else, if t is a *BPMN Concept* (rule 4b), p is denoted as an association navigable from the element matching c to the element matching t. Instead, if t is an *Extension Concept* (rule 4c), t is specified by an ExtensionElement and p by an association navigable from the element matching c to the element matching t. This is illustrated in Figure 7 by the representation of the *distributionAgent*, *name* and *granted* (rule 4a), *distributionTrigger* (rule 4b) and *taskPrivileges* (rule 4c) properties defined in Figures 4b and 4c.

In addition to the analysis of properties, it is also necessary to analyze the generalization relationships between the concepts of a CDME. Let g be a generalization relationship from a class c to a super class s. The representation of g, c and s in a BPMN+X model depends on the characterization of c and s and on whether g is original or new. Table 2 summarizes the rules for representing g in a BPMN+X model based on these parameters. The representation of c and s is then inferred based on the representation of g.

Rule 5 is valid when g is an original generalization relationship from a *BPMN Concept* c to another *BPMN Concept* s. In this case, g is represented as a generalization relationship from the BPMNElement matching c to the BPMNElement matching s in the BPMN+X model. This is illustrated in the BPMN+X model of Figure 7 by the representation of the generalization relationship from *UserTask* to *Task* defined in all CDMEs of Figure 4.

Table 1. Rules to represent a CDME class property in a BPMN+X model

	Class(c)	Property(p)	Type(t)	Representation of p
1a	BPMN Concept	Original	Data Type	BPMNElement Property
1b	BPMN Concept	Original	BPMN Concept	BPMNElement Property
2a	BPMN Concept	New	Data Type	ExtensionAttributeDefinition
2b	BPMN Concept	New	BPMN Concept	ExtensionAttributeDefinition
2c	BPMN Concept	New	Extension Concept	ExtensionAttributeDefinition
3	BPMN Concept	New	Extension Concept	ExtensionRelationship
4a	Extension Concept	New	Data Type	ExtensionElement Property / ExtensionAttributeDefinition
4b	Extension Concept	New	BPMN Concept	ExtensionElement Property / ExtensionAttributeDefinition
4c	Extension Concept	New	Extension Concept	ExtensionElement Property / ExtensionAttributeDefinition

Rule 6 applies when g is a new generalization relationship from a *BPMN Concept* to another *BPMN Concept*. At this stage, g is considered to be invalid so it is not represented in the BPMN+X model as it is not supported by the BPMN extension mechanism.

Rule 7 is applicable when g is a generalization relationship between a *BPMN Concept* and an *Extension Concept*. The BPMN extension mechanism enables the approach of extension by addition. It only enables attaching domain-specific elements to the original BPMN elements. It does not allow representing a new taxonomic relationship between a more specific *BPMN Concept* and a more general *Extension Concept* (rule 7a) or vice versa (rule 7b). Hence, g would have to be considered as invalid. However, as a best-effort solution, the *Extension Concept* can be represented as an ExtensionDefinition element and g as an ExtensionRelationship from the BPMNElement matching the *BPMN Concept* to the created ExtensionDefinition element. In this way, the additional properties defined by the *Extension Concept* can be added to the *BPMN Concept*. The representation of the generalization relationship from TaskWithDistributionStrategy to UserTask defined in Figure 4c as the ExtensionRelationship from UserTask to DistributionStrategy of Figure 7 illustrates rule 7b.

The use of other mechanisms like Profiles or MOF would have to be considered to extend BPMN when rule 7 is not suitable or the rule 6 applies.

Finally, rule 8 is valid when g is a generalization relationship from an *Extension Concept* c to another *Extension Concept* s. A prerequisite for the application of rule 8 is the previous classification of s as an ExtensionDefinition or as an ExtensionElement. This is done by applying rules 2c, 3 or 4c to the properties typed as s, and by applying rules 7 or 8 to generalization relationships involving s. Then, c is represented as an ExtensionElement element (rule 8a) or as an ExtensionDefinition element (rule 8b) depending on whether s is an ExtensinElement or an ExtensionDefinition, respectively and g is represented as a generalization relationship from the element matching c to the element matching s in the BPMN+X model.

Table 2. Rules to represent a CDME generalization relationship in a BPMN+X model

	Class(c)	Generalization(g)	Super Class(s)	Representation of g
5	BPMN Concept	Original	BPMN Concept	BPMNElement Generalization
6	BPMN Concept	New	BPMN Concept	Invalid
7a	BPMN Concept	New	Extension Concept	ExtensionRelationship
7b	Extension Concept	New	BPMN Concept	ExtensionRelationship
8a	Extension Concept	New	Extension Concept	ExtensionElement Generalization
8b	Extension Concept	New	Extension Concept	ExtensionDefinition Generalization

3.3 Transformation of the BPMN+X Model into an XML Schema Extension Definition Model

The third step consists of transforming the BPMN+X model into an XML Schema Extension Definition Model that is an instance of a MOF metamodel representing the concepts of the XML Schema specification [9]. Figure 8 illustrates the transformation rules.

An *ExtensionModel* element is transformed into a *Schema* element. An *ExtensionDefinition* element is transformed into a *ModelGroupDefinition* element. An *ExtensionElement* element is transformed into a *ComplexTypeDefinition* element. An *ExtensionEnum* element is transformed into a *SimpleTypeDefinition* element. *BPMNElement* and *BPMNEnum* elements are not transformed into any kind of XML Schema element. This is because the generated *Schema* imports the BPMN specification so the BPMN elements can be referenced by the other elements defined in the ExtensionModel.

Figure 9 shows the result of applying the transformation to the BPMN+X model shown in Figure 7. It consists of a *Schema* containing a *GroupDefinition* called DistributionStrategy that has three element declarations. The first one is distributionAgent that is typed tDistributionAgent as it was generated from an

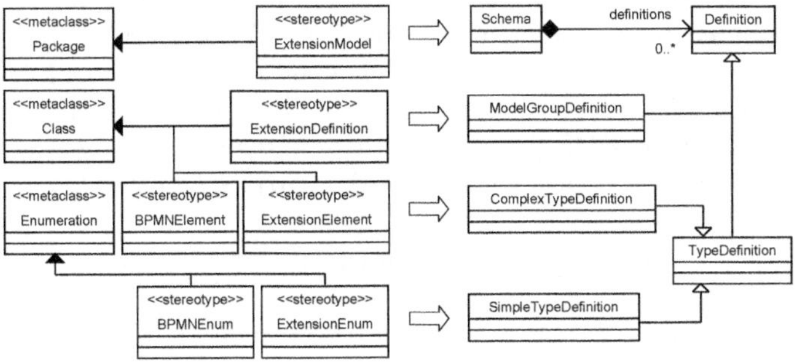

Fig. 8. BPMN+X to XML Schema Extension Definition Model transformation

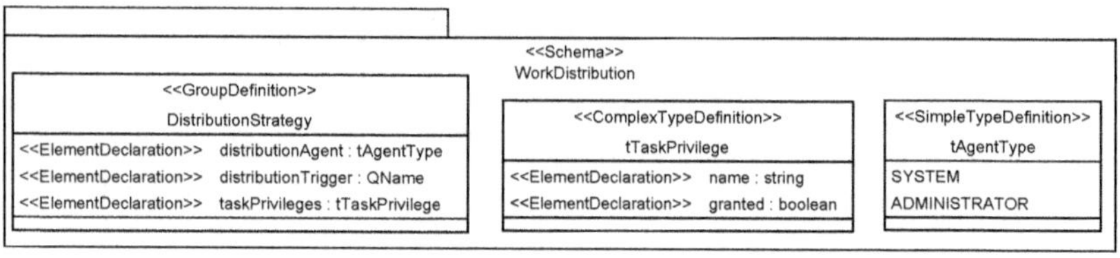

Fig. 9. Example of an XML Schema Extension Definition Model

attribute. The second one is distributionTrigger that is typed QName because it was generated from a reference association. The last one is taskPrivileges that is typed tTaskPrivilege as it was generated from a composite association. The tTaskPrivilege *ComplexTypeDefinition* element represents the TaskPrivilege ExtensionElement element of Figure 7. The tAgentType *SimpleTypeDefinition* element represents the AgentType ExtensionEnum.

3.4 Transformation of the XML Schema Extension Definition Model into an XML Schema Document

The last step of the method consists of generating an XML Schema document representing the elements of the XML Schema Extension Definition Model resulting of the third step. This document is produced by means of a straightforward model-to-code transformation producing one element in the resulting document per each element in the input model. The *Schema* elements are transformed into <xsd:schema> elements. The *GroupDefinition* elements are translated into <xsd:group> elements. The *ComplexTypeDefinition* elements result in <xsd:complexTypeDefinition> elements. Finally, *SimpleTypeDefinition* elements are converted into <xsd:simpleTypeDefinition> elements. The result of this step is called *XML Schema Extension Definition Document* (see Figure 10).

An *XML Schema Extension Definition Document* is imported by one or more *XML BPMN Model Definition Documents*, which are XML documents describing BPMN models. An *XML BPMN Model Definition Document* is an instance of the *XML Schema BPMN Metamodel Definition Document*, which specifies the XML Schema representation of BPMN. An *XML BPMN Model Definition Document* must define one Extension element to bind each of the imported extension definitions to the elements of the model being defined.

Figure 3a shows an *XML Schema Extension Definition Document* resulting of applying the described transformation to the *XML Schema Extension Definition*

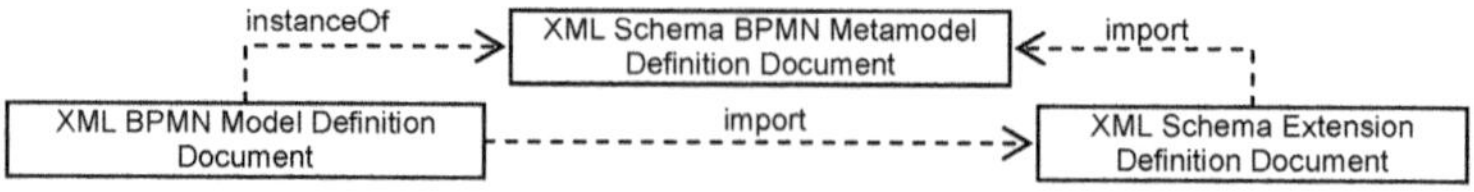

Fig. 10. Structure of the resulting documents

Model shown in Figure 9. Figure 3b shows an *XML BPMN Model Definition Document* importing the *XML Schema Extension Definition Document.*

4 Tool Support

The method described in the above section is supported by a tool developed on the Eclipse platform. The tool is available at `http://code.google.com/p/bpmnx/`. It has the structure shown in Figure 11.

The first step of the proposed method can be accomplished by creating UML models with the Eclipse UML2 and UML2 Tools plugins. The second step is supported by the BPMN+X plugin developed on the UML2 plugin which allows creating and validating BPMN+X models based on the conceptual domain model resulting of the first step. The third step of the method is supported by a model-to-model transformation developed by using the QVT plugin. This transformation takes a BPMN+X model and returns an XML Schema Extension Definition Model that is an instance of an Ecore representation of XML Schema [9]. The last step is supported by a model-to-code transformation developed using the JET plugin. It produces one XML Schema element in the resulting XML Schema Extension Definition Document for each element in the input XML Schema Extension Definition Model.

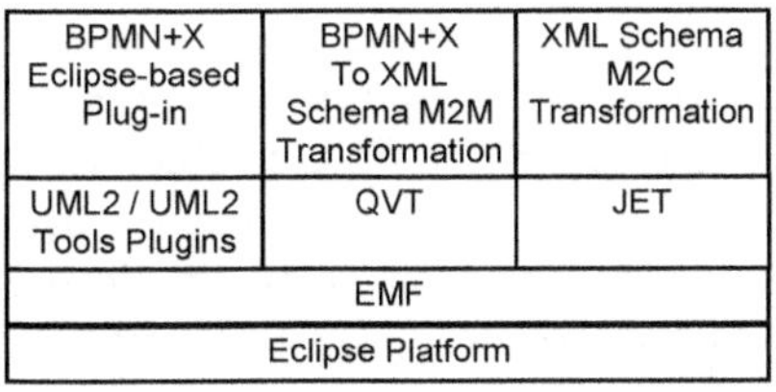

Fig. 11. Structure of the developed tool

5 Related Work

To date, there is a lack of works providing systematic approaches for the development of extensions to the BPMN 2.0 metamodel. However, there are previous works providing approaches to extend UML by developing UML Profiles. Fuentes et al [7] propose an approach consisting of five steps which starts with the definition of conceptual models of the profile to be developed. Selic [5] provides a similar step based approach starting with the construction of a conceptual model. That work also provides a checklist for the revision of profiles in order to ensure they do not contradict any restriction imposed by the extension mechanism. Lagarde et al [8] identify a set of patterns which can be identified in conceptual models of extensions to UML and how they can be traduced in terms of the UML Profile extension mechanism. The method proposed in the present work considers some of the practices recommended in these articles.

In a previous work [10], we proposed a BPMN extension to support the resource perspective of business process models. Its conceptual model was defined with UML and stereotypes were used to match its elements with the elements of the BPMN extension mechanism. Another work by Saeedi et al [11], proposed an extension for representing quality requirements. It was also defined with UML and the extension concepts were linked to the BPMN concepts by composite associations. A third work by Schleicher et al [12] proposed a BPMN extension to specify compliance requirements. It also defined the conceptual model of the extension with UML, but specified an extension definition as a subclass of the BPMN ExtensionDefinition element. The differences between the aforementioned works unveil the need for a unified method for the conceptual modeling of extensions and their representation in terms of the BPMN extension mechanism.

6 Conclusions

This work presented an MDA-based method and a tool supporting the development of extensions to the BPMN 2.0 metamodel. The method takes into account the BPMN extension mechanism. It guides the development of extensions from their representation in conceptual models to their codification as XML Schema documents. The method encourages starting from a UML conceptual domain model of the extension (CDME) and provides guidelines to derive a BPMN extension model (BPMN+X) representing it. The remaining steps of the method can be performed automatically with the aid of the provided tool.

This work also proposed the BPMN+X profile. It enables defining BPMN extensions graphically. It is better suited for use by people than XML Schema as it avoids them having to deal with implementations issues. It includes OCL constraints to validate the extensions against the BPMN extension mechanism.

A procedure was also defined for creating a BPMN+X model from a CDME. It includes a set of rules to create BPMN+X elements from the concepts of the CDME by analyzing its properties and generalization relationships.

The resulting BPMN+X model can be automatically transformed into an XML Schema document that can be processed by BPMN tools. This is done in two steps. First, it is transformed into an XML Schema Extension Definition Model. Second, the XML Schema Extension Definition Model is transformed into an XML Schema Extension Definition Document. These transformations guarantee the generated document can be used by compliant BPMN tools and avoid introducing errors by the manual definition of this document.

A tool based on the Eclipse platform implementing and supporting the method was also presented. It makes use of different plugins provided by that platform such as UML2, UML2 Tools, QVT and JET. Thus, it was demonstrated that the method can be implemented by using currently available tools.

The use of ontologies to conceptualize extensions and define CDMEs, as well as the development of approaches for extending the BPMN notation to depict instances of extensions in BPMN diagrams are considered as future work.

References

1. OMG: Business Process Model and Notation (BPMN), V.2.0 (2011), http://www.omg.org/spec/BPMN/2.0
2. OMG: MDA Guide Version 1.0.1 (2003), http://www.omg.org/cgi-bin/doc?omg/03-06-01.pdf
3. OMG: Unified Modeling Language (UML) Infrastructure, V.2.2 (February 2009), http://www.omg.org/spec/UML/2.2/Infrastructure
4. OMG: Unified Modeling Language (UML) Superstructure, V.2.2 (February 2009), http://www.omg.org/spec/UML/2.2/Superstructure
5. Selic, B.: A Systematic Approach to Domain-Specific Language Design Using UML. In: ISORC 2007: Proceedings of the 10th IEEE International Symposium on Object and Component-Oriented Real-Time Distributed Computing, pp. 2–9. IEEE Computer Society, Los Alamitos (2007)
6. Routledge, N., Bird, L., Goodchild, A.: UML and XML schema. Aust. Comput. Sci. Commun. 24(2), 157–166 (2002)
7. Fuentes-Fernández, L., Vallecillo-Moreno, A.: An Introduction to UML Profiles. UPGRADE, European Journal for the Informatics Professional 5(2), 5–13 (2004)
8. Lagarde, F., Espinoza, H., Terrier, F., Gérard, S.: Improving UML Profile Design Practices by Leveraging Conceptual Domain Models. In: International Conference on Automated Software Engineering (ASE) (November 2007)
9. WRC: XML Schema Part 1: Structures Second Edition (October 2004), http://www.w3.org/TR/xmlschema-1/
10. Stroppi, L.J.R., Chiotti, O., Villarreal, P.D.: A BPMN 2.0 Extension to Define the Resource Perspective of Business Process Models. In: CIbSE 2011: Proceedings of the XIV Iberoamerican Conference on Software Engineering (April 2011)
11. Saeedi, K., Zhao, L., Falcone Sampaio, P.R.: Extending BPMN for Supporting Customer-Facing Service Quality Requirements. In: Proceedings of the 2010 IEEE International Conference on Web Services, pp. 616–623. IEEE Computer Society, Washington, DC, USA (2010)
12. Schleicher, D., Leymann, F., Schumm, D., Weidmann, M.: Compliance scopes: Extending the bpmn 2.0 meta model to specify compliance requirements. In: 2010 IEEE International Conference on Service-Oriented Computing and Applications (SOCA), pp. 1–8 (December 2010)

BPMN for REST

Cesare Pautasso

Faculty of Informatics
University of Lugano (USI)
via Buffi 13, CH-6900 Lugano, Switzerland
http://www.pautasso.info/
c.pautasso@ieee.org

Abstract. The *Representational State Transfer (REST)* architectural style has seen substantial growth and adoption for the design of modern Resource-Oriented Architectures. However, the impact of fundamental constraints such as stateful resources, stateless interactions, and the uniform interface have had only limited uptake and impact in the *Business Process Modeling (BPM)* community in general, and in the standardization activities revolving around the BPMN notation. In this paper we propose a simple and minimal extension of the BPMN 2.0 notation to provide first-class support for the concept of resource. We show several examples of how the extended notation can be used to externalize the state of a process as a resource, as well as to describe process-driven composition of resources.

1 Introduction

Whereas the BPMN notation has been originally developed for modeling complex message-based interactions between process-backed services [3], in the last few years a novel abstraction has emerged (the resource [5]) which changes some of the assumptions and gives new constraints for the design of service oriented architectures [21]. Since business process modeling is one of the foundations for service reuse and composition [9], it becomes important to study how modeling techniques and notations developed for message-based service choreography and orchestration can also be applied to resource-based (or RESTful [16]) Web services.

In this paper, we take a look at the general problem of how to combine *Business Process Modeling (BPM)* with the REpresentational State Transfer (REST [5]) architectural style within the specific context of the BPMN notation [11]. The goal is to study how well the basic modeling concepts and constructs of the BPMN notation fit with the resource abstraction and to propose a lightweight, minimalistic and simple extension to fill the current gap between BPMN and REST. The proposed extension aims at reusing the existing graphical elements of BPMN as much as possible in order to avoid to further increase its visual complexity [10]. With it, it becomes possible to model so-called RESTful business processes, which can be both used to orchestrate and compose a set

R. Dijkman, J. Hofstetter, and J. Koehler (Eds.): BPMN 2011, LNBIP 95, pp. 74–87, 2011.

of distributed and independent resources, as well as to give a high level representation of the behaviour of stateful resources [12]. Whereas some BPMN engines[1] are starting to feature experimental support for REST, with an HTTP-based API to deploy, manage and execute processes, current solutions are still experimental and incomplete. Thanks to our approach, modelers can use BPMN for REST to give an explicit representation of the resources involved in the business process at design-time and precisely control which process elements should be published through a RESTful Web service API at run-time.

The rest of this paper is organized as follows. In Section 2 we give some background on REST and discuss why BPMN as-is should be extended to natively support RESTful Web services. In Section 3 we give an informal definition of the proposed extensions to the BPMN, while in Section 4 we show how these extensions can be used to model three non-trivial RESTful business processes. Related work is cited in Section 5, before we draw some conclusions in Section 6 and outline some future work in Section 7.

2 Background and Motivation

The REST architectural style [4] was introduced to give a principled design of the architecture of the World Wide Web and to explain its quality attributes (loose coupling, scalability, resilience to long-term change, intrinsic interoperability). Whereas most of these quality attributes are also shared by service-oriented architectures, it is under debate whether the corresponding message-based, publish-subcribe technologies are fully capable of enabling them [18]. In the past few years, REST (or more precisely its underlying HTTP protocol [1,19]) was rediscovered and proposed as an alternative way to approach the design of such service-oriented architectures, which – according to some – could be renamed as resource-oriented architectures [16].

More in detail, a RESTful Web service publishes to its clients a number of resources, which are globally addressable by means of URIs. Clients employ a stateless communication protocol to access the uniform interface associated with each resource. The uniform interface defines a standard and common set of verbs (or methods) which can be performed on a resource. Resources are dynamically discovered by means of decentralized referral and can have multiple representations, which can be negotiated by clients. These three basic constraints (resource identification, uniform interface and multiple representations) are usually visualized as the "REST triangle", which we use (Figure 1) as an inspiration for the resource icon used in the BPMN for REST extension.

Due to the emphasis placed on the reliable transfer of state between clients and resources, RESTful services significantly differs from the basic service abstraction supported by WS-* [6,20]. For example, the WS-Resource Framework [7]) provides an additional layer of complexity by extending the SOAP protocol to build stateful services. While it borrows the notion of resources from REST, it

[1] `http://www.activiti.org/userguide/index.html#N12156`

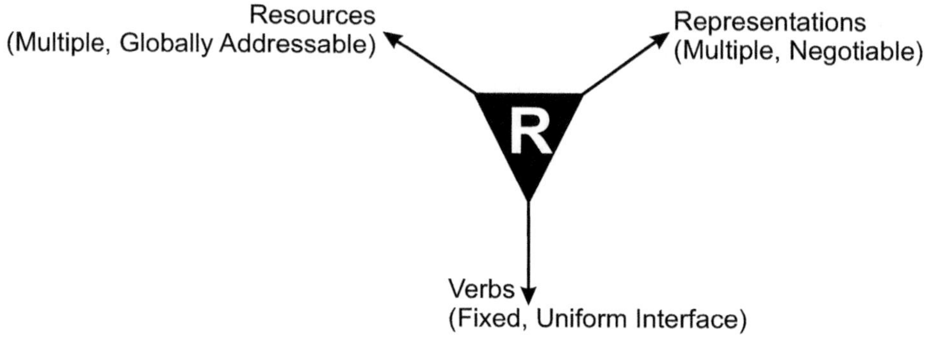

Fig. 1. The REST triangle and the Resource symbol

fails to provide a simple solution for the corresponding notions of uniform interface and global addressability of resources. Thus, it is still remains a challenge to completely wrap the resource abstraction within a traditional service-based interface [15,14]. As a consequence, there is some mismatch between the REST architectural style (originally developed for the design of distributed and decentralized hypermedia systems) and SOA technologies (such as BPEL/BPMN) addressing the needs for describing distributed systems built out of the integration and reuse of interoperable services.

In this paper we are concerned with one particular mismatch, which concerns the reuse of services by means of process-based composition, orchestration and choreography. This was originally achieved with the BPEL standard [13] and today with the latest version of the BPMN standard. These languages and the corresponding notations make a strong assumption about the set of composition techniques [2] that are available to compose services. For example, the languages provide specific constructs for message-based interaction (e.g., send/receive message icons which can be associated with tasks and events, as well as message-flow edges which literally visualize the communication between different processes). Whereas it is possible to attempt to mimick the synchronous client/server interactions of the HTTP protocol using the same elements of the notation (Figure 2 a) — after all SOAP originally proposed as a transport-independent envelope format that can wrap arbitrary content in XML so that it can be sent in terms of messages over any kind of transport protocol [17] — we believe that a more abstract and expressive notation is needed to represent at a higher level of abstraction the semantics of such interactions (Figure 2 b). Following the spirit of BPMN, the challenge consists of hiding such low-level communication details of the HTTP protocol, which are the concern of technical people. On the contrary, the goal is to let the business process modeler focus on capturing the more fundamental RESTful interactions at a higher level of abstraction without having to specify them as exchanges of HTTP request/response messages.

In particular, it should be possible to use a BPMN model to answer the following modeling questions:

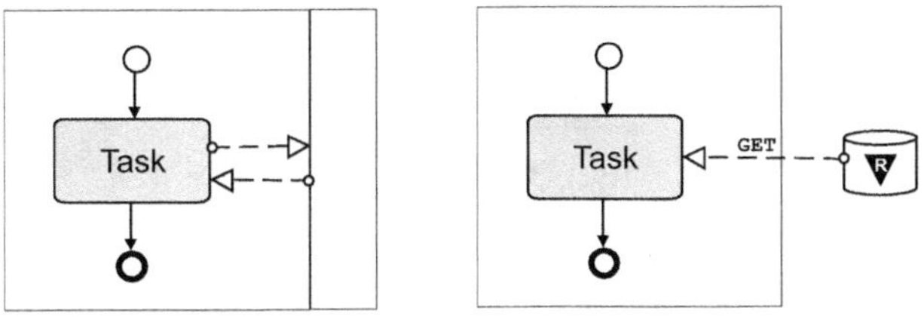

(a) BPMN 2.0 (b) BPMN for REST

Fig. 2. Modeling a task which performs a read-only GET request on a resource using BPMN (a) and BPMN for REST (b)

- Which are the resources that a process depends upon for a successful execution?
- Which are the resources that are affected by the execution of a process?
- Can we reason about the behavior of stateful resources using a process model?
- Which are the tasks of a process that have been made accessible to clients as a resource?
- Which are the possible requests that can be sent to a resource whose behavior is specified by a process?

The goal of this paper is to start a discussion on a possible minimal extension to BPMN to be able to answer these and other similar questions. We will use several examples in Section 4 to show that there is indeed a benefit of directly and natively including in a BPMN model information suitable to answer these modeling questions.

3 Notation

The BPMN for REST extension augments a small number of BPMN stencils with the resource icon (Figure 3 a). The goal is to keep the extension as minimal and lightweight as possible in order to avoid adding too many new graphical symbols to an already complex notation. In order to avoid confusing the resource icon shape with the existing signal shape, which also uses a triangle, the orientation

(a) (b) (c) (d)

Fig. 3. The resource icon (a) applied to tasks published as a resource (b) and the new resource request event (c) which should be distinguished from the standard signal event (d)

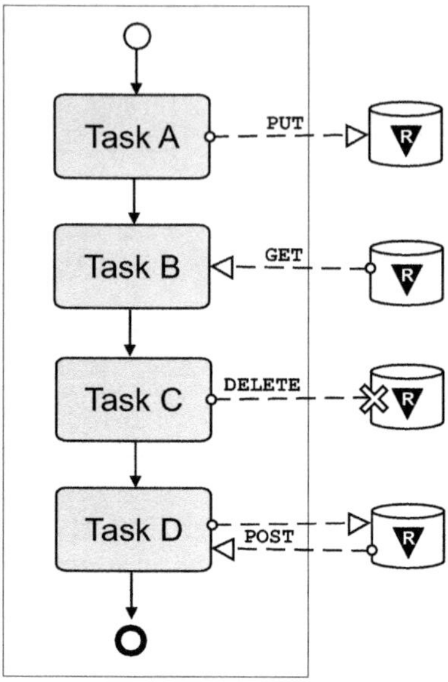

Fig. 4. Interaction with external resources

of the triangle used for the resource icon has been reversed (compare Figure 3 c vs. d).

In this section we describe the notation for modeling the interaction between processes and external resources (i.e., resource orchestration). Additionally, we also show two different ways for processes to publish resources and handle requests directed to their resources.

3.1 Modeling External Resources

Resources whose lifecycle is independent of a specific processe instance (e.g., a remote RESTful Web service API) are represented using the data store symbol refined with the resource icon (Figure 4). The intention is to depict an external place where processes can read or write persistent data, with the additional constraint that this place is a resource: the data store is addressed with a unique identifier (a URI which is not shown in the diagram, but kept as a property attribute of the shape) and it is accessed using the uniform interface (which is more expressive than basic read/write operations as in the current BPMN standard).

To specify the kind of interactions of tasks with such external resources we suggest to use the message flow edges (since the intention is to model information flowing across organizational boundaries) and to annotate the edges with the actual verb to be invoked on the resource's uniform interface. This way a precise model of the interaction can be visualized. In particular, the direction of the

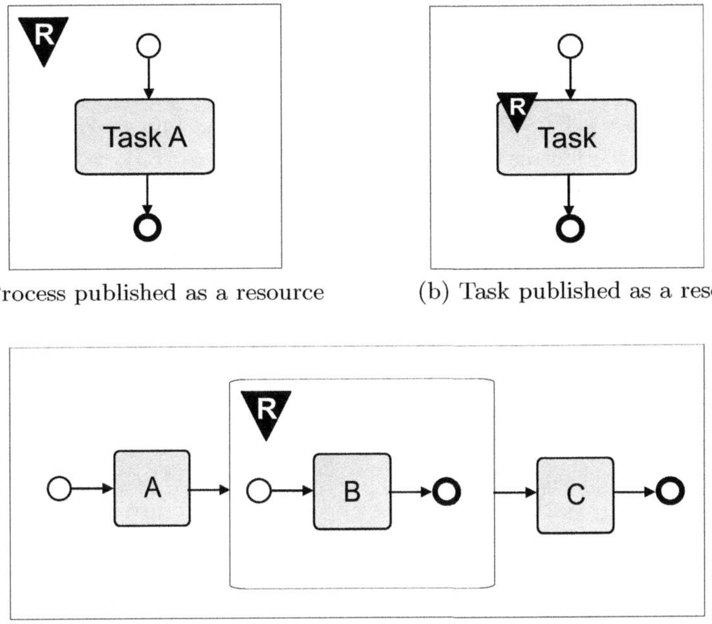

(a) Process published as a resource

(b) Task published as a resource

(c) Sub-process published as a resource

Fig. 5. Publishing processes, tasks and sub-processes as resources

message flow edge reflects the information flow associated with the method[2]. GET requests fetch information from the resource into the task consuming it; PUT requests are symmetric since they allow tasks to update the state of a resource, thus the information flows from the task into the external resource; POST requests enable bi-directional information flow (thus the double message flow edges). DELETE requests do not model any message flow, thus the edge head shape has been slightly modified to visualize the "destructive" effect on the resource targeted by the request.

3.2 Publishing Process Elements as Resources

Publishing process elements as resources entails defining a mapping between the resource abstraction and some BPMN constructs so that modelers can declaratively specify which process elements should be published as a resource. To do so, we propose to visually tag with the resource icon the processes, tasks, or sub-processes which should correspond to a resource (Figure 5). The lifecycle of such resource, as opposed to an external resource, will be implicitly entangled with the lifecycle of the process instance.

[2] Whereas in the notation examples used throughout the paper we chose to include specific HTTP methods, the notation would work in a similar way for resources having methods defined as part of a different, non-HTTP-based uniform interface.

More specifically, processes published as a resource get their own URI (e.g., `/{process}`) and follow a predefined behavior when handling requests through the resource uniform interface. Processes which are not published as a resource use an implementation-specific mechanism for their execution, which may or not involve the use of a RESTful Web service interface. The `/{process}` resource acts as a "resource factory" [1] as it allows clients to initiate the execution of new process instances by sending POST requests to it. Following the POST-REDIRECT-GET pattern[3], the client will receive an identifier of the newly started process instance (e.g., (`POST /{process}; 302 Redirect, Location: /{process}/{instance}`)) and the execution of the process will continue in the background. The clients may then use such identifier to safely retrieve (with `GET /{process}/{instance}`) the result of the process once it completes its execution. Process instances may still be created using the other mechanisms (message events, receive tasks, event-based gateways) foreseen by BPMN. Also in this case process instances get their own URI, which however has to be discovered by clients through a channel which should be independent of the instantiation mechanism (e.g., by asking the process engine to enumerate the URIs associated with the process instances of a certain user).

At any time, clients can also use the process instance resource identifier to retrieve a global view over a running process instance by GETting its representation, which – depending on the chosen media type – may contain links to the individual tasks which have been published as a resource. A client may be interested in only listing all active tasks of a process instance, as opposed to retrieving links to all tasks and then having to poll each task to determine its state. By default task URIs can be automatically generated by concatenating the process instance resource idenfier with the name of the task BPMN element (i.e., (`/{process}/{instance}/{task}`). It may be possible to override such default naming convention with a manually defined URI associated with the task. As shown in [8], a more complex URI template would be necessary to distinguish multi-instance tasks (in case those are published as resources). Concerning tasks which are found within loops, the URI would point to the most recent state of the loop, i.e., so that clients can bookmark and retrieve a representation of the state associated with the task most recent iteration.

Once a task URI has been retrieved, a client may perform a GET request on it to read task-specific information (e.g., its state, its input/output parameter values). Clients may also perform a PUT request to change the state of a task (i.e., to indicate that its execution has completed) and set the value of its output parameters. Clients are not allowed either to POST or DELETE individual task resources. Once all tasks have completed their execution, their final state remains associated with the corresponding resources until a `DELETE /{process}/{instance}` request is performed. Only then, all information associated with all tasks of a process instance is removed.

[3] This could also be implemented using the 201 Created status code, which however is not yet fully supported by Web browsers, which will not continue the navigation to the URI found in the Location header unless the 302 Redirect code is used instead.

As shown in Figure 5 (c), it is also possible to associate resources with subprocesses. The idea is that these resources become visible to clients only during the execution of the sub-process. Once the execution leaves the sub-process block, then the resources are not longer visible. Clients may perform GET requests on the corresponding identifier (`/{process}/{instance}/{sub-process}`) to retrieve the state of the resource associated with the sub-process. PUT requests can also be allowed so that information from clients can flow into the sub-process and affect the behaviour of the tasks found within. In general, POST and DELETE are not allowed. In fact, DELETE requests could be used to allow clients to trigger the cancellation of the sub-process block (assuming that the corresponding cancellation handlers have been attached to the sub-process block).

Whereas the details of how to map processes/tasks to resources can be further refined, the main goal is to abstract the complexity of the interactions here described and very simply depict the difference between private tasks of the process model from tasks that become accessible from clients through a predefined RESTful Web service interface.

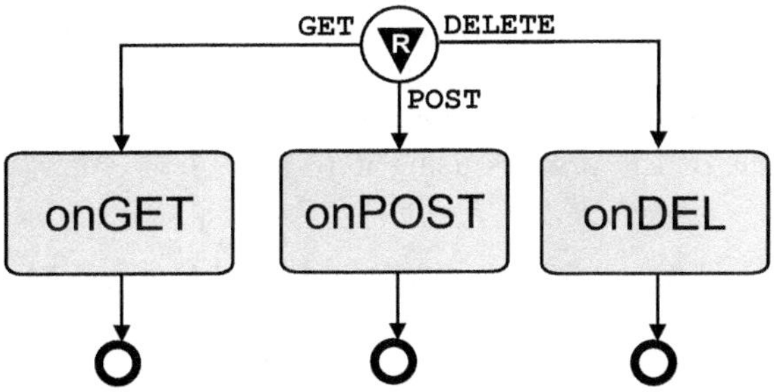

Fig. 6. Handling different request methods (e.g., GET, POST, DELETE) with the resource request event. Methods which are not explicitly modeled (e.g., PUT) will result in a `205 method not allowed` response status code.

3.3 Modeling Internal Resources: The Resource Request Event

For a more detailed and fine-grained model of how processes can be used to specify what happens inside resources, we propose to introduce a new kind of top-level event (Figure 6). This event is triggered whenever a client performs a request on the corresponding resource. The event can discriminate the different verbs associated with the request so that different tasks of the process can be activated depending on whether a GET or a POST request was received by the resource. Graphically, we associate the verbs with the control flow edges outgoing from the event. For simplicity and consistency the resource request event reuses the same resource icon as before.

The execution semantics of the resource request event is analogous to existing BPMN events. A process may accept a request sent to a resource even if the execution path triggered by previous requests has not yet completed. Multiple execution of the tasks associated with the resource request event can be serialized for POST, PUT, DELETE requests, while read-only safe GET requests may be executed concurrently for optimization purposes. It is important that the tasks associated with the request handling paths of a request event conform to the safety and idempotency properties of the corresponding methods.

4 Examples

4.1 Local Search Mashup

The local search mashup process models how information from an external RESTful API can be processed in order to be visualized on a map widget. The process contains three tasks: 1) retrieve the search results with a GET request on an external resource representing, e.g., the Google Search API; 2) process the results (Geocode) so that they can be converted to a format which is suitable for plotting them on a map; 3) generate an HTML page with the map and the results.

The two versions of the process shown in Figure 7 differ in terms of how they model how the result of the process is made available to its clients. Version (a) makes explicit use of an external resource to store (with a PUT request) the results of the mashup. The lifecycle of the resource is completely decoupled from the one of the process using it to store its results, meaning that the

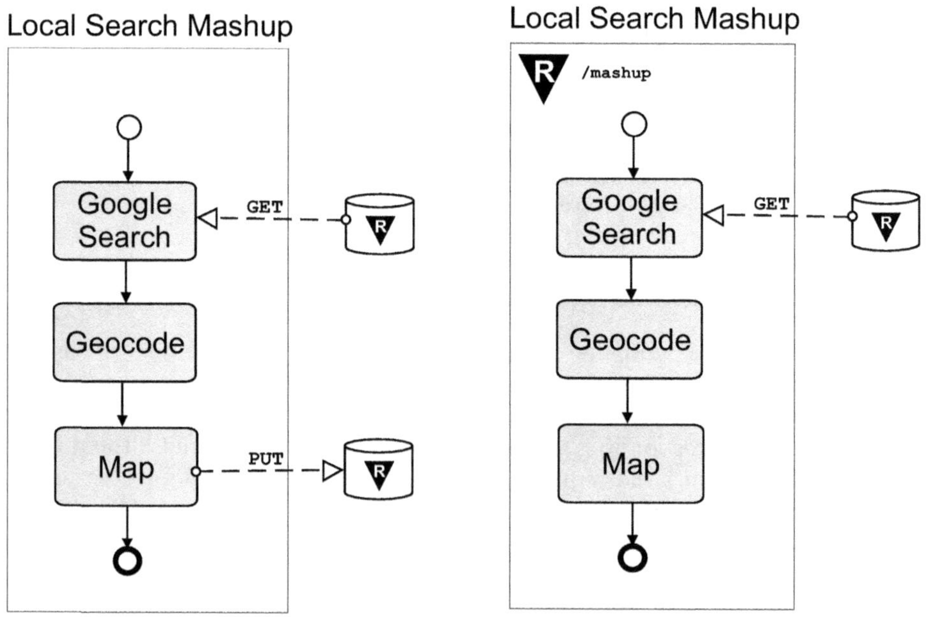

(a) Result published to external resource (b) Process published as a resource

Fig. 7. Local Search Mashup example

BPMN engine can use its own mechanism to start the process and manage its state. Once the state of the process instance is cleaned up, the external resource carrying its results is still available. Conversely, in Version (b) the mashup process model is published as a resource. Therefore clients can retrieve (`GET /mashup/{instance}`) at any time its execution state, as this is associated with the corresponding process instance resource. Once the execution reaches the final Map task, the state of the process resource will also include the output of this task, which thus can be retrieved by clients (even if the task is not explicitly published as a resource). Once clients DELETE the process instance resource, the output of the mashup will no longer be available.

4.2 Loan Approval

We use the classical loan approval process to illustrate how a business process model can make use of the proposed notation to publish some of its tasks as a resource and to interact with external resources. The process as a whole is published as a resource, which is identified by the `/loan` URI. Two of its tasks (called `choose` and `approve`, marked with the resource symbol in Figure 8) are published as resources. The other tasks are not visible from clients but carry out important back-end activities, such as checking the validity of incoming loan applications, contacting different banks for the latest rates as well as confirming the loan, if an offer has been chosen by the customer and approved by management. Both the retrieval and the confirmation tasks are backed up by an external resource which belongs to the Bank Web Services swimlane.

The notation helps to distinguish that the first interaction (getting the current rate) is a single read-only GET request, while the final confirmation is an idempotent PUT request. The notation could be further refined to indicate that

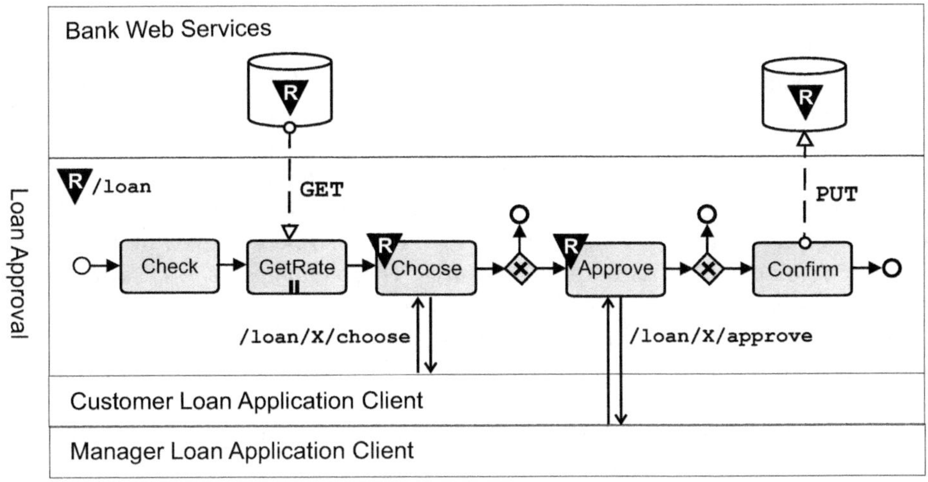

Fig. 8. The Loan approval process example

the confirmation URI was dynamically discovered by the loan approval process, as it could have been provided by the Bank Web Service as a hyperlink found in the response to the GET rate request.

The interaction between the choose and approve tasks with the corresponding clients happens through several request-response rounds as described in the semantics of the "task published as a resource" extension. The pair of edges going from the task to the swimlane representing the client abstract an arbitrary number of requests to the task resource (i.e., GET the current state of the task, or PUT the task in another state) which can happen during the entire lifecycle of the whole process. Such interactions may be allowed or disallowed depending on the current state of the tasks (e.g., once a task has been PUT into a completed state, further state changes will be restricted). This should explain why the shape of the edges is different than the "message flow" edges chosen to represent a single request-response interaction with an external resource.

4.3 RESTBucks

The RESTBucks example is adapted from [19]. It was one of the original case studies advocating the practical usage of REST and hypermedia to guide clients in discovering and following complex distributed workflows. As shown in Figure 9, the BPMN for REST extensions are also suitable to visualize the interaction between a customer and the RESTBucks order management process.

Clients can download a menu (with GET), choose a flavour of coffee (local decision task) and follow a hyperlink to place an order with a POST request to the RESTBucks process, which has been published as a resource. The newly started process instance collects the order request and uses it to compute a price, which is passed to the payment task. The customer can retrieve the price to be paid with a GET request on the payment task, since this has been published as a resource. The response also contains the form to be filled out with the payment details, which can then be submitted with a PUT request also to the same Payment task. Once the PUT request reaches the payment task, its execution completes and the payment information can be validated. If the payment validation is successful, a receipt is produced and stored in the corresponding resource. The client can track the status of the order by GETting the corresponding process instance resource at any time, eventually this status will also contain a link to the receipt resource, which can also be retrieved by the client. Since it is modeled as an external resource, the payment resource will remain available even if the process instance is deleted.

The model of the RESTBucks process also includes the ability to handle updates to the order once it has been created. These can be submitted by clients using a PUT request on the order process instance resource. Such requests will trigger the recalculation of the price by making use of the new resource request event. However, once the payment is received, it is no longer possible to change the order, as modeled with the event sub-process handling the PUT request (which will exit as soon as the Payment task completes).

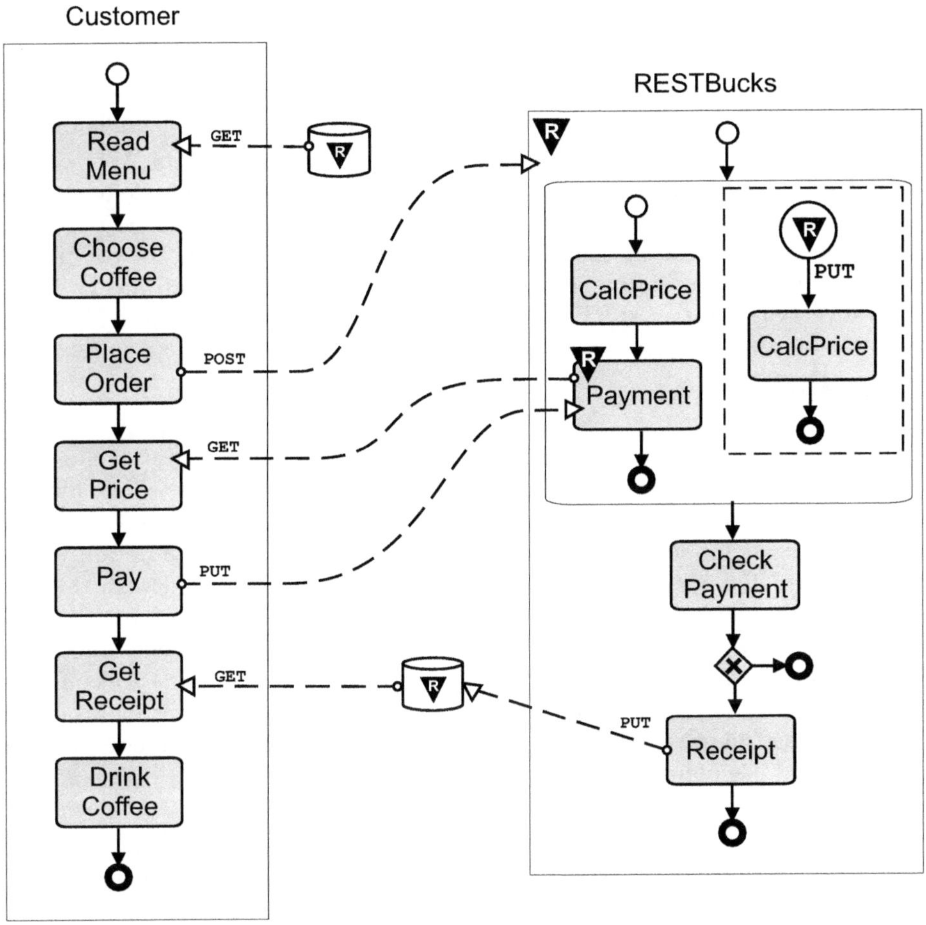

Fig. 9. The RESTBucks order management process example

5 Related Work

This paper shares a similar motivation with our previous work on the BPEL for REST [14] extensions. The concept of using the BPEL language to control the state of resources was first proposed in R-BPEL [12]. The idea of a RESTful Web service API to access the state of workflow instances has been also described in [22], where similar predefined interaction patterns to instantiate new processes where described. A similar idea has been followed in the implementation of the HTTP API of the Activiti BPMN engine.

6 Conclusion

This paper informally sketches the graphical syntax and extended semantics of an proposal for applying the BPMN notation to model RESTful business processes. The goal is to give a precise, expressive yet simple representation of processes which interact with external resources (such as RESTful Web services APIs), and to specify with various degrees of refinement which elements of a process model (tasks, sub-processes or even entire processes) can be published as a resource. Whereas the extensions have a minimal impact on the complexity of the visual syntax of the standard notation, they can already be useful to express several non-trivial RESTful business process model examples.

7 Future Work

Further research is needed to refine the extension to support more dynamic aspects of RESTful business processes, which include features such as: late binding of tasks to dynamically discovered resource identifiers, content-type negotiation and generalized support for hypermedia protocol design. More in detail, we are working on defining the specific meta-model elements associated with the proposed notational elements and have started to look into the problem of how to verify that tasks associated with request events can satisfy the safety and idempotency properties of the corresponding methods. We particularly welcome the feedback from the community concerning the specific advantages or disadvantages of using the proposed notation extension in order to set up a more detailed usability and usefulness analysis.

Acknowledgements. The authors would like to thank the anonymous reviewers for their positive and constructive feedback. This work is partially supported by the S-CUBE network of excellence (EU-FP7-215483) and by the Swiss National Science Foundation with the CLAVOS - Continuous Lifelong Analysis and Verification of Open Services project (Grant Nr. 200020_135051).

References

1. Allamaraju, S.: RESTful Web Services Cookbook. O'Reilly & Associates, Sebastopol (2010)
2. Assmann, U.: Invasive Software Composition. Springer, Heidelberg (2003)
3. Barros, A.P., Dumas, M., ter Hofstede, A.H.M.: Service Interaction Patterns. In: van der Aalst, W.M.P., Benatallah, B., Casati, F., Curbera, F. (eds.) BPM 2005. LNCS, vol. 3649, pp. 302–318. Springer, Heidelberg (2005)
4. Fielding, R.T.: Architectural Styles and the Design of Network-based Software Architectures. Ph.D. thesis, University of California, Irvine, California (2000)
5. Fielding, R.T., Taylor, R.N.: Principled Design of the Modern Web Architecture. ACM Transactions on Internet Technology 2(2), 115–150 (2002)
6. Foster, I., Parastatidis, S., Watson, P., McKeown, M.: How Do I Model State? Let Me Count the Ways. Communications of the ACM 51(9), 34–41 (2008)

7. Humphrey, M., Wasson, G.S., Jackson, K.R., Boverhof, J., Rodriguez, M., Gawor, J., Bester, J., Lang, S., Foster, I.T., Meder, S., Pickles, S., McKeown, M.: State and events for Web services: a comparison of five WS-resource framework and WS-notification implementations. In: Proceedings of the 14th IEEE International Symposium on High Performance Distributed Computing (HPDC-14), pp. 3–13 (2005)
8. Lessen, T.V., Leymann, F., Mietzner, R., Nitzsche, J., Schleicher, D.: A Management Framework for WS-BPEL. In: Proc. of the Sixth European Conference on Web Services (ECOWS 2008), pp. 187–196 (2008), `http://dl.acm.org/citation.cfm?id=1488724.1488774`
9. Leymann, F., Roller, D., Schmidt, M.T.: Web services and business process management. IBM Systems Journal 41(2), 198–211 (2002)
10. zur Muehlen, M., Recker, J.: How Much Language Is Enough? Theoretical and Practical Use of the Business Process Modeling Notation. In: Bellahsène, Z., Léonard, M. (eds.) CAiSE 2008. LNCS, vol. 5074, pp. 465–479. Springer, Heidelberg (2008), `http://dx.doi.org/10.1007/978-3-540-69534-9_35`
11. OMG: BPMN: Business Process Modeling Notation 2.0. Object Management Group (2010)
12. Overdick, H.: Towards Resource-Oriented BPEL. In: Proc. of the 2nd ECOWS Workshop on Emerging Web Services Technology (WEWST 2007) (November 2007)
13. Pasley, J.: How BPEL and SOA Are Changing Web Services Development. IEEE Internet Computing 9(3), 60–67 (2005)
14. Pautasso, C.: RESTful Web Service Composition with BPEL for REST. Data & Knowledge Engineering 68(9), 851–866 (2009)
15. Pautasso, C., Zimmermann, O., Leymann, F.: RESTful Web Services vs. "Big" Web Services: Making the Right Architectural Decision. In: Huai, J., Chen, R., Hon, H.W., Liu, Y., Ma, W.Y., Tomkins, A., Zhang, X. (eds.) 17th International World Wide Web Conference, pp. 805–814. ACM Press, Beijing (2008)
16. Richardson, L., Ruby, S.: RESTful Web Services. O'Reilly & Associates, Sebastopol (2007)
17. Vinoski, S.: RPC and REST: Dilemma, Disruption, and Displacement. IEEE Internet Computing 12(5), 92–95 (2008)
18. Vinoski, S.: Serendipitous Reuse. IEEE Internet Computing 12(1), 84–87 (2008)
19. Webber, J., Parastatidis, S., Robinson, I.: REST in Practice: Hypermedia and Systems Architecture. O'Reilly & Associates, Sebastopol (2010)
20. Weerawarana, S., Curbera, F., Leymann, F., Storey, T., Ferguson, D.: Web Services Platform Architecture. Prentice Hall (March 2005)
21. Wilde, E., Pautasso, C. (eds.): REST: From Research to Practice. Springer, Heidelberg (2011)
22. zur Muehlen, M., Nickerson, J.V., Swenson, K.D.: Developing Web Services Choreography Standards — The Case of REST vs. SOAP. Decision Support Systems 40(1), 9–29 (2005)

A Notation for Supporting Social Business Process Modeling

Marco Brambilla, Piero Fraternali, and Carmen Vaca

Politecnico di Milano, Piazza L. da Vinci 32, Milano, Italy
name.surname@polimi.it

Abstract. Social networking is more and more considered as crucial for helping organizations harness the value of informal relationships and weak ties, without compromising the consolidated business practices embedded in conventional BPM solutions. However, no appropriate notation has been devised for specifying social aspects within business process models. In this paper we propose a first attempt towards the extension of business process notations with social features. In particular, we devise an extension of the BPMN notation for capturing social requirements. Such extension does not alter the semantics of the language: it includes a set of new event types and task types, together with some annotation for the pool/lane levels. This notation enables the description of social behaviours within BPMN diagrams. To demonstrate the applicability of the notation, we implement it within the WebRatio BPM editor and we provide a code generation framework that automatically produces a process enactment Web application connected with mainstream social platforms.

Keywords: BPM, BPMN, Social Software, Social Network, Enterprise 2.0, Code Generation.

1 Introduction and Motivation

The growing interest towards social interactions within the enterprise is leading to a new discipline called Social BPM, which fuses BPM with social software. Its aim is to enhance the enterprise performance by means of a controlled participation of external stakeholders to process design and execution [5,10,15].

The motivation of the social extension to BPM is to improve the organization efficiency. Depending on the context and on the kind of processes, this can be obtained by:

- Exploiting *weak ties* between people and *implicit enterprise know-how* to improve activity execution and disseminating of knowledge. This could also entail fostering mutual support among users.
- Increasing *transparency and participation* to the decision procedures, so as to raise awareness of the processes and acceptance of the outcomes. This also increases the possibility of collecting feedbacks that may contribute to the process improvement.

R. Dijkman, J. Hofstetter, and J. Koehler (Eds.): BPMN 2011, LNBIP 95, pp. 88–102, 2011.

- Involving (informal) *communities in activity execution*, thus assigning the execution to a broader set of performers or to find most appropriate contributor within a group.

In classical BPM, processes are defined centrally by the organization and deployed for execution by *internal performers*, i.e., actors formally entitled to execute the activities and directly produce the advancement of a process case. This closed-world approach can be opened with social features at different levels of control [2]: *Participatory Design* opens the process design to multiple actors, including end users; the resulting process is then executed in the traditional way; *Participatory enactment* shifts socialization from design to execution, allowing limited user communities to gain visibility and limited participation to the process; and *Social enactment* opens the process execution to open communities of actors dynamically signed-up to the process.

The coverage of these aspects imposes new requirements to business process notations and design tools, which are well suited for classical business process model descriptions, but fall short when dealing with social aspects describing informal interactions among people. This poses a linguistic problem (how to express socialization in the process model) and a procedural problem (how to design the process model so that it fulfills the socialization goals). BPMN 2.0 native extension mechanism can be exploited to provide a quite natural answer to the former issue: the main concepts of the language can be stereotyped to convey their social extension.

In this paper we propose a first attempt towards extending the Business Process Modeling Notation (BPMN) with new items that enable the coverage of the social aspects. In particular, the contribution of the paper include:

- An extension of BPMN enabling the specification of social roles, activities, events, and process flows. Such extension does not alter the semantics of the language but provides some stereotypes that make explicit the role of user communities within the processes.
- A gallery of design patterns representing archetypal solutions to recurrent process socialization problems (social process patterns).
- A technical framework for generating Social BPM applications from the BPMN specifications covering also the social aspects, implemented in a commercial tool suite called WebRatio BPM [1].

The paper is organized as follows: Section 2 discusses the aspects that need to be socialized in BPM; Section 3 describes the proposed extensions to the BPMN language; Section 4 shows some examples; Section 5 presents some social BPM design patterns; Section 6 describes the technical framework for social process modeling and application generation; Section 7 discusses the related work; and Section 8 concludes.

2 Dimension of Socialization

The introduction of social features in business processes requires some modifications in the notation and in the design practices from various perspectives.

The main perspectives that are affected are: the actor categorization, the level of visibility of the process status, and the level of user participation.

2.1 Actor Categorization

The participants to a business process can be categorized based on the level of formality at which they engage in the process. Three broad categories can be recognized: 1) *internal performers* belong to the organization(s) owning the process, are formally registered before process deployment and directly affect case and activity advancement; 2) *internal observers* belong to the organization(s) owning the process, are formally registered before process deployment but cannot directly affect case and activity advancement; however, they can be notified of selected aspects of a case (e.g., events, artifacts, activity status) and may produce events and artifacts that indirectly affect case and activity advancement; 3) *external observers* do not belong to the organization(s) owning the process and may not be formally registered a priori; they can login into the process through third party identification services (e.g., through accounts at public social networks or standard open accounts); they can perform the same tasks as the internal observers and influence case advancement only indirectly. A summary of these three categories is provided in Figure 1.

2.2 Visibility of the Process Status

The interaction with cases and activity instances can occur at different levels of control: an actor can interact via the explicit publication and manipulation of the case and activity status (direct access); via the right of publication and manipulation of a restricted set of case- and activity-related parameters (view access); or in an implicit and indirect way, via the publication and manipulation of objects or other derived information (artifact-mediated access). When the access to process status is indirect, the influence on activity advancement can still take place, via the mediation of a human task executed by an internal performer or a decision gateway testing some condition formally expressed in the process model

2.3 Level of Social Participation

The interaction of external social actors with a business process can produce different impacts on case advancement; external users can: be informed about the progress of a case or an activity; create comments used for (offline) process evaluation; create events that trigger the state transition of activities; create data objects or modify parameter values that alter the status of activities or the control flow of the case.

3 Social BPMN Extensions

Process design benefits from visual languages that convey the process structure and constraints in an clear way, immediately communicable also to non-technical

Role type	Icon	User Provenance	Description
Internal performer		Formal roles in the BPM definition, specified at design time	Directly affect case and activity advancement
Internal Observer		Communities of users known at design time (e.g., members of the organization)	May produce events and artifacts that indirectly affect case and activity advancement
External Observer		Communities of users not known a priori, dynamically registered in the process	Can be informed and participate through social network platforms

Fig. 1. BPMN lanes and pools stereotyped to denote social actors

stakeholders. Social process design should preserve the intuitiveness and expressivity of state-of-the-practice visual languages and possibly be based on standard notations. To this end, social extensions of business processes can be conveyed using the BPMN standard[1] as a linguistic base. BPMN 2.0 incorporates a native extension mechanism that makes the language well suited for the adaptation to special process requirements, like those arising in Social BPM. By enriching the existing BPMN concepts with a social meaning, it is possible to achieve a visual language that is both familiar to BPMN practitioners and possess enough expressive power to convey social behaviours.

3.1 Notation for Community Lane and Actor Categorization

The main extension that is needed for the notation is the concept of Community Pool, which is defined as the pool devoted to social activities: it may represent a public social networks or an enterprise social network. It grants the possibility of assigning work to users different from internal performers, i.e., to internal or external observers. Community pools shall be annotated with the user icons representing the category of users involved in the social tasks. Figure 1 shows the notations we allow for community pools: social users are denoted by a stereotype icon adorning the BPMN pool, so to distinguish internal performers (corresponding to the standard semantics of BPMN pools) and the pools formed by the social communities of internal and external observers, according to the description provided in Section 2.1.

3.2 Notation for Socialization of Activities and Decisions

We propose three design practices to increase the efficiency of social interactions design. The corresponding notation is summarized in Figure 2.

First of all, we propose to allow the hierarchical definition of user roles. Accordingly, a role may comprise several sub-roles. The super-role is assigned to

[1] http://www.bpmn.org/

Requirement	BPMN notation	Comment
Choices performed by users or automatically		Gateways can be annotated with the user or automatic symbol, as one can for tasks
Avoid duplication of lanes and tasks	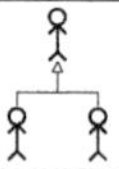	User roles can be defined as a hierarchy
Activities performed by the community		A sub-process delegated to a community is marked as *ad hoc* to denote the non-structured nature of interactions

Fig. 2. Extended notation to efficiently represent social activities

one lane, while the sub-roles to others. However, sub-roles can perform both the tasks in their own lane and tasks in the lane of the super-role. This is meant to avoid duplication of activities across lanes. This is a general requirement and we think it should be considered in general for BPMN, but it gets particularly critical in social applications where multiple roles may perform social tasks; to avoid specifying activities repeatedly in every lane, a parent role factoring out the activities common to multiple sub-roles can be used, which makes the specification of social behavior more compact.

Secondly, we introduce the concept of user gateways to express human choices. The specification of human-executed choices in BPMN is an open issue currently under discussion in the BP analyst community. Social applications corroborate the need of a better way to explicitly model human decisions, which can be achieved simply by distinguishing user gateways, which entail a user's decision; and automat-ic/service gateways, which entail a decision taken according to a rule (this is the standard semantics for BPMN gateways) or performed by a service.

Finally, the BPMN concept of *ad hoc task* is proposed as an effective solution for describing social activities, which are inherently unstructured. This highlights the flexible and sometimes uncontrollable nature of the interactions when dealing with the social execution of tasks.

Notice that the other issues discussed in Section 2 (i.e., visibility of process status and level of social participation) do not require a specific notation because they can be inferred from the BPMN diagram by looking at the flow, task, and event definitions.

3.3 Notation for Social Tasks

While most social interaction may be described with standard message flows within the community pool or between the community and the enterprise pool, a simplified notation may be convenient in several cases. *Social tasks* specialize the BPMN task concept to denote a process action with a social semantics: they are denoted by an icon that suggest the social meaning of the task, as exemplified by the annotations reported in figure 3. These annotations are a

Task type	Annotation icon	Description
Social broadcast		Data flow to a community pool
Social posting		Data flow to a single user in a community pool
Invitation to activity		Dynamic enrolment to a task in the process case
Commenting		Comment the activity
Voting		Voting (y/n) on an activity, either within a social network platform or directly in the BPM system
Login to join		Login using a social profile
Invitation to join a network		Invitation between community users
Search for actor's information		Lookup query to the community to search for an actor with specific profile attributes

Fig. 3. BPMN tasks stereotyped to denote social activities

shortcut for social activities: they respectively express the broadcasting of messages/contents from a task to the entire social network (or a subset thereof), the posting of messages/contents to one member of the network, the invitation of people from the social network to perform a specific task, the invitation to comment or vote on a task or on its outcomes, the login of users in the BPM system using credentials from a social network, and the search for user's skills or reputation within a social network (e.g., for checking recommendations before assigning tasks to users). The control of social tasks is based on the standard BPMN control flows, either within a social pool or between a social and a normal pool.

Requirement	BPMN notation	Comment
Community-generated events		(Generic) events raised by the community
Event: New user engaged in the social community		An event is raised when a user dynamically enrolls to the process case
Event: New social relationship link		An event is raised when a user establishes a social relationship with another user
Event: Invitation acceptance/rejection		An event is raised when a user accepts/rejects an invitation

Fig. 4. BPMN event types supporting social interactions

3.4 Notation for Social Events

As shown in Figure 4, specialized event types can be used to denote case advancement triggered by social interactions. A generic social event concept represents any kind of occurrence within the social network; this can be specialized to express more detailed event types like: the addition of a new user to the community, the establishment of a new social relationships, the notification of acceptance/rejection of a social request (e.g., for friendship, invitation to groups or applications), and so on. Once again, these represent only stereotypes of the classical BPMN event concept, whose semantics is not changed.

4 Usage Examples

To demonstrate the use of social tools to support common tasks on a process execution, we report here three different examples of Social BPM applications designed with our notation.

4.1 Scheduling a Meeting

The first example focuses on the social scheduling of a meeting. Imagine a scenario in which the director of a public government office needs to look for stakeholders in an specific area and define a time to meet all of them. It is necessary to socialize the process in such a way that everyone is able to select the dates when he/she will be available. The director logs in into the application by using one of his social network credentials (e.g., LinkedIn credentials). Then, he can search for professionals in some industry area among his contacts. The search activity is supported by the social platform he is connected to, so he can use a great amount of social data without leaving the application and loosing context. Using the results of the query, the director selects the people to whom invitations will be sent to setup the meeting date.

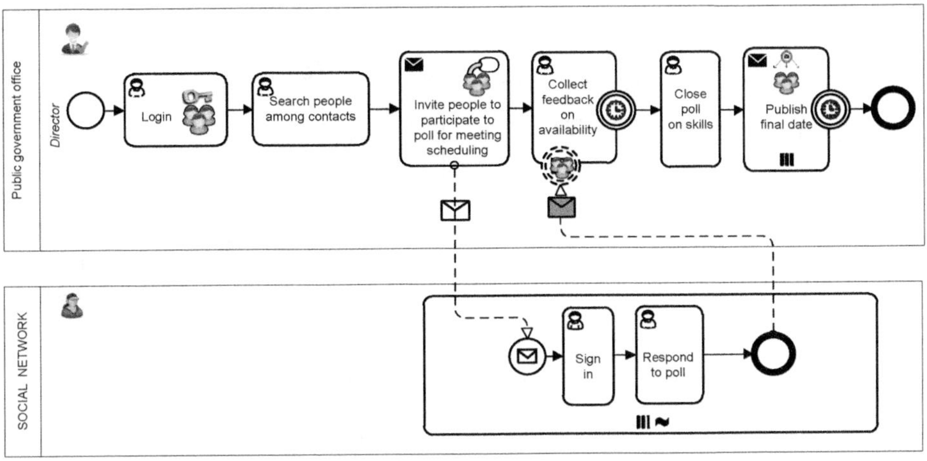

Fig. 5. The socialized Meeting coordination process

Once the professionals to be invited are selected, a poll is created and the people are invited to mark their preferences among a predefined list of dates. The Director introduces the information needed to automatically generate a poll within a free online application (e.g., the popular Doodle platform) and the system generates a message sent to all of the social (LinkedIn) inbox of all participants. The message contains all the details to participate in the poll. This activity is represented as a message to a social pool where actors are enrolled dynamically and are able to create input in the process without being previously registered in the system. The process finishes when the Director chooses the final date for the meeting and publishes it.

The implemented prototype of this application is available online at: `http://www.bpm4people.org/demo`.

4.2 Thesis Approval

The second example reports a process model to approve proposals of undergraduate students' theses within a university. The actors involved in the process are: the student submitting the proposal, the Vice-Dean and the Professors (evaluators). To avoid students making errors in the presentation of the documents, the university defines a social support to the process, allowing students to get support and advice from their colleagues.

The student login into the application using his social network credentials (e.g., Facebook), and publishes his thesis proposal inviting his peers to comment. Once his "friends" on the social networking site send their suggestions, he can fix the proposal accordingly and he can ask for approval to the academic authority, i.e. the Vice-Dean. The Vice-Dean selects teachers to evaluate the proposal based on the topic and field. Teachers are able to ask colleagues to rate the document

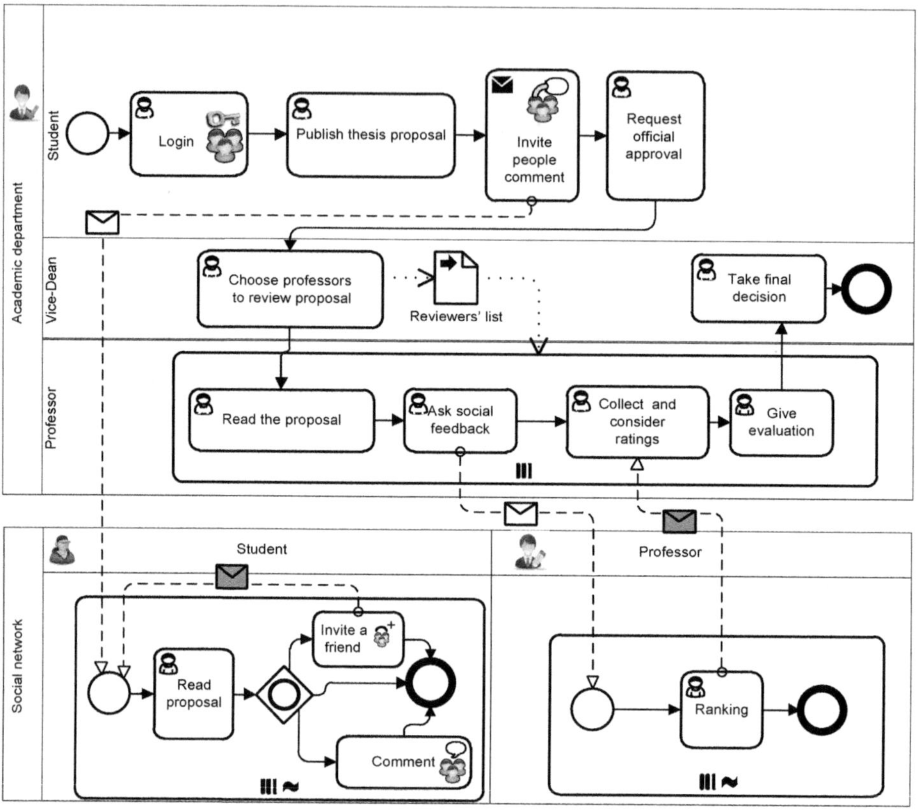

Fig. 6. The socialized Thesis approval process

and consider this feedback when submitting the final evaluation. Finally, the evaluations are sent to the Vice-Dean, who takes the final decision.

Figure 6 shows the process described including the interaction with the social pool. Students who make comments on the thesis are considered *External Observers* because they are registered users of the chosen social network platform; they could even be students from other universities or professionals working in the industry. The pool for the Professors is labeled using the *Internal Observer* icon because the system allows sending invitations to rate the proposal only to the internal social network of professors of the current university.

4.3 Social BPM in a B2C Scenario

Let's consider now a B2C scenario, in which a multinational company that sells consumer electronics products (PCs, small appliances, mobile devices) wants to setup some social process within its web portal, for launching a new product line and testing the social marketing potentials. In particular, the company wishes to support the sales of collateral services (e.g., guarantee extensions and premium

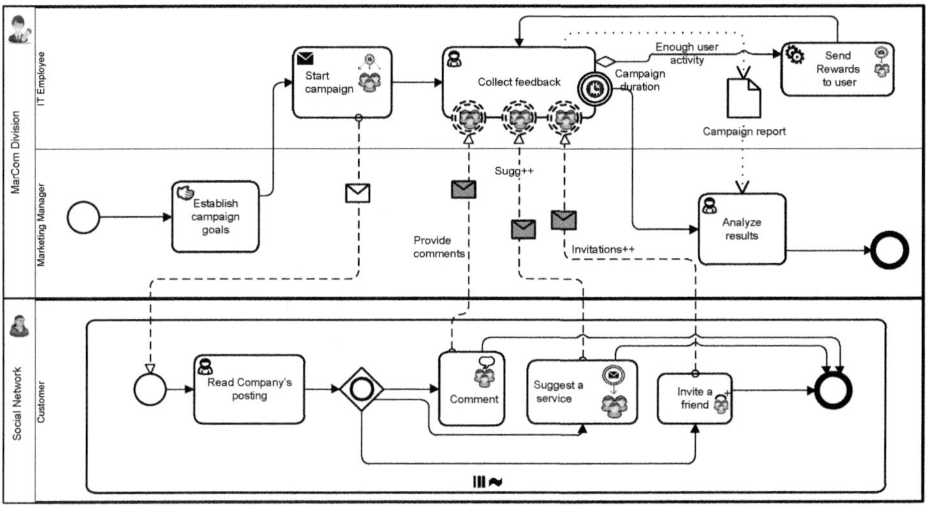

Fig. 7. The Social Campaign Management process

technical support) by letting customers enroll in the company portal through an existing social network account (e.g., Twitter, Facebook or others) and asking them to authorize the company to post on their wall and/or to become friend. Periodically, the company launches new promotions, by posting announcements to registered customers. Customers can take active part in the campaign by proactively inviting friends to join the company's portal, by suggesting the services, voting on the promotions, and so on. The number of successful invitations and induced sales of a user is tracked and a bonus program grants discounts when certain objectives are met. The campaign closes after a predetermined period of time and a post-campaign report is produced with performance data (new enrolled customers, online purchases in the period, and so on).

Figure 7 shows the Social Campaign Management process. The process actors comprise world-wide managers, country managers and employees of the Marketing and Communication (MarCom) department. The process implies an explicit interaction between the company's MarCom personnel and the observer users clustered in a social pool. The process initiates when the company's marketing manager decides that a new campaign has to be launched; a marketing employee prepares the campaign content and broadcasts the event (together with the content) to the social pool with an explicit message flow; as a consequence, each user that previously accepted to receive campaign announcements will get a message in her favorite social network applications.

Then, the process continues within the social pool. A social network member may comment back to the company, suggest the service/product to his own friends, or invite new friends to the company network or social group. As a result, new actors can enroll to the company's portal and dynamically become part of the social pool. Each action from a social pool actor is notified to the company, which in turn registers the events for the whole duration of the campaign. If the user reaches the agreed objectives, a task is activated to notify the reward from the company to the user in the community pool, by means of an individual communication in the user's preferred social network(s). The campaign terminates at the end of a designated time interval; after the temporal event, the marketing manager can analyze the final report on the campaign results.

Notice that the social community pool is marked as external observer and includes a parallel ad hoc task to describe the social action, possibly repeated for every message sent out. Message flows are also shown explicitly to describe the message sources and contents. On the other hand, the "send rewards to user" activity is specified using the task stereotype notation, because the task behavior is standard and the message follows can be deduced from the short notation and from rest of the process diagram.

5 Social Design Patterns

Social pools, actor categories, social tasks and events are the linguistic building blocks for expressing the design of social features within BPMN models. In line with the software engineering and the business process modeling practices, we also tried to identify the most common social scenarios in BPM and we defined the corresponding design patterns, i.e., archetypal or best practice solutions to recurrent scenarios where cooperative tasks are executed using social software.

Notice that the patterns we identify are application-level patterns. As such, they may exploit control-flow level patterns (e.g., the ones defined by van der Aalst et al. [17]) in their definition, but do not aim at substituting or complementing them.

This section illustrates an initial gallery of design patterns, collected from an ongoing experience of analysis with process owners in companies and public administrations. In this first proposal, every pattern is described by a statement of the problem it addresses and a short description explaining the supported social interaction. The current list of patterns comprises the following ones:

- **Dynamic enrollment:** the aim is to support the involvement of people external to the process. Platforms like enterprise and public social networks[2] are exploited for dynamically adding new actors to social activities.
- **Poll:** the aim is to collect input from a community of users cooperating to a social decision. An internal performer publishes to a social platform a question (e.g., an open or closed list of options to choose from). Internal/external observers receive an invitation to participate in the poll and contribute with their choices.
- **People/skills search:** this pattern focuses on finding the right competencies for performing an activity. A social community is exploited to find people with required expertise, considering the trade-off between level of expertise

[2] Example of enterprise social network are Yammer and Jive; of public ones are Facebook, LinkedIn and Twitter.

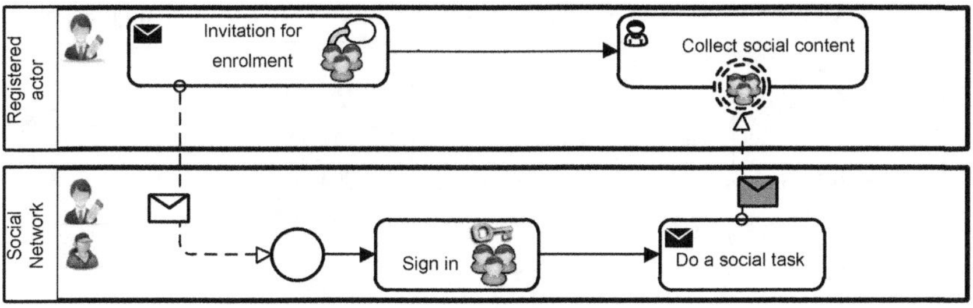

Fig. 8. Dynamic enrolment pattern

and social distance. The process usually consists in publishing a call for people, to which internal/external observers respond.
- **Social publication:** this aims at making a process artifact visible to social actors, e.g., by posting a document to a social platform [8]. Artifacts contain limited views of the process status or of the associated content, which is shared with the community.
- **Social sourcing:** the purpose is delegating an activity to one or more social actors. Internal performers publish the description of the work and share a resource link to start contributions. Internal/external observers contribute to the execution of an activity, e.g., by co-authoring or enriching socially produced documents [15], e.g., through tagging [6,14].
- **Advancement notification:** this pattern aims at informing social actors about process advancement, for instance by using micro-blogging platforms [13] to keep the users updated, thus increasing transparency and involvement.
- **Feebdack:** this pattern focuses on acquiring qualitative/quantitative feedback from social actors by asking internal/external observers to rate some content or to insert comments into the social platform.

As an example of pattern, Figure 8 shows the BPMN representation of the dynamic enrollment pattern, implementing an open invitation to users using the annotation icons to denote social activities. Internal performers generate an invitation by sending a message to a social pool, and internal/external observers sign up and start contribute to some social task.

6 Implementation Experience

To validate the viability and usability of our notation, we have implemented it within WebRatio [1], a Model-Driven Web application development tool allowing one to edit BPMN models and automatically transform them into running JEE applications. The code generation exploits an intermediate platform-independent application model, expressed in the WebML language [3], so that application developers can fine-tune the Web application for enacting the process, by enriching the skeleton application model produced automatically from the BPMN process diagram.

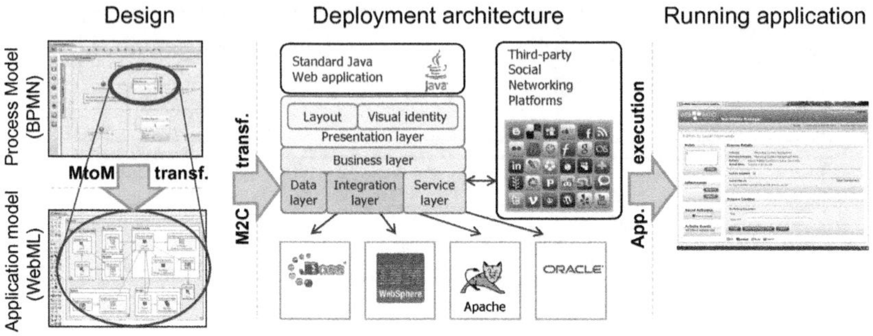

Fig. 9. Overview of the implementation of the approach within WebRatio

A set of new WebML components and transformation rules have been implemented to realize the social BPM patterns and connect the resulting enactment application to the social networking platforms needed for social behavior.

In our extended version, a rapid prototyping function applies directly to the social process model and lets a business analyst or a stakeholder: 1) impersonate any actor of the process, at all the levels of social interaction; 2) start/suspend/resume/terminate the process activities; 3) create and inspect project artifacts and parameters, according to the process specification; 4) impersonate external user roles and play social actions.

The prototype can be refined at the Web application modeling level by editing WebML models and then re-executing the model transformations, until the resulting application meets the requirements for deployment.

Figure 9 provides an overview of the implementation framework. At design time, the analyst creates the Social BPMN process models. Then, the automatic transformation from BPMN to WebML generates a Web application model for process enactment. In particular, social BPMN tasks are transformed into WebML application-level patterns, which make use of components for connecting to the social software. Process deployment exploits the transformation from WebML to the Java code, which is already implemented in WebRatio [1] and has been extended to support the social BPM patterns.

7 Related Work

Social BPM goals and impact have been deeply investigated in a variety of business sectors. For instance, people tagging has been applied to BluePages, the corporate directory at IBM, to improve information quality on people and skills ; similarly, [14] proposes an approach for building competence ontologies in a collaborative way for a repository of people's skills.

Previous works on tools for social BPM focus on supporting the process modeling phase [4,11,16] and the execution phase [9,12,15,16]. For example, [8,11] discuss how social modeling tools allow multiple designers to register the design interactions so to produce recommendations for future projects. In the execution phase instead, the goal is to make information available to the users affected by the process even if these users were not identified at the definition stage [15].

The social BPM problem at large has been recently tackled by the recent book [7] published by WfMC, gathering several contributions by BPM practitioners from the field.

In the process deployment field, social and business process integration is emerging also in the industry, as several vendors are proposing integrated social BPM suites. Among them, Appian, IBM BlueWorks Live, Oracle BPM Suite 11g, Software AG AlignSpace, Intalio and a few others.

The approach illustrated in this paper focuses on socializing process execution, and is the first attempt at devising an extended notation for expressing social process models. With respect to existing design and deployment tools, the architecture and toolsuite illustrated in Section 6 apply for the first time the pattern-driven development paradigm to the life-cycle of social BPM solutions.

As already mentioned, the patterns we study are at the application level and do not compete with control-flow level patterns (e.g., the ones defined by van der Aalst et al. [17]).

8 Conclusions

This paper proposed an extension to the BPMN notation to tackle the domain of social BPM solutions. The core idea is to extend the BPMN visual language for process design with primitives expressing social interactions, thus providing a domain-specific set of annotations to the BPMN elements. We also provided a first set of application-level design patterns that provide a systematic way of turning the typical socialization requirements into the model of a social process, which blends centralized process execution with controlled interactions with social users.

Our implementation experience consists in extending a BPM design tool suite called WebRatio, equipped with code generators and a runtime architecture, to cope with the social BPM requirements.

Ongoing work is focusing on the collection of a large gallery of social design patterns, on the implementation of tighter integration between the BPM platforms and the social services, and on the experimentation of the methodology and of the technical approach in real-world scenarios in the enterprise and public administration.

Acknowledgements. This work is partially funded by the BPM4People project within the EU Capacities program of the 7th FP. Further information on the project can be found at: `http://www.bpm4people.org`.

References

1. Brambilla, M., Butti, S., Fraternali, P.: Webratio BPM: A Tool for Designing and Deploying Business Processes on the Web. In: Benatallah, B., Casati, F., Kappel, G., Rossi, G. (eds.) ICWE 2010. LNCS, vol. 6189, pp. 415–429. Springer, Heidelberg (2010)

2. Brambilla, M., Fraternali, P., Vaca, C.: A model-driven approach to social BPM applications. In: Social BPM Handbook, pp. 95–112. Future Strategies - WfMC (2011)
3. Ceri, S., Fraternali, P., Bongio, A., Brambilla, M., Comai, S., Matera, M.: Designing Data-Intensive Web Applications. Morgan Kaufmann Publishers Inc. (2002)
4. Dengler, F., Koschmider, A., Oberweis, A., Zhang, H.: Social Software for Coordination of Collaborative Process Activities. In: zur Muehlen, M., Su, J. (eds.) BPM 2010 Workshops. LNBIP, vol. 66, pp. 396–407. Springer, Heidelberg (2011)
5. Erol, S., Granitzer, M., Happ, S., Jantunen, S., Jennings, B., Johannesson, P., Koschmider, A., Nurcan, S., Rossi, D., Schmidt, R.: Combining BPM and social software: contradiction or chance? J. Softw. Maint. Evol. 22, 449–476 (2010)
6. Farrell, S., Lau, T., Nusser, S., Wilcox, E., Muller, M.: Socially augmenting employee profiles with people-tagging. In: Proceedings of the 20th Annual ACM Symposium on User Interface Software and Technology, pp. 91–100 (2007)
7. Fischer, L. (ed.): Social BPM. Work, Planning and Collaboration Under the Impact of Social Technology. Future Strategies - WfMC (2011)
8. Holtzblatt, L., Tierney, M.L.: Measuring the effectiveness of social media on an innovation process. In: Proceedings of the 2011 Annual Conference Extended Abstracts on Human Factors in Computing Systems, CHI EA 2011, pp. 697–712. ACM (2011)
9. Huiming, Q., Sun, J., Jamjoom, H.T.: SCOOP: Automated social recommendation in enterprise process management. In: IEEE SCC, vol. 1, pp. 101–108 (2008)
10. Johannesson, P., Andersson, B., Wohed, P.: Business Process Management with Social Software Systems-A New Paradigm for Work Organisation. In: Ardagna, D., Mecella, M., Yang, J. (eds.) BPM 2008 Workshops. LNBIP, vol. 17, pp. 659–665. Springer, Heidelberg (2009)
11. Koschmider, A., Song, M., Reijers, H.A.: Social Software for Modeling Business Processes. In: Ardagna, D., Mecella, M., Yang, J. (eds.) BPM 2008 Workshops. LNBIP, vol. 17, pp. 666–677. Springer, Heidelberg (2009)
12. Neumann, G., Erol, S.: From a Social Wiki to a Social Workflow System. In: Ardagna, D., Mecella, M., Yang, J. (eds.) BPM 2008 Workshops. LNBIP, vol. 17, pp. 698–708. Springer, Heidelberg (2009)
13. Riemer, K., Richter, A.: Tweet inside: Microblogging in a corporate context. In: Proceedings 23rd Bled eConference, eTrust, BLED 2010, paper 41 (2010)
14. Schmidt, A., Braun, S.: People tagging & ontology maturing: Towards collaborative competence management. In: 8th International Conference on the Design of Cooperative Systems (COOP 2008), Carry-le-Rouet (2008)
15. Schmidt, R., Dengler, F., Kieninger, A.: Co-creation of Value in IT Service Processes Using Semantic MediaWiki. In: Rinderle-Ma, S., Sadiq, S., Leymann, F. (eds.) BPM 2009 Workshops. LNBIP, vol. 43, pp. 255–265. Springer, Heidelberg (2010)
16. Silva, A.R., Meziani, R., Magalhães, R., Martinho, D., Aguiar, A., Flores, N.: AGILIPO: Embedding Social Software Features into Business Process Tools. In: Rinderle-Ma, S., Sadiq, S., Leymann, F. (eds.) BPM 2009 Workshops. LNBIP, vol. 43, pp. 219–230. Springer, Heidelberg (2010)
17. van der Aalst, W.M.P., ter Hofstede, A.H.M., Kiepuszewski, B., Barros, A.P.: Workflow patterns. Distributed and Parallel Databases 14, 5–51 (2003), doi:10.1023/A:1022883727209

Evaluating Choreographies in BPMN 2.0 Using an Extended Quality Framework

Mario Cortes-Cornax[1], Sophie Dupuy-Chessa[1], Dominique Rieu[1], and Marlon Dumas[2]

[1] University of Grenoble, CNRS, LIG
{Mario.Cortes-Cornax,Sophie.Dupuy,Dominique.Rieu}@imag.fr,
http://sigma.imag.fr/
[2] University of Tartu, Estonia
marlon.dumas@ut.ee

Abstract. The notion of choreography has emerged over the past years as a foundational concept for capturing and managing collaborative business processes. This concept has been adopted as a first-class citizen in the latest version of the Business Process Modeling Notation (BPMN 2.0). However, it remains an open question whether or not BPMN 2.0 is actually appropriate for capturing choreographies. In this paper, we shed light into this question by extending an existing language evaluation framework in order to cover the specificities of choreographies, and applying the extended evaluation framework to BPMN 2.0. Among others, the evaluation identifies a number of issues in BPMN 2.0 that affect the perceptual discriminability of certain choreography modelling constructs. These deficiencies could potentially affect the comprehensibility of models and lead to confusion, particularly among novice users. Recommendations for addressing these deficiencies are put forward.

Keywords: Choreography, Quality Framework, BPMN 2.0.

1 Introduction

A *choreography* is a global representation of the interactions between multiple organizations or organizational units involved in a common business process [1]. Choreographies provide analysts with a basis for understanding, analyzing and optimizing cross-organizational business processes .

Choreography modeling has not achieved standardization despite W3C's efforts within the context of the Web Service Choreography Description Language proposal (WS-CDL [2]). Various research projects [3,4,5,6,7] have proposed different languages for choreography modeling. More recently, the notion of choreography diagram has been incorporated into the latest version of the Business Process Model and Notation (BPMN version 2.0 [8]). The goal of this paper is to evaluate the adequacy of the constructs for choreography modeling introduced in BPMN 2.0. The catalogue of identified requirements might be a starting point for further (empirical) evaluation on choreographies. Also, it represents a clear overview on possible criteria for evaluating a choreography's quality.

R. Dijkman, J. Hofstetter, and J. Koehler (Eds.): BPMN 2011, LNBIP 95, pp. 103–117, 2011.

There have been several previous evaluations of BPMN. Wohed et al. [9] evaluated BPMN (v.1.1) in terms of the workflow patterns [10]. Recker et al. [11] have evaluated BPMN (also v.1.1) in terms of the Bunge-Wand-Weber ontology. This latter analysis highlighted a certain level of construct redundancy and overload. Meanwhile, Wahl & Sindre [12] conducted an evaluation of BPMN using a Semiotic Quality Framework [13] – the same framework we use (with some extensions) as the basis of our evaluation. Like Recker et al., Wahl & Sindre's conclusions put into evidence some construct overload in BPMN that could potentially have a negative effect on comprehensibility. These previous evaluations focused on earlier versions of BPMN, which did not include the choreography subset. Hence, our evaluation complements the above ones.

This paper is structured as follows. After an overview of the choreography subset of BPMN 2.0 (Section 2), we introduce the language quality framework upon which we base our evaluation (Section 3). This framework is very general and can be adapted/extended to fit the requirements of specific domains. Accordingly, we identify and analyze a set of requirements for choreography modeling, leading to an extended language quality framework tailored to the evaluation of choreography modeling languages (Section 4). Next, Section 5 summarizes the results of the analysis of BPMN 2.0 choreography subset using the extended quality framework. Finally, Section 6 puts the results into a broader perspective.

2 Choreographies in BPMN 2.0

A choreography in BPMN 2.0 formalizes the way business *participants* coordinate their *interactions*. In a choreography, the focus is not on the work performed internally by each participant, but rather on the *exchange of information* (e.g. messages) between participants. Another way to look at choreography in BPMN 2.0 is to view it as a type of *business contract* between two or more organizations.

In previous versions of BPMN the only way to represent choreographies was via *collaboration diagrams*. This new version allows modelers describing both choreography and collaboration approaches together or individually. Actually, a global view of interactions is represented in addition to the participants' view given by collaborations which enriches the expressiveness of the language. Figure 1 illustrates how choreographies are represented in BPMN 2.0. This figure captures a manufacturing process inspired by one of the examples in the BPMN specification [8]. In this choreography diagram, interactions between participants are explicitly represented by means of *choreography tasks*. The fact of explicit interactions' sequencing, avoids possible misunderstandings and deadlock errors when capturing choreographies in collaboration diagrams [14].

In each interaction we might find at least two *participants*. One of them (the white band) is the *initiating participant* of the interaction (the one who sends the *initiating message*) while the shaded one is the receiver. The latter could respond with a *response message* (the shaded message). For example, in the first interaction, the *Customer* participant sends an *Order Request* to the *Manufacturer*

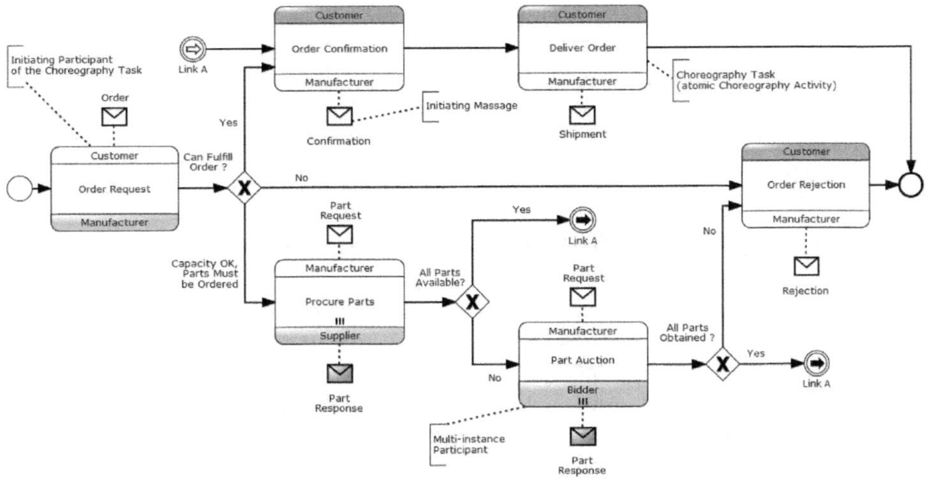

Fig. 1. The manufacturing process represented in a choreography diagram

participant. When the *Manufacturer* contacts the *Supplier* to procure missing parts, a request-response interaction takes place. The *control flow arrows* and *gateways* determine the sequencing of the choreography elements. For further details on BPMN choreography diagrams, the reader is referred to the "Choreography" chapter of the BPMN standard specification [8].

3 The Language Quality Framework

We choose to base our evaluation of BPMN 2.0 on a semiotic quality framework proposed by Kogstie [13] which allow us to assess a broad spectrum of characteristics of a language. Accordingly, in this paper we extend this semiotic quality framework with the aim of framing it in the specific context of choreographies.

Krogstie's framework for language quality is based on a number of characteristics that depend on the technical actors (i.e. tools), stakeholders and modelers such as *"Comprehensibility Appropriateness"*. We do not consider *"Externalizability Appropriateness"* and *"Participant Language Knowledge Appropriateness"* of Krogstie's framework as these characteristics only make sense when evaluating a language relative to a given set of stakeholders. We evaluate some aspects of the *"Domain Appropriateness"* based on criteria found in the literature. Below, we summarize the areas of Krogstie's framework employed in our evaluation:

Domain Appropriateness (D). This area relates to the quality of the language semantics. The key underpinning idea is that the conceptual basis of the language must be powerful enough to express anything in the domain but no more.

Comprehensibility Appropriateness (C). This area relates the language to the social actor interpretation. It considers the concepts of the language and the notation.

Technical Actor Interpretation Appropriateness (T). This area relates the language to the tool. The syntax and the semantics of the language must be formal enough so that tools can automate some treatments on models.

In the following section, we refine these three areas based on a set of requirements for choreography modeling.

4 Choreography Modeling Requirements

Our starting point to evaluate the appropriateness of BPMN 2.0 for choreography modeling has been to identify a set of requirements. We surveyed several previous research works [15,6,16,7,17]. One of the most detailed prior evaluations of choreography definition languages is based on the *Service Interaction Patterns* [18], but these patterns only cover one perspective of the requirements for choreography definition languages. Accordingly, in this paper we complement this patterns-based evaluation framework with other perspectives paying special attention to graphical notation, since the graphical notation is a key ingredient of BPMN.

To organize and categorize the identified choreography modeling requirements, we extend the *Language Quality Framework*, previously described in Section 3, placing the requirements in the different dimensions of the framework (Fig. 2). The following sections detail each dimension adapted to choreographies.

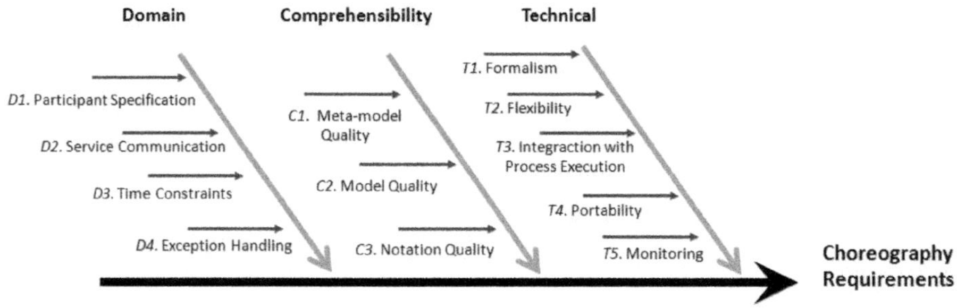

Fig. 2. The requirements axis extending the language quality framework

4.1 Domain Appropriateness Requirements (D)

The following requirements are mainly extracted from the service interaction patterns [18] and from the choreography requirements identified by Decker et al. in [6]. These requirements are summarized below and they are extended in Section 5.1:

D1. Participant Specification. A choreography language should support the representation of more than one participant (service) and more than one instance of the same participant.

D2. Service Communication. A choreography language should support the representation of communication between participants as there is no central coordinator in choreographies.

D3. Time Constraints. A choreography language should allow participants to agree upon how long a given message is being waited for and during what period a participant is expected to transmit a message.

D4. Exception Handling (Fault Paths). Messages may not be sent on time or may represent faults. Thus, modelers should be able to define paths in a choreography that handle such negative scenarios.

4.2 Comprehensibility Appropriateness Requirements (C)

We consider three "Comprehensibility Appropriateness" requirements. The first one establishes that the meta-model of a choreography modeling language should allow modelers to gradually comprehend and design choreographies (*C1. Meta-model Quality*). The second requirement deals with readability and simplicity [19] (*C2. Model Quality*). Finally the third requirement, namely *C3. Notation Quality*, establishes that the concrete syntax of a choreography modeling language should be cognitively effective (optimized for human communication and problem solving [20]), which can be achieved by abiding to the *Principles of Graphical Notations* [20]. These requirements are summarized below and are extended in Section 5.2:

C1. Meta-model Quality. A choreography language must allow modelers to gradually comprehend and design choreographies.

C2. Model Quality. A language must guide modelers to produce appropriate models.

C3. Notation Quality. The language must be cognitively effective.

4.3 Technical Appropriateness Requirements (T)

We consider five important points when analyzing the technical level of choreographies. Firstly, we find the necessity to formalize both syntax and semantics [15] (*T1. Formalism*). Accordingly, a choreography diagram should have a precise semantics, which can be specified for example by means of a mapping to a formal notation (e.g., colored petri nets or pi-calculus).

Secondly, in line with previous work [6,7], we adopt the requirement that choreographies should be independent from specific communication technology (e.g. independent from physical endpoints definitions) (*T2. Flexibility*).

Thirdly, adequate alignment between choreographies and process execution is necessary in order to bridge the "Business-IT gap" [21] and to avoid inconsistencies between process modeling and execution [16] (*T3. Integration with Process Execution*). This can be achieved by aligning (though not necessarily mapping) the choreography language to an executable process definition language such as the Business Process Execution Language (BPEL) [22] (cf. the approach taken in BPEL4Chor [6]) or by aligning choreographies with executable BPMN models.

The possibility to exchange models between tools is another important requirement [15,23] (*T4. Portability*). Accordingly, a choreography language should define an interchange format covering both the language itself as well as graphical data attached to the model elements.

Finally, previous work [17] has highlighted the usefulness of monitoring in the context of choreographies (*T5. Monitoring*). Thus, a choreography language should be defined in a way that choreography monitoring is possible.

These requirements are summarized below and are extended in Section 5.3:

T1. Formalism. Precise/formal definition or mapping into a well-established formalism.
T2. Flexibility. Decoupling from Web Services Extension point to plug in different technical configurations might be supported.
T3. Integration with Process Execution. Alignment with executable processes.
T4. Portability. Model interchange support.
T5. Monitoring. Introduction of monitoring mechanisms.

5 Evaluation of BPMN 2.0 for Choreographies

In this section, we evaluate the choreography proposal presented in BPMN 2.0. We use the language quality framework described in Section 3 extended with the requirements identified in Section 4. We go through the scenario on Fig. 1 to illustrate some of the evaluation points.

5.1 Domain Appropriateness Evaluation

In this section we analyze the domain requirements' support in BPMN 2.0.

D1. Participant Specification. We consider two specific requirements in this section:

D1.1 Multi-lateral Interactions. More than two participants (services) can be involved in choreography.
D1.2 Service Sets. Several participants (services) of the same type might be involved in a choreography.

As Fig. 1 illustrates, more than two participants can be involved in the choreography model (*D1.1. Multi lateral interactions*). In the example of Fig. 1, participants are the *Customer*, the *Manufacturer*, the *Supplier* and the *Bidder*. BPMN 2.0 also supports multi-instance participants (*D1.2 Service sets*). The example shows that several instances of the participant *Bidder* might be involved in the choreography. BPMN 2.0 allows defining how many participants of one type will be involved (*ParticipantMultiplicity*). However, this multiplicity is only supported in an implementation level, but not represented graphically.

D2. Service Communication. When analyzing the service communication requirements, we identify the following three cases:

D2.1 Selection of Services and Reference Passing. Selection (of a service) can be done in design, deployment or execution time. A reference of a selected participant(service) may be passed to another participant as there is no central coordinator in choreography.

D2.2 Service Correlation. Possibility to distinguish different conversations as well as relating an incoming message to the previously sent or received must be supported.

D2.3 Message Multiplicity. Possibility to define the number of messages sent from one (or more) participant(s) to other(s).

One potential deficiency in BPMN relates to the absence of a notion of *channel* as in WS-CDL (*D2.1 Selection of Services and Reference Passing*). A channel is a reference that allows one participant to communicate with one other participant. Importantly, channels can be created by one participant and passed to other participants, thereby enabling dynamic message destinations [2]. For example, in Fig. 1 a *Customer* could create a channel to exchange delivery information. In this scenario, the *Customer* sends the channel to the *Manufacturer* who forwards it to the *Supplier*. The *Supplier* then sends delivery information directly to the *Customer* using the channel originally created by the *Customer*. Potentially, the customer could communicate with multiple suppliers and give a separate response channel to each of them.

The concepts of *Correlation Key* and *Participant References* in BPMN 2.0 address this need to some extent. However, these concepts constitute one particular way of implementing a channel, based on the idea that every message contains an explicit identifier. In practice, this is not the only mechanism for implementing channels. For example, Uniform Resource Locators (URLs) are often used to represent communication channels between web services, especially in RESTful services [24]. URLs allow one to encode both the participant reference, and the correlation key together. When using URLs, the separation between correlation key and participant reference is irrelevant. The concept of channel abstracts away from such details, while the concepts of correlation keys and participant keys do not provide this level of abstraction. A possible way to address this deficiency in BPMN might be to replace participant references/correlation keys with a single concept of channel. In this extension, interactions in a BPMN choreography diagram would have channels attached to them in order to capture channel creation, passing and use. Additionally, channel details could be captured using textual annotations, following the principle of *Dual Coding* [20].

BPMN 2.0 uses the mechanism of *Correlation Key* to link messages with process instances (*D2.2 Service Correlation*). Correlation can be applied to *Message Flows* in collaboration and choreography. A conversation represents a set of *Message Flows* grouped together based on a concept and/or a correlation key. It is however not clearly specified in the standard how this correlation is graphically represented. Semantically, several correlation keys could be related to a choreography but not explicit representation is considered. Nevertheless, *Function-Based* correlation patterns (e.g., property-based correlation) described in [25] could be explicitly represented in choreography diagrams so as to render clearer possible labeling or special treatment to group of messages.

Now, if we look at communication between services, we should take into account several scenarios listed below (*D2.3 Message Multiplicity*).

1. A participant X sends one message to a participant of type Y.
2. A participant X sends multiple messages to a participant of type Y.
3. A participant X sends one message to multiple participants of type Y.
4. A participant X sends multiple messages to each participant of type Y.

Other scenarios might also be possible by reversing the direction of the message flow. BPMN 2.0 does not distinguish between these cases. This distinction is important to strictly define choreographies and avoid inconsistencies when participant processes are implemented. The point here is that BPMN captures the concept of *Participant Multiplicity*, but it does not capture the concept of *Message Multiplicity*. Perhaps the concept of *Message Flow* should be extended so that the message multiplicity and the concept of participant multiplicity can be made visible in the message flows. This may be more appropriate than having a concept of *ParticipantMultiplicity* attached to the participants.

In addition to the above, the lack of visual representation of the notion *Service Correlation* affects our assessment of *Service Communication* support. In this respect, we propose to recover the concept of *Channel* used in WS-CDL for reference passing and to assign a graphical notation to it.

D3. Time Constraints and D4. Exception Handling. BPMN 2.0 allows the definition of time constraints (*D3. Time Constraints*) as well as the definition of fault paths or exception handling (*D4. Exception Handling (Fault Paths)*). Choreography diagrams maintain this aspect from classical process diagrams.

Table 1. Domain requirements in BPMN 2.0 (for choreographies)

Level	Requirement	Refinement	Support
Domain	D1. Participant Specification	D1.1 Multi-lateral Interactions	2
		D1.2 Service Sets	2
			4 (4)
	D2. Service Communication	D2.1 Selection of Services and Reference Passing	1
		D2.2 Service Correlation	1
		D2.3 Message Multiplicity	0
			2(6)
	D3. Time Constraints		**2(2)**
	D4. Exception Handling		**2(2)**

Synthesis. *Table 1* summarizes the support of domain requirements in BPMN 2.0 for choreographies. In similar evaluations, a three-valued scale [–, +/– , +] is used to indicate whether a requirement has *no direct support*, *no complete support*, or *full support* respectively. We choose a similar but numerical scale [0, 1, 2] to have a better overview of the requirements that have sub-requirements. The sum of the sub-requirements's score is presented with the possible maximum score in parenthesis (e.g., **2 (6)** means that two out of six of the possible score is achieved). We wish to underscore however that in this evaluation, the numeric score is not the main purpose, but rather a by-product. The main purpose of the evaluation is to identify limitations and areas for improvement in the language.

5.2 Comprehensibility Appropriateness Evaluation

We analyze here the comprehensibility requirements' support in BPMN 2.0.

C1. Meta-model Quality Three important points are considered when analyzing meta-model quality. They are listed below:

C1.1. Abstraction Levels. Different levels of abstraction might be presented. This gradual presentation would improve comprehensibility and understanding of the meta-model.
C1.2. Views-Perspectives. Different perspectives are identified and shown in different diagrams (e.g., structural and behavioral views).
C1.3. Presentation. Meta-model's diagrams (e.g., UML class diagrams) must be cognitive effective tools.

BPMN 2.0 does not specify different dialects or levels of abstractions when defining choreographies [23](*C1.1. Abstraction Levels*). Propositions as the 3-leveled models presented by Silver in [23] should be present in the standard to help in the construction of choreographies.

The presentation of different perspectives should also be a main concern when defining choreographies (*C1.2. Views-Perspectives*). In [26,27,6] the authors contend that different perspectives when modeling are required. In the standard, the use of different diagrams (e.g., choreography and collaboration) is called perspectives but this concept is not clearly explained. The new *conversation diagram* could be exploited when defining choreographies. Figure 3 shows how it represents the manufacturing process of the example. The conversation diagram could be considered as the *structural view* as it models relationships between participants and the choreography diagram the *behavioral view* (models interactions between participants). Currently, it is not required for choreography conformance [8] but we suggest it.

When analyzing the meta-model, several style guidelines described in [19,23] as well as the WS-CDL critics taken from [15] are taken into account. In the standard, numerous complex and not effective meta-models are found (*C1.3. Presentation*). For example, choreography meta-model has 18 elements and 25

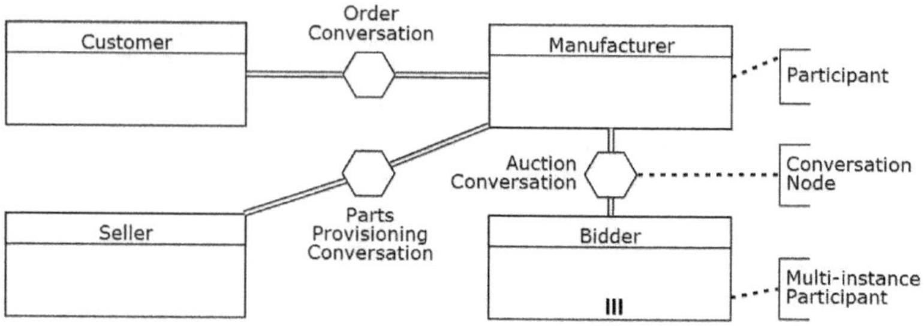

Fig. 3. The manufacturing process represented in a conversation diagram

relationships. It is not easy to understand the choreography concept just regarding the meta-model despite it should be one of its goals. Symmetry, exhaustive multiplicity definition and avoiding cross lines seems to be prior issues in the standard's meta-model style. However, the use of color, coherent sized elements, placing subclasses below super classes or the fact of avoiding redundant information could simplify meta-model's comprehension and make them much more effective [28,19,20].

C2. Model Quality. We identify two main points when looking at model quality. We focused on the capacity of the language to produce good models and to avoid producing bad ones. The model quality can be induced by the language. Here, we consider a very simple vision of model quality which is limited to the readability (*C2.1. Readability*) , the simplicity (*C2.2. Simplicity*) and the guidance (*C2.3. Guidance*) encouraged by the language.

C2.1. Readability. Readability facilitates diagram comprehension (crossing lines, sized symbols, use of color, symmetric, ...).

C2.2. Simplicity. Simplicity must be encouraged as an effective cognitive method (show indispensable, reorganization, diagram size, ...).

C2.3. Guidance. Guidance should be given in order to encourage useful models.

Readability (*C2.1. Readability*) and simplicity (*C2.2. Simplicity*) will depend mostly on the modeler's skills as well as the tools. The standard provides mechanisms as *Sub-process* or *Link events* to deal with these requirements [8]. However, the standard lacks of guidelines to produce good models (*C2.3. Guidance*). All diagrams can be combined and fulfilled at different level of details. Very complex as well as too simple diagrams can be produced. This flexibility and the lack of orientation could be disturbing factors for modelers specially novices.

C3. Notation Quality. In [29], the authors analyze the cognitive effectiveness of the BPMN 2.0 visual notation through a set of Principles of Notations. They focus on BPMN business process diagrams but several of their observations are also applicable to BPMN choreographies. The Principles of Notations considered in this prior work are:

C3.1 Semiotic Clarity. One-to-one correspondence between symbols and concepts.

C3.2 Perceptual Discriminability. The easy and accuracy with which different symbols are clearly distinguishable from each other.

C3.3 Semantic Transparency. Visual representation whose appearance suggests their meaning.

C3.4 Cognitive Integration. Inclusion of explicit mechanisms to support integration of information from different diagrams.

C3.5 Visual Expressiveness. Use the full range and capacities of visual variables (shape, texture, brightness, size, color and orientation).

C3.6 Dual Coding. Use text to complement graphics. Textual encoding is most effective when it is used in a supporting role.

C3.7 Graphical Economy. The number of different graphical symbols has to be cognitively manageable.

C3.8 Cognitive Fit Expert-Novice Difference. Take into account difference between practitioners and novices.

C3.9 Complexity Management. Include explicit mechanisms for dealing with complexity.

One of the major problems detected in [29] is the lack of a scientific background in notation design. This problem applies to the choreography subset of BPMN 2.0. In particular, there is not always one-to-one correspondence between symbols and concepts (*C3.1 Semiotic Clarity*). For example, the service correlation or the participant's multiplicity are just declared in an implementation level. In other cases such as for instance, timer event, this requirement is fulfilled. The perceptual discriminability can also be criticized. The difference between call-choreographies and sub-choreographies by its line width its an example of this lack (*C3.2 Perceptual Discriminability*). The concept of message flow in BPMN is perhaps overloaded. Specifically, if one participant creates an instance of another participant ("instantiation"), it will use a message flow. But also, if one participant wants to send a message to an existing instance of another participant, it will also use a message flow. This lack of perceptual discrimination in BPMN 2.0 might lead to comprehensibility issues.

In some cases the notation is intuitive, e.g. envelopes are used for symbolizing message events and clocks are used for symbolizing timer events. In other cases, especially those regarding the minimal differences between the process activities and choreography activities, less transparency is achieved (*C3.3 Semantic Transparency*). It is not always intuitive the integration between the different BPMN diagrams, in particular between collaboration and choreography diagrams. In choreography diagrams, the sending participant band is shaded in white and the receiving participant band is shaded in gray. In collaboration diagrams the sending event is marked with a black envelope, whereas the receiving event is marked with a white envelope. Thus, gray corresponds to white and white corresponds to black. It is not always evident how to match send tasks in collaborations to response messages in choreography tasks (*C3.4 Cognitive Integration*).

Visual expressiveness will depend on implementors as the standard suggests flexibility in this aspect (*C3.5 Visual Expressiveness*). Dual coding is supported and recommended and will also depend on modelers and implementations (*C3.6 Dual Coding*). The number of graphical symbols is cognitively manageable as the use of event and gateway symbols is considerably reduced w.r.t. process diagrams (*C3.7 Graphical Economy*). Due to the simplicity of choreography notation, there is arguably no need for multiple dialects as proposed by Moody [20](*C3.8 Cognitive Fit*). Instead, we propose to adopt conversation diagrams to complement choreographies. Finally BPMN 2.0 allows one to declare sub-choreographies that can be expanded or hidden (*C3.9 Complexity management*).

Table 2. Comprehensibility requirements in BPMN 2.0 (for choreographies)

Level	**Requirement**	**Refinement**	**Support**
Comprehensibility	C1. Meta-model Quality	C1.1 Abstraction Levels	0
		C1.2 Views-Perspectives	1
		C1.3 Presentation	1
			2 (6)
	C2. Model Quality	C2.1 Readability	2
		C2.2 Simplicity	2
		C2.3 Guidance	0
			4 (6)
	C3. Notation Quality	C3.1 Semiotic Clarity	1
		C3.2 Perceptual Discriminability	1
		C3.3 Semantic Transparency	1
		C3.4 Cognitive Integration	1
		C3.5 Visual Expressiveness	2
		C3.6 Dual Coding	2
		C3.7 Graphical Economy	2
		C3.8 Cognitive Fit	1
		C3.9 Complexity Management	2
			13 (18)

Synthesis. *Table 2* resumes the support of comprehensibility requirements in BPMN 2.0. Regarding to this level, the major lack is detected in the *Meta-model Quality.* This point is clearly improvable introducing abstraction levels and different viewpoints when presenting choreography concepts. The meta-model presentation can also be improved, simplifying diagrams and eliminating superfluous terms. However, model quality and graphical notation are remarkable strengths in BPMN 2.0 for choreographies. When looking to notation we criticized the choice of keeping the rounded rectangle form to represent choreography activities as well as the use of term *Activity* when referring to an interaction.

5.3 Technical Actor Interpretation Appropriateness Evaluation

We consider BPMN 2.0 for choreographies well integrated with process execution due to its good alignment to process orchestrations (BPMN's process diagrams) and consequently to BPEL (*T3. Integration with Process Execution*).

This fact will depend on the accuracy of choreography models to achieve a good integration with final execution process. BPEL is based on process algebra formalism (pi-calculus). Therefore, choreographies in BPMN 2.0 can be considered to have a well-established formalism (*T1. Formalism*). A more detailed analysis of BPMN 2.0 execution semantics is found in [30]. Other related works are also surveyed in the latter article.

Choreography diagrams are decoupled from technical configurations (*T2. Flexibility*). As depicted in [31], BPMN is considered as an implementation independent language. In addition, it permits WSDL easily plug in which allows a simple transition to web service technology. Portability will strongly depend on vendors (*T4. Portability*). In [32] Silver states: "It seems that vendors, in particular the ones that drove the standard, do not really care about this most fundamental user expectation of any standard". Nevertheless, BPMN 2.0 standard specifies the meta-model and schema for BPMN 2.0 Diagram Interchange (BPMN DI) [8]. Monitoring is out of the scope of the standard but they envisage however a monitoring extension (*T5. Monitoring*).

Synthesis. *Table 3* resumes the support for technical requirements in BPMN 2.0. We observe that these requirements are much better supported than both domains' and participants' requirements which are similarly supported. It is clear, as remarked Silver in [32] that the OMG has done a big effort in the technical aspects in this new version. We hope that implementations take into account all these improvements presented in the standard.

Table 3. Technical requirements in BPMN 2.0 (for choreographies)

Level	Requirement	Refinement	Support
Technical	T1. Formalism		**2(2)**
	T2. Flexibility		**2(2)**
	T3. Integration		**2(2)**
	T4. Portability		**2(2)**
	T5. Monitoring		**1(2)**

6 Discussion and Conclusions

We have evaluated the appropriateness of the new BPMN's diagram to capture choreographies. Before it, we could represent them using collaboration diagrams, but this new representation depicts interactions in a truly global view. BPMN 2.0 also permits the combination of both collaboration and choreography diagrams so alignment between both representations could be achieved. We conclude that it is a good choreography language but there are still some limitations described in the previous section. As a new representation, extensions might be surely introduced as the ones suggested in the different evaluation points in Section 5.

The limited size of the paper did not permit a more exhaustive evaluation of BPMN 2.0 choreography diagrams. However, we have analyzed some important axes in a more detailed way than other evaluation works' based on the Semiotic Quality Framework.

A limitation of our work is the lack of empirical validation of our suggestions with real BPMN users. We consider experimentations with service and business specialist to validate and to complete our requirements proposal. We should also work about defining more measurable scales to validate the evaluation. These measures will also be useful to compare with other choreography proposals.

We considered to review and improve the choreography requirements so they could be used as source of inspiration and reference to evaluate choreography languages, as well as to better understand this currently emerging concept. However, we hope that this work will help designers in understanding the potential of BPMN 2.0 for choreographies.

References

1. Peltz, C.: Web services orchestration and choreography. Computer, 46–52 (2003)
2. W3C: Web services choreography description language version 1.0 (ws-cdl) - w3c candidate recommendation (2005)
3. Ross-Talbot, S., Brown, G., Honda, K., Yoshida, N., Carbone, M.: Pi4soa technologies fundation, `http://sourceforge.net/apps/trac/pi4soa/wiki`
4. Decker, G., Kirov, M., Zaha, J., Dumas, M.: Maestro for Lets Dance: An Environment for Modeling Service Interactions. BPM Demo Session, p. 32 (2006)
5. Nitzsche, J., Van Lessen, T., Leymann, F.: Extending bpellight for expressing multi-partner message exchange patterns. In: 12th International IEEE Enterprise Distributed Object Computing Conference, pp. 245–254. IEEE (2008)
6. Decker, G., Kopp, O., Leymann, F., Weske, M.: Interacting services: from specification to execution. Data & Knowledge Engineering 68(10), 946–972 (2009)
7. Barker, A., Walton, C., Robertson, D.: Choreographing Web Services. IEEE Transactions on Services Computing 2(2), 152–166 (2009)
8. OMG: Business process model and notation (bpmn 2.0) (2011), `http://www.omg.org/spec/BPMN/2.0/`
9. Wohed, P., van der Aalst, W.M.P., Dumas, M., ter Hofstede, A.H.M., Russell, N.: On the Suitability of BPMN for Business Process Modelling. In: Dustdar, S., Fiadeiro, J.L., Sheth, A.P. (eds.) BPM 2006. LNCS, vol. 4102, pp. 161–176. Springer, Heidelberg (2006)
10. van der Aalst, W., Ter Hofstede, A., Kiepuszewski, B., Barros, A.: Workflow patterns. Distributed and Parallel Databases 14(1), 5–51 (2003)
11. Recker, J., Indulska, M., Rosemann, M., Green, P.: Do process modelling techniques get better? A comparative ontological analysis of BPMN. In: Proceedings of the 16th Australasian Conference on Information Systems, Sydney, Australia. Citeseer (2005)
12. Wahl, T., Sindre, G.: An analytical evaluation of BPMN using a semiotic quality framework. Advanced Topics in Database Research 5 (2006)
13. Krogstie, J., Sindre, G., Jørgensen, H.: Process models representing knowledge for action: a revised quality framework. European Journal of Information Systems 15(1), 91–102 (2006)
14. Decker, G., Weske, M.: Interaction-centric modeling of process choreographies. Inf. Syst. 36, 292–312 (2011)

15. Barros, A., Dumas, M., Oaks, P.: A critical overview of the web services choreography description language. BPTrends Newsletter 3 (2005)
16. Ross-Talbot, S., Brown, G., Honda, K., Yoshida, N., Carbone, M.: Soa best practices: Building a soa using process governance. JBoss (2009)
17. Wetzstein, B., Karastoyanova, D., Kopp, O., Leymann, F., Zwink, D.: Cross-organizational process monitoring based on service choreographies. In: Proceedings of the 2010 ACM Symposium on Applied Computing, pp. 2485–2490. ACM (2010)
18. Barros, A., Dumas, M., ter Hofstede, A.H.M.: Service Interaction Patterns. In: van der Aalst, W.M.P., Benatallah, B., Casati, F., Curbera, F. (eds.) BPM 2005. LNCS, vol. 3649, pp. 302–318. Springer, Heidelberg (2005)
19. Ambler, S.: The elements of UML 2.0 style. Cambridge Univ. Pr. (2005)
20. Moody, D.: The Physics of Notations: Toward a Scientific Basis for Constructing Visual Notations in Software Engineering. IEEE Transactions on Software Engineering, 756–779 (2009)
21. Weidlich, M., Barros, A., Mendling, J., Weske, M.: Vertical Alignment of Process Models–How Can We Get There? In: Halpin, T., Krogstie, J., Nurcan, S., Proper, E., Schmidt, R., Soffer, P., Ukor, R. (eds.) Enterprise, Business-Process and Information Systems Modeling. LNBIP, vol. 29, pp. 71–84. Springer, Heidelberg (2009)
22. OASIS: Web services business process execution language v2.0 (ws-bpel 2.0) (2007)
23. Silver, B.: BPMN Method and Style: A levels-based methodology for BPM process modeling and improvement using BPMN 2.0. Cody-Cassidy Press, US (2009)
24. Fielding, R.: Architectural styles and the design of network-based software architectures. PhD thesis, Citeseer (2000)
25. Barros, A., Decker, G., Dumas, M., Weber, F.: Correlation Patterns in Service-Oriented Architectures. In: Dwyer, M.B., Lopes, A. (eds.) FASE 2007. LNCS, vol. 4422, pp. 245–259. Springer, Heidelberg (2007)
26. Dijkman, R., Dumas, M.: Service-oriented design: A multi-viewpoint approach. International Journal of Cooperative Information Systems 13, 337–368 (2004)
27. Barros, A., Decker, G., Dumas, M.: Multi-staged and multi-viewpoint service choreography modelling. Technical report (2006)
28. Evitts, P.: A UML pattern language. New Riders Publishing, Thousand Oaks (2000)
29. Genon, N., Heymans, P., Amyot, D.: Analysing the Cognitive Effectiveness of the BPMN 2.0 Visual Notation. In: Malloy, B., Staab, S., van den Brand, M. (eds.) SLE 2010. LNCS, vol. 6563, pp. 377–396. Springer, Heidelberg (2011)
30. Dijkman, R., Van Gorp, P.: BPMN 2.0 Execution Semantics Formalized as Graph Rewrite Rules. In: Mendling, J., Weidlich, M., Weske, M. (eds.) BPMN 2010. LNBIP, vol. 67, pp. 16–30. Springer, Heidelberg (2010)
31. Decker, G., Kopp, O., Barros, A.: An introduction to service choreographies. Information Technology 50(2), 122–127 (2008)
32. Silver, B.: Bpmn model interchange: Update (2011), `http://www.brsilver.com/2011/02/26/bpmn-model-interchange-update/`

A Lightweight Approach for Designing Enterprise Architectures Using BPMN: An Application in Hospitals

Oscar Barros[1], Ricardo Seguel[2], and Alejandro Quezada[1]

[1] University of Chile, Santiago, Chile
obarros@dii.uchile.cl
[2] Eindhoven University of Technology, The Netherlands
r.e.seguel@tue.nl

Abstract. An Enterprise Architecture (EA) comprises different models at different levels of abstraction. Since existing EA design approaches, e.g. MDA, use UML for modeling, the design of the architecture becomes complex and time consuming. In this paper, we present an integrated and lightweight design approach for EA that uses a generic architecture and patterns, expressed in BPMN. The approach facilitates the modeling between the different levels. This has been applied in real cases in hospitals and other domains, demonstrating its feasibility and usability, reducing complexity and time for modeling.

Keywords: Enterprise Architecture, Process Architecture, Business Process Management, Process Pattern, BPMN.

1 Introduction

Companies using EA as a management method have found that different representations of processes are needed according to the level of detail that managers want to know. Based on the reported experience of many companies [12,18] and our own experience with hundreds of redesign projects through the collaboration with industry [3,4], the following levels of detail can be identified:

I. Process Architecture, which is a high-level representation for communicating to executives
II. Business Design based on the process representation of value chains for its presentation to process managers and business executives.
III. Process Logic that is a detailed representation of the process models for simulation and implementation for communicating to process specialists.
IV. IT Process Support that is the representation of the system supporting the execution of the processes for process and IT specialists.

Different modeling schemes and tools can be used for each of these levels for process analysis and design. For example, for Level I, we can use simple diagrams as the one that are part of the first level of SCOR [7] or eTOM [9]. Next, for Level

R. Dijkman, J. Hofstetter, and J. Koehler (Eds.): BPMN 2011, LNBIP 95, pp. 118–123, 2011.

II we can draw informal Porter Value Chain diagrams [15] or more formal IDEF0 models [8]. Then, for Level III, we can use BPMN [19] or EPC [16] for more detailed models. For Level IV, depending on the type of implementation, we can use alternatives such as UML, Workflow diagrams or BPMN for implementing the supporting software application into a process-aware information system. Therefore, differences and inconsistencies appear as the models are designed by using different modeling languages at the different levels. In this paper, we propose an integrative approach in which all the models are designed with BPMN and the process models are implemented in a BPMN-based system. We use a real case that is being developed in a hospital to exemplify our ideas..

Existing frameworks for designing Enterprise Architecture [14] use a similar approach to the one we propose. MDA [13] is based on UML for modeling the complete architecture, from business requirements to software architecture for implementing the supporting system. Since UML is not broadly used at the business level, the modeling becomes complex for non UML experts and hard to communicate to business executives. An analysis of a complex architecture, using MDA in combination with the Zachman Framework [20] has been developed for investigating this gap and defining a mapping between them with a three-dimension approach [17]. TOGAF is a comprehensive framework for designing an EA, based on a iterative life-cycle which architecture modeling method (ADM) uses the Archimate language [12]. Although TOGAF does not force the use of Archimate, other modeling language can be used such as UML or even combining ADM with MDA [5]. In practice, TOGAF is generic and it can be used for any company in any industry. Since TOGAF does not have any design pattern [6] for developing an architecture in a given domain, this process becomes complex and slow. In previous research [1,3,4], we have developed patterns for designing an Enterprise Architecture and processes in different industries such as healthcare. By using the patterns, the design process becomes faster than just using a generic framework as TOGAF or MDA. In this paper, we present an EA design approach, which uses BPMN to model designs based on our patterns at the four levels in an integrative way. We concentrate on the Process Architecture, but other architectures such as the application, data and technical architectures are present in design levels Levels III and IV defined above. The remainder of this paper is as follows. Section 2 explains the solving approach of the problem. Section 3 describes the approach for designing an EA with BPMN in a hospital. Finally, Section 4 describes the conclusions and future work.

2 Problem Solving Approach

In this paper, we propose a scheme that uses BPMN as a unique technique for designing and modeling all the four levels (I-IV) defined above. For this, we take the best of the different methods in which we have experience: Business Process Patterns (BPP) [1,3] that are in line with the purpose of SCOR [7] or eTOM [9] but valid for different industries; BPMN modeling language, and process-aware information systems for implementing BPMN models. The key ideas of our approach are:

1. In order to drive modeling at all levels of detail, predefined general process patterns are used. The patterns, which are based on what we call macroprocesses, provide templates or general structures of activities and flows about how a process should be performed. Each macroprocess is itself, a layered normative structure of processes. A macroprocess gives, in several levels of detail, the processes, sub processes and activities plus the relationships that should be executed in order to produce a desired result.
2. Using these patterns, ad-hoc for different industries, the design or re-design process is accelerated.
3. We adopt a simple information flow representation and hierarchical decomposition of activities for gradually giving details of the process for Levels I and II, using some of the simplest BPMN constructs to represent levels I and II, for flow type models.
4. We keep consistency and traceability with hierarchical decomposition: all the elements of any level should be details of an element at a higher level.

Other authors such as Freund and Rücker[10] have proposed the use of BPMN for process modeling; they only concentrate on Levels III and IV of our approach. They do not consider the process architecture design of Level I by using frameworks as SCOR [7] or eTOM [9], nor the business design of Level II by using Porter Value Chain or IDEF0 diagrams. Therefore, their approach lacks the strategic and business alignment for designing processes. According to the design guidelines of Hevner et al. [11], we propose an approach that produces an artifact that can be used by practitioners to provide solutions in a given domain. Our design domain is stated above and goes from strategy based process architectures to information systems that support such processes. This problem is very relevant since most organizations deal with process and information system design on a piecemeal basis, without considering the integration that we propose.

3 Designing the EA with BPMN

We now explain how each level defined above is modeled for the case of a hospital. For the sake of space, we give a more details in [2].

3.1 Process Architecture Modeling (Level I)

We base the modeling of this level on general process architecture patterns reported on our previous research [1,3,4]. The patterns are based on the thesis that the architecture of any enterprise can be modeled by means of four general Business Process Patterns, which we call macroprocesses. In Figure 1, we show the resulting architecture for the domain of hospitals we are working with. From the architecture we select the macroprocess that is to be designed in detail, which is Service Lines to Patients , since the business goal in this case is to improve the service to patients and make a better use of resources and it is considered that it can be done by designing this macroprocess. Such services lines or value chains are then detailed, by hierarchical decomposition.

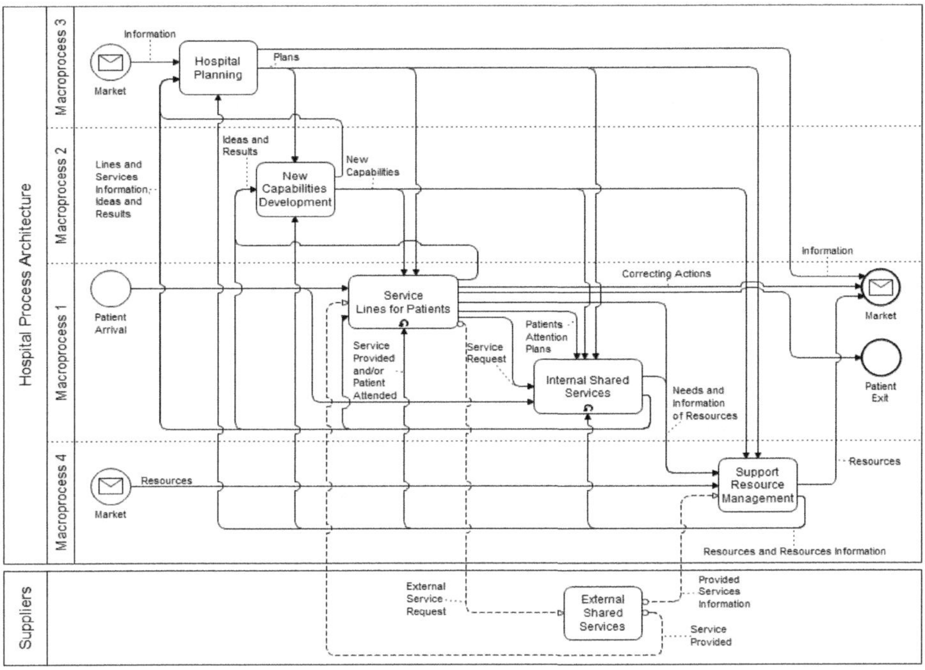

Fig. 1. Process Architecture for Hospitals (Level I)

3.2 Business Design Using Patterns (Level II)

The basic rule that we apply for designing in this level is to take the structure of processes provided by the architecture of the previous level and design each of its components by using the process pattern corresponding to the value chain. This provides a set of sub processes that are necessary to execute. Then, the component are specialized to the particular case; i.e. to establish how every sub process of the pattern is currently executed, if at all, and then evaluating technically and economically the feasibility of performing it according to what the pattern prescribes.

3.3 Process Logic Design (Level III)

The basic rule is that each of the sub processes designed in the previous level should be detailed in terms of who is responsible for each activity of the sub process, the business logic that will be executed by people or the information system and the workflow that establishes the relationships among activities. This should be consistent with the previous level in that all the functionality that a sub process provides at such level and the relationships it supports must be provided by the design. For our running example, we detail the BPMN model for the sub process Attendance Control shown in Figure 2. This tries to solve one important problem currently observed at a given hospital, which is that

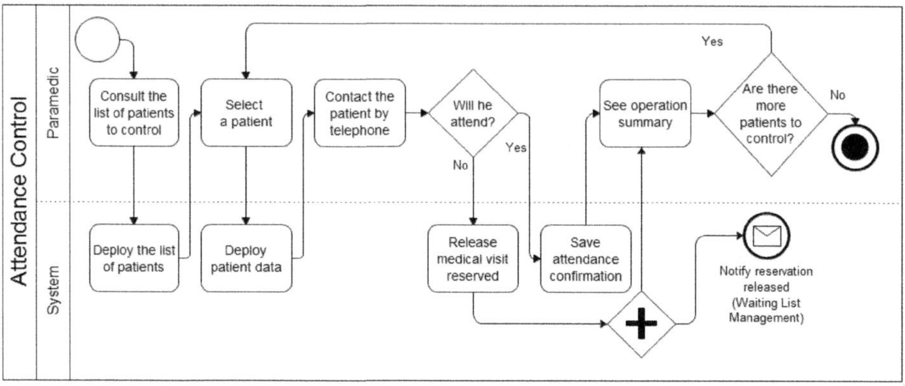

Fig. 2. BPMN diagram for Attendance Control (Level III)

20% of medical visits fail because of patient absenteeism. We aim to improve the performance of medical booking service to reduce the waiting list of patients. This is done by introducing a logic that detect patients that are likely not to attend and calling them to check them up. This generates the possibility of assigning liberated medical hours to patients in a waiting list that otherwise will not get attention.

3.4 IT Process Support (Level IV)

We illustrate this level with the case in which we want to automatically generate the supporting system for the processes models in BPMN. The BonitaSoft system is used to demonstrate the easy implementation of the processes from the models designed in Level III.

4 Conclusions

All the steps performed from Level I to Level IV have taken just 4 weeks for implementing the processes in the prototype for our running example. This means that in this period we have designed the architecture of the hospital, developed the redesign of the critical processes, implemented the redesigned processes in the supporting system and communicated all the changes to the different stakeholders at every level (I-IV). Compared to other EA design approaches as Zachman [20], MDA [13] and TOGAF [12] that take long and become complex due to the generic guidelines, our approach accelerates the design process of the EA by using process patterns and BPMN as the only modeling language. So, our approach represents an integrated and lightweight design process for an Enterprise Architecture. Although this is preliminary result and need much more success cases, we have shown in a real case that indeed our approach is less complex, much easier to use and faster than existing approaches.

References

1. Barros, O., Julio, C.: Enterprise and process architecture patterns. Business Process Management Journal 17(4), 598–618 (2011)
2. Barros, O., Seguel, R., Quezada, A.: A lightweight approach for designing enterprise architectures using BPMN: an application in hospitals (long version). University of Chile (2011)
3. Barros, O.: Business process patterns and frameworks: Reusing knowledge in process innovation. Business Process Management Journal (January 2007)
4. Barros, O.: Business processes architecture and design. BPTrends (May 2007)
5. Blevins, T.J., Spencer, J., Waskiewicz, F.: TOGAF ADM and MDA - Revision 1.1. The Open Group (2004)
6. Buckl, S., Ernst, A.M., Matthes, F., Ramacher, R., Schweda, C.M.: Using enterprise architecture management patterns to complement TOGAF. In: IEEE International Conference on Enterprise Distributed Object Computing (2009)
7. Supply Chain Council. SCOR: Supply-Chain Operations Reference model; version 9.0 (2008)
8. Feldmann, C.G.: The practical guide to business process reengineering using IDEF0. Dorset House Publishing Co., Inc., New York (1998)
9. TM Forum. eTOM: enhanced Telecom Operations Map; release 8.0 (2008)
10. Freund, J., Rücker, B.: Praxishandbuch BPMN 2.0. Hanser Fachbuchverlag (2010)
11. Hevner, A.R., March, S.T., Park, J., Ram, S.: Design science in information systems research. MIS Quarterly 28(1), 75–105 (2004)
12. Lankhorst, M.: Enterprise Architecture at Work: Modelling, Communication and Analysis, 2nd edn. Springer, Heidelberg (2009)
13. Mellor, S.J.: MDA distilled: principles of model-driven architecture. Addison-Wesley, USA (2004)
14. Minoli, D.: Enterprise architecture A to Z: frameworks, business process modeling, SOA, and infrastructure technology. CRC Press (2008)
15. Porter, M.E.: What is strategy? Harvard Business Review (1996)
16. Scheer, A.-W.: ARIS – Business Process Frameworks. Springer, Germany (1999)
17. Seguel, R., Grefen, P., Eshuis, R.: Design of complex architectures using a three dimension approach: the crosswork case. BETA WP309, Eindhoven University of Technology, The Netherlands (2010)
18. van't Wout, J., Waage, M., Hartman, H., Stahlecker, M., Hofman, A.: The Integrated Architecture Framework Explained: Why, What, How. Springer, Heidelberg (2010)
19. White, S.A., Miers, D.: BPMN Modeling and Reference Guide: Understanding and Using BPMN. Future Strategies, Inc., FL (2008)
20. Zachman, J.: The Zachman framework for enterprise architecture. In: Zachman International (2002)

Implementing the Semantics of BPMN through Model-Driven Web Application Generation

Marco Brambilla and Piero Fraternali

Politecnico di Milano, Dipartimento di Elettronica e Informazione
P.za L. Da Vinci, 32. I-20133 Milano - Italy
{marco.brambilla,piero.fraternali}@polimi.it

Abstract. We describe a pragmatic approach based on Model Driven Engineering (MDE) principles for implmenting the execution semantics of BPMN. The approach is based on a two-step model transformation that transforms BPMN models into Web application models specified according to the WebML notation and then into running Web applications. Thanks to the proposed chain of model transformations it is also possible to fine tune the final application in several ways by refining the intermediate WebML application models.

1 Introduction

Turning a business process model into the specification, design and implementation of a software solution for process enactment is a non trivial task: the semantics of the adopted business process modeling notation is not always well defined, the specified processes can be a mix on new functionality to be developed and interactions with pre-existing systems and the user's activities must be supported through effective and usable interfaces, possibly compliant with the visual identity and interaction style of other corporate applications. Furthermore, the business requirements embodied in the process models, as well as the technical context in which the underlying applications are deployed, are subject to evolution. This may cause severe alignment problems when trying to keep the business process and the application in sync.

In this short paper we propose a pragmatical yet very precise implementation of the execution semantics of BPMN through a model transformation and code generation approach. We show how the gap between process modeling and application development can be alleviated by increasing the degree of automation in the design, implementation and maintenance of applications derived from process models.

The automation framework we propose supports the automatic translation of BPMN process models into running applications. Aside, we note that the approach is flexible enough to incorporate different architectural and interaction requirements, and can be applied also to application evolution and maintenance.

R. Dijkman, J. Hofstetter, and J. Koehler (Eds.): BPMN 2011, LNBIP 95, pp. 124–129, 2011.

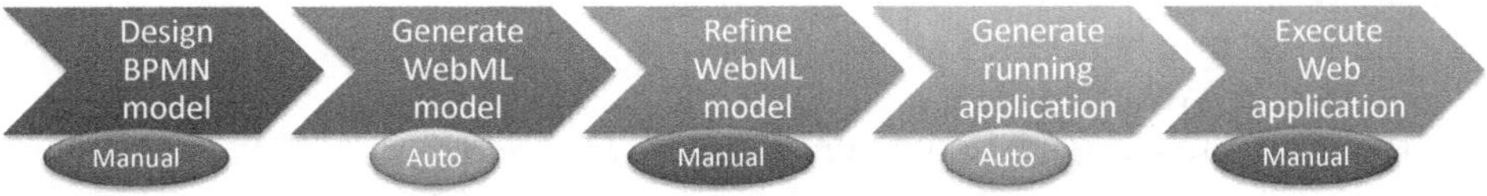

Fig. 1. Overview of the approach: the manually developed BPMN model is transformed into the WebML application model, which in turn can be manually refined. Finally, the running application is automatically generated and then executed.

2 Challenges and Contributions

The BPM community recognizes the conceptual distance between the process model and the the running application: the former dictates roles, activities and business constraints at a very abstract level, irrespective of how these are supported by computing tools; the latter embodies very low-level details, where business, architecture, and interaction aspects are blended together and hard to customize and evolve separately. As an example, the same user's activity specified in the process model could be enacted in a variety of ways: by means of a wizard, by form editing, by using a legacy application interface.

In the scientific community, several works have addressed the binding of BPM and Model Driven Development of Web applications: PML [6], YAWL [5], OOHDM [8], WSDM [9] and a few others. Our previous work [3] established the theoretical basis of the implementation described in here; with respect to that early idea, now the BP model and the application model are treated as orthogonal and independent models, which can evolve and interact in parallel throughout the entire application development lifecycle.

Based on these premises, our original contributions are: (i) a model-driven approach to the definition of the execution semantics of BPMN; (ii) a practical approach to business process-based software application development, which leverages the integrated use of two orthogonal models (BP and application models); (iii) a generative framework for producing the executable code from the process and application model, and a one-click, zero-coding generation of a running prototype on an enterprise class standard architecture; (iv) the implementation of the model editor and transformations in a commercial tool suite called WebRatio [1], which supports all the steps of the proposed approach.

The proposed approach and the associated toolsuite have been validated on some large-scale industrial applications in various fields (finance, utilities, marketing, and public administration) [2].

3 Model Driven Engineering Applied to Process Models

Our approach applies Model Driven Engineering (MDE) principles and organizes the specifications of process-oriented applications at three levels:

1. the business model (specified with BPMN [7]);
2. the structure, behavior and user interaction of the software application (expressed in WebML [4]);
3. the executable application running code.

Given that the WebML execution semantics has been already defined in the past, and a full-fledged code generation approach has been in place for several years now, the challenge becomes to define an appropriate mapping between BPMN models and WebML models.

In this way, the application execution can be enabled through two consecutive transformations: the *Process Model to Application Model transformation*, and the *Application Model to Running Code transformation.* Figure 1 shows an overview of the approach, highlighting the phases that need human intervention (tagged as "manual") and the completely automated ones (tagged as "auto").

The introduction of the application modeling layer increases the complexity of the conceptual architecture, but brings fundamental advantages: there is one place (the application model), where it is possible to reason about the distinct aspects of the application separately; the BPM to Application transformation can be supplied with transformation rules capable of producing alternative ways of encoding an activity, by using different patterns; automatically generated application models can be fine tuned, to introduce usability patterns, without breaking the application compliance to the process model; application evolution can be performed independently of the technical platform, by updating the application model and then regenerating the application code.

4 Model Transformations

The core of our contribution stands in the transformation from BPMN models to WebML models. *WebML* is a visual language for designing data- and service-centric Web applications, that allows specifying the conceptual model of applications built on top of a data schema and composed of one or more hypertexts used to publish or manipulate data.

In our approach the process state is encoded as instances of a specific data model and the execution, including the checks of the constraints imposed by the business process, is defined as a set of application rules upon the data.

Hence, starting from a BPMN specification, the automatic transformation produces the logical representation of the process metadata and a WebML Application Model, comprising a Data Model dictating the application-specific concepts and a collection of hypertext models, including the primitives for the user interaction and Web service orchestrations.

4.1 Process Data Model Generation

The transformation from BPMN to the process data model consists of an encoding of the BPMN concepts in a relational database structure: the BPMN

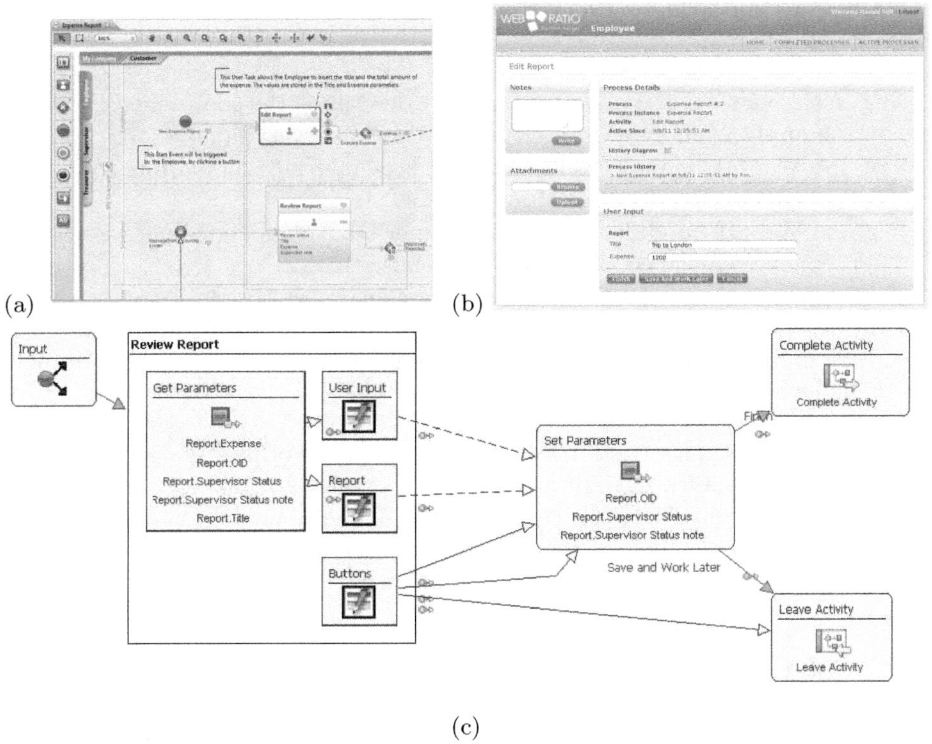

Fig. 2. The WebRatio BPMN editor interface (a); the automatically generated prototype Web interface (b); the WebML application model of a generic task module comprising data object retrieval from the workflow, input forms for the users, and data object update before completion of the task (c).

precedence constraints and gateways are transformed into instances of a relational representation. At runtime, the BPMN constraints, stored in the Process Metadata Schema, are exploited by the components of the Application Model for enacting the precedences among human-executed tasks and executing the service invocations.

4.2 Application Model Generation

The transformation from BPMN to WebML considers the type of the gateways and of the tasks, as well as the information on the control and data flows. The generated application models consist of a coarse set of user interfaces and prototype business operations.

Process control is encapsulated thanks to the automatically generated process data model: the computation of the next enabled activities given the current state of the workflow is delegated to a specific WebML component, which factors out the process control logic. It exploits the information stored in the process data model to determine the current process status and the enabled state transitions.

The basic transformation rules from BPMN to WebML include the generation of:

- of on site view (i.e., the WebML concept describing the comprehensive vision of the application by a user, once logged in) for every lane;
- of one WebML module containing the user interface model for submitting or visualizing data (in case of manual tasks);
- of one WebML module containing a generic business logic operation, to be subsequently specified (in case of automatic tasks);
- of one process branching control unit for every gateway. Basic gateways conditions based on single-valued guard conditions are supported automatically, while more complex behaviour need manual refinement at the WebML modeling level.

Every module includes the retrieval of the relevant workflow data objects and their update, as shown in Figure 2(c).

The tool also automatically generates the WebML model for managing the tasklist, for checking the process execution status, and the interface for a basic Business Activity Monitoring (BAM) dashboard.

5 Tool Implementation

The proposed generative framework has been implemented as an extension of WebRatio, a Model-Driven Web application development tool allowing one to edit WebML models and automatically transform them into a running applications for JEE and Service Oriented Architectures. For supporting BPM design, the following extensions have been devised. The *model editing GUI* has been extended with a new BPMN editor. The *code generator* has been extended with the transformation from BP model to application model; furthermore, the JEE code generation has been augmented to produce the relational instance of the Process Metadata and the Java code of novel WebML components. Moreover, a one-click publishing function has been added to the BPMN editor, thus allowing the immediate generation of a rapid prototype of the BPMN process. This functionality invokes in sequence the two transformations from BPMN to WebML and from WebML to JEE, yielding a dynamic, multi-actor application with a default look & feel. The generator creates a few exemplary users for each BPMN actor, which allows the analyst to impersonate each role in the process. Figure 2 shows the BPMN editor (a), the generated application interface (b), and a piece of WebML model (c).

6 Conclusion

We presented a pragmatic, Model-driven approach for the implementation of BPMN process models. Thanks to the associated tool suite, visual model design and model transformations allow designers to produce both as early prototypes and final applications without coding.

The approach does not cover the entire expressive power of BPMN: we support manual and automatic activities and the basic process design patterns; and the basic gateways (AND, XOR, Event), events and roles. Furthermore, we do not support choreography and conversation models. Future work aims at increasing the coverage of the BPMN model in the transformations to WebML.

References

1. Acerbis, R., Bongio, A., Brambilla, M., Butti, S., Ceri, S., Fraternali, P.: Web applications design and development with webml and webratio 5.0. In: TOOLS Conference (46), pp. 392–411 (2008)
2. Brambilla, M., Butti, S., Fraternali, P., Borrelli, S. In: BPM 2010 - Industrial Experiences Track (2010)
3. Brambilla, M., Ceri, S., Fraternali, P., Manolescu, I.: Process Modeling in Web Applications. ACM TOSEM 15(4), 360–409 (2006)
4. Ceri, S., Fraternali, P., Bongio, A., Brambilla, M., Comai, S., Matera, M.: Designing Data-Intensive Web Applications. Morgan Kaufmann, USA (2002)
5. Hofstede, A.H.M., van der Aalst, W.M.P., Adams, M., Russell, N. (eds.): Modern Business Process Automation, YAWL and its Support Environment. Springer, Heidelberg (2010)
6. Noll, J., Scacchi, W.: Specifying process-oriented hypertext for organizational computing. J. Netw. Comput. Appl. 24(1), 39–61 (2001)
7. OMG, BPMI. BPMN 1.2. Technical report (2009), http://www.bpmn.org/
8. Schmid, H.A., Rossi, G.: Modeling and designing processes in e-commerce applications. IEEE Internet Computing 8(1), 19–27 (2004)
9. De Troyer, O., Casteleyn, S.: Modeling complex processes for web applications using wsdm. In: Ws. on Web Oriented Software Technology (IWWOST), Oviedo, pp. 1–12 (2003)

Layout Patterns with BPMN Semantics

Philip Effinger

Wilhelm-Schickard-Institut für Informatik,
Eberhards Karls Universität Tübingen, Germany
philip.effinger@uni-tuebingen.de

Abstract. BPMN is a notation language that provides visual elements for modeling business processes. The resulting BPMN diagrams that represent BPMN models follow rules concerning their layout for creating a common understanding among all BPMN designers. A subset of the rules is determined by the BPMN standard. Other rules evolved when the BPMN community gained experience in the usage of its notation language. From a layout algorithmic perspective, the rules are formalized as so-called aesthetics. Until today, aesthetics for BPMN are mostly limited to the underlying graph structure of a BPMN process model diagram.

In this work, we present new layout patterns that can be applied in layout applications of BPMN and its modeling tools. The new layout patterns support BPMN semantics and address layout issues that are not covered by aesthetics so far. The patterns can be combined to achieve positive effects on multiple a) layout issues and b) BPMN semantics at a time. We also give detailed algorithmic descriptions for our patterns.

1 Motivation

For many users of BPMN ($> 50\%$, according to a survey among experts[1]), the main purpose of BPMN is *Process Description*. The description of a process employs the graphical notation of BPMN. As BPMN specifies graphical representations for its elements, these given representations quickly allow simple diagramming in modeling tools when developing a model.

Our focus in this work is on the support of a user when graphically developing a process model. We aim to provide features in tools that can create a layout for a given process diagram. The layout of a diagram should be created automatically (by a single mouse-click) and it is expected to appeal to the user. The layout methods are based on graph-drawing algorithms.

In previous work, we presented a survey on user requirements towards BPMN diagrams and specific layout properties of BPMN models [1]. From the survey, we can derive important expectations and criteria for layout, so-called aesthetics. Also, there exist approaches for layout support in BPMN ([2,3]). The existing layout approaches are based on the structure of a BPMN diagram. The structure is considered to be a graph with nodes (BPMN elements) and edges connecting

[1] `http://bpex.blogspot.com/2011/05/bpmn-usage-survey-results.html`

R. Dijkman, J. Hofstetter, and J. Koehler (Eds.): BPMN 2011, LNBIP 95, pp. 130–135, 2011.

the nodes (in BPMN: sequence flow, conditional flow, default flow). However, the graph structure does not consider the types of the nodes (BPMN semantics).

In this work, we present patterns that are designed to overcome the gap between graph structure and semantics of BPMN diagrams when creating a layout. The patterns aim to a) reduce cluttering in diagrams (primarily around gateways), b) highlight the logical structure of a BPMN diagram (induced by gateways) and c) accentuate the process flow.

2 Layout Patterns

The new layout patterns aim to reduce the lack of BPMN semantics in existing BPMN layout approaches [2,3]. Inspecting the list of standard layout aesthetics of [1], it is easy to observe that BPMN semantics in terms of element types are not taken into account in any of the aesthetics. The lack of support for BPMN element types is a gap between the graph structure and BPMN semantics. By introducing new layout patterns in the next section, we try to take a first step to overcome this syntax-semantics gap in BPMN layout. The patterns should be considered as a starting point for BPMN semantics in layout approaches and cannot be considered to be complete. For instance, one pattern might, on the one hand, enlarge the area size of the diagram and insert a new crossing between two flows, but on the other hand, three bends are removed and the length of a flow is reduced. This shows the tradeoff between an aesthetically optimal solution and consideration of semantics.

2.1 Geometric Pattern (GeoP)

Description: The Geometric Pattern (GeoP) aims at reducing visual cluttering. Cluttering describes the occurrence of many elements in a small amount of the diagram area (high element-density). For instance, around gateways with multiple connected elements, the cluttering is higher than the cluttering around a start event with a single outgoing sequence flow. Therefore, reducing the visual cluttering demands a reduction of density.

As a pre-processing step, we will show how the density of a BPMN diagram is determined. Density values can be visualized as depicted in Figure 1a). The calculation defines densities diametrically opposed to the flow in the model for each swimlane. The density values are derived by performing a sweep-line algorithm [4] call for each swimlane individually. In a single sweep, an event handler changes the density counter depending on incoming events. In our case, events are left/right geometric sides of boxes representing BPMN elements.

After the detection of dense areas, we insert temporary edges (marking edges) in the center of each dense area. The edges mark these areas for the algorithm. The pre-processing step ends with the edges' insertion orthogonally to the swimlane orientation, see Figure 1b). The algorithm of the pattern then aims at resolving the introduced overlaps by moving (sifting) nodes affected by marking edges.

Algorithm: Our algorithm for GeoP is related to the *Sifting Algorithm (SA)* [5,6]. In general, SA tries to move one element at a time along an ordering of

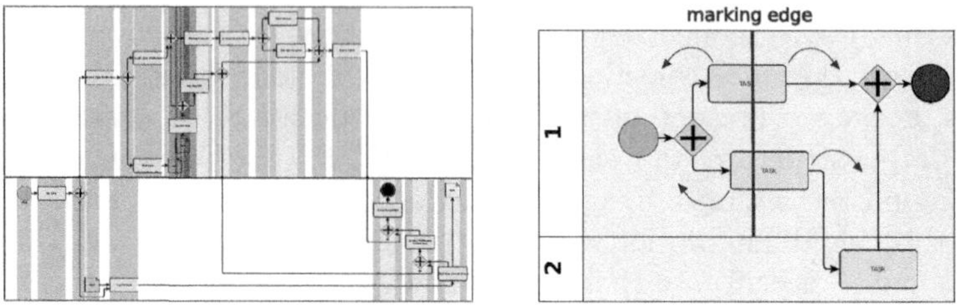

(a) Density visualization **(b)** GeoP-Sifting

Fig. 1. (a) Visualization of densities (red = high, green = low). (b) Schematic view of the algorithm for the GeoP. Red arrows depict the direction of possible sifting moves.

other elements until a goal function reaches a (local) minimum. In our case, we move all elements sequentially that are overlapped by a temporary marking edge. An element can be moved in parallel to its swimlane. Therefore, other than in the general SA, we have two orderings that an element can be moved along, see Figure 1b). Thus, we have more freedom and move an element in either direction until the overlap with the marking edge is prevented. This spreads the original density center and the cluttering is reduced.

To reduce cluttering in several dense areas, the algorithm allows to insert multiple temporary edges that are processed sequentially.

2.2 Gateway Pattern (GaP)

Description: The Gateway Pattern (GaP) aims at highlighting the logical structure of a BPMN process model. The logic structure is defined by the combination of gateways. Gateways determine the process flow based on logical expressions that are evaluated when a gateway is passed. Evaluations of gateways may cause split/joins of process flow(s). Since BPMN is not a block-structured notation language, but a graph-based notation language [7], the underlying logic structure is not trivial. In [8], the challenges of 'unraveling' (transforming) a non well-structured process model to a well-structured model are described. In general, if a process model is not well-structured, determination of corresponding pairs of opening split and closing joins is not unique. We call such a pair 'GaP-pair'.

If we can find such a GaP-pair that encloses a block structure, GaP is implying that no element of this block is placed 'before' the opening split gateway (with respect to the process model flow orientation) or 'after' the closing join gateway. Thus, the goal of GaP is to highlight the semantic block structure by a visual block structure that is surround by the GaP-pair.

In most process models, we cannot find well-structured parts when analysing the gateways. Therefore, we apply a method that allows the construction of blocks that do not require well-structured processes. The details of this algorithm are described in the following.

Algorithm: For our approach, we use the concept of a path in a graph: A path is a sequence of consecutive edges in a graph and the length of the path is the number of edges traversed. Since we also want to handle non-well-structured models, we define a GaP-pair as follows: A split-gateway $G1$ and a join-gateway $G2$ form a GaP-pair, if, for all possible paths starting at $G1$, the size of the subset of paths arriving at $G2$ is maximal among all gateways. In other words, we count the number of paths arriving at any gateway, where $G1$ is the root node in the path; then, for $G2$, the counter reaches its maximum and $G1$ and $G2$ form a GaP-pair.

Counting paths is executed using a variant of depth-first-search (DFS) [9]: we start a DFS-run from every split-gateway (or other gateways that perform process flow split, e.g. complex gateways). Since DFS is able to handle cycles (by storing visited nodes) and we employ our path counting method, we are able to find GaP-pairs in non-well-structured models.

If, for a split-gateway $G1$, there are two join-gateways $G2a$ and $G2b$ with the same path counter, the minimum distance between $G1$ and either $G2a$ or $G2b$ is taken as criteria for determining the GaP-pair.

After finding GaP-Pairs, we insert surrounding temporary edges (skeleton edges), analogously to the GeoP, orthogonally to the flow orientation. Skeleton edges are inserted into the swimlane(s) of the gateways forming the GaP-pairs, see Figure 2. For every pair, one skeleton edge is introduced before the split-gateway and a second skeleton edge after the join-gateway. The skeleton edges delimit the surrounding box representing the block that is formed by the GaP-pair. When performing a layout (for instance with the approach presented in [3]), the skeleton edges prevent nodes to be moved to the outside of the block.

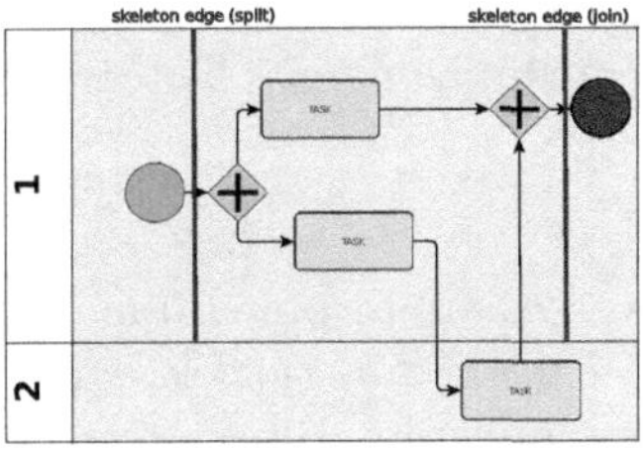

Fig. 2. Insertion points of skeleton edges in GaP

2.3 Start-End-Pattern (SEP)

Description: The Start-End-Pattern (SEP) formalizes the compliance of placing start- and end-events considering aesthetics FLOW [1]. These elements should be placed such that they follow the orientation of the process flow (or 'reading' direction of the user). When SEP is activated, it ensures that a start-event is moved to the 'beginning' (left side) of its assigned swimlane, and an end-events is set to the 'end' (right side) its swimlane. Performing SEP might affect lengths of edges: edges connected to moved events might increase severely in length. In order to possibly reduce the increase of edge length or prevent bends, we support two variants of SEP:

1. **Dynamic:** Events affected by SEP are set to the left/right border of the swimlanes but may move in parallel to the swimlane orientation in order to reduce unnecessary long edges or prevent bends, see Figure 3a).

2. **Locking:** All (start/end) events of a swimlane are aligned in the beginning/end of the swimlane, see Figure 3b). The events are locked in a box surrounded by skeleton edges that guarantee that they do not move to the outer side of the box when performing a new layout.

The second variant is more appropriate for process models that have highly parallel process flow and, thus, several starting/terminating events.

Algorithm: As mentioned in the two variants, we employ for SEP the idea of skeleton edges that was also used in GaP. The skeleton edges ensure the structure of the locking box and keep the nodes aligned in the beginning/end of the swimlanes. The alignment of the event node of one swimlane is done such that overlapping of nodes is prevented and the size of an element is kept.

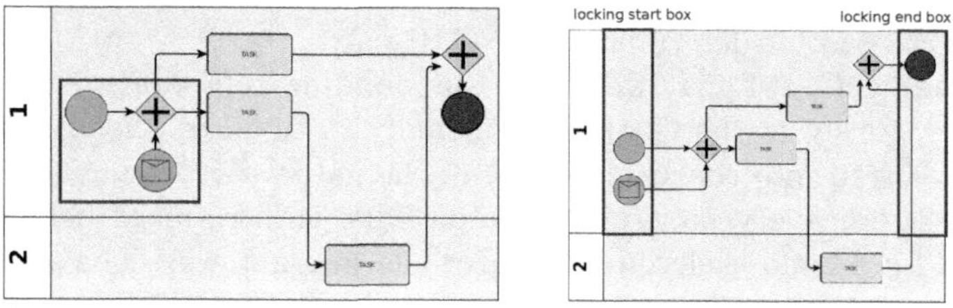

(a) SEP dynamic (b) SEP locking

Fig. 3. (a) Start- and End-events are allowed to optimize their position, e.g. see the node MESSAGE_START_EVENT that moved in order to prevent a bend in a flow. (b) Start- and End-events are kept static in boxes built by skeleton edges.

3 Related Work

Patterns in (business) processes are a common method to express abstract similarities in process models, e.g., *action patterns* are used to formalize semantic analysis of BPMN process models in [10] or for organization in large business process model repositories [11]. The term 'layout patterns' is used in [12] for expressing layout constraints that represent conditions for layout algorithms.

For model decomposition that was performed in Section 2 when analysing the graph for GaP-pairs, a preferred decomposition for process models is often using SPQR-trees for a subsequent analysis of the structure or application of rules for abstraction [13].

4 Conclusion

In this work, we introduce new layout patterns for BPMN diagrams. The layout patterns allow to include BPMN semantics in layout algorithms for BPMN process models. The layout patterns take into account common rules of BPMN diagrams, so-called aesthetics. The patterns address the following issues in BPMN diagrams: a) Cluttering of nodes in diagrams, b) Perceiving the logical structure of a BPMN diagram (induced by gateways) and c) Accentuate the process flow at start events and process' termination in end events.

The presented set of layout patterns is not to be considered complete but constitutes a starting point for rising interest in BPMN semantics in layout approaches in future (commercial) applications. At the moment, we are conducting an empirical evaluation with an available set of more than 750 process models [14]. Furthermore, it will be an interesting task for the future to conduct a user study in order to receive feedback on the human aesthetics' perspective on the drawbacks/benefits of the presented patterns. Also, statements from users might lead to additional patterns that incorporate more BPMN semantics in layouts.

References

1. Effinger, P., Jogsch, N., Seiz, S.: On a Study of Layout Aesthetics for Business Process Models Using BPMN. In: Mendling, J., Weidlich, M., Weske, M. (eds.) BPMN 2010. LNBIP, vol. 67, pp. 31–45. Springer, Heidelberg (2010)
2. Kitzmann, I., König, C., Lübke, D., Singer, L.: A Simple Algorithm for Automatic Layout of BPMN Processes. In: CEC, pp. 391–398 (2009)
3. Effinger, P., Siebenhaller, M., Kaufmann, M.: An Interactive Layout Tool for BPMN. In: IEEE Internat. Conference on E-Commerce Technology, vol. 1, pp. 399–406 (2009)
4. Bentley, J.L., Ottmann, T.: Algorithms for reporting and counting geometric intersections. IEEE Trans. Computers 28(9), 643–647 (1979)
5. Matuszewski, C., Schönfeld, R., Molitor, P.: Using Sifting for k -Layer Straightline Crossing Minimization. In: Kratochvíl, J. (ed.) GD 1999. LNCS, vol. 1731, pp. 217–224. Springer, Heidelberg (1999)
6. Rudell, R.: Dynamic variable ordering for ordered binary decision diagrams. In: Proceedings of the IEEE/ACM International Conference on Computer-Aided Design (ICCAD 1993), pp. 42–47 (1993)
7. Kopp, O., Martin, D., Wutke, D., Leymann, F.: The difference between graph-based and block-structured business process modelling languages. Enterprise Modelling and Information Systems Architectures 4(1), 3–13 (2009)
8. Dumas, M., García-Bañuelos, L., Polyvyanyy, A.: Unraveling Unstructured Process Models. In: Mendling, J., Weidlich, M., Weske, M. (eds.) BPMN 2010. LNBIP, vol. 67, pp. 1–7. Springer, Heidelberg (2010)
9. Cormen, T.H., Leiserson, C.E., Rivest, R.L., Stein, C.: Introduction to Algorithms, 2nd edn. The MIT Press (September 2001)
10. Smirnov, S., Weidlich, M., Mendling, J., Weske, M.: Action Patterns in Business Process Models. In: Baresi, L., Chi, C.-H., Suzuki, J. (eds.) ICSOC-ServiceWave 2009. LNCS, vol. 5900, pp. 115–129. Springer, Heidelberg (2009)
11. Smirnov, S., Weidlich, M., Mendling, J., Weske, M.: Object-sensitive action patterns in process model repositories. In: BPM Workshops, pp. 251–263 (2010)
12. Maier, S., Minas, M.: Interactive diagram layout. In: Proceedings of the 28th Internat. Conference on Human factors in Computing systems, CHI EA 2010, pp. 4111–4116. ACM, NY (2010)
13. Polyvyanyy, A., Smirnov, S., Weske, M.: The Triconnected Abstraction of Process Models. In: Dayal, U., Eder, J., Koehler, J., Reijers, H.A. (eds.) BPM 2009. LNCS, vol. 5701, pp. 229–244. Springer, Heidelberg (2009)
14. Fahland, D., Favre, C., Jobstmann, B., Koehler, J., Lohmann, N., Völzer, H., Wolf, K.: Instantaneous Soundness Checking of Industrial Business Process Models. In: Dayal, U., Eder, J., Koehler, J., Reijers, H.A. (eds.) BPM 2009. LNCS, vol. 5701, pp. 278–293. Springer, Heidelberg (2009)

Integration of BPM and BRM

Jörg Hohwiller[1], Diethelm Schlegel[1], Gunter Grieser[2], and Yvette Hoekstra[3]

[1] Capgemini, CSD Research, Berliner Str. 76, 63065 Offenbach, Germany
[2] Capgemini, GB CSD MRDT, Berliner Str. 76, 63065 Offenbach, Germany
[3] Capgemini, Public Sector, Papendorpseweg 100, 3528 BJ Utrecht, Netherlands

Abstract. The *Business process modelling notation* (BPMN) is used for modelling and automating business processes. The resulting process models contain all details that define the process flows from the high level scope up to technological aspects. Often, the readability decreases due to complex flow decisions and computations. While the models could be simplified from the business perspective they must be precise enough when they are executed later on. This paper proposes to use *business rule management* (BRM) in addition to *business process management* (BPM) to overcome these drawbacks. It shows best practices for a proper integration of BPM and BRM with regard to modelling and a seamless system integration.

Keywords: BRM, BPM, BPMN, integration, business process, rule.

1 Introduction and Motivation

In this paper, we want to focus on *modelling* and *execution* of business processes using the *Business process modelling notation* (BPMN). Thereby, modelling is more business-oriented and primarily focuses on the visualization and notation of processes for the purpose of documentation and transparency. On the other hand, for the execution of processes a more technical view on processes is required with focus on syntax and semantics.

The use of BPMN for both aspects improves efficiency and flexibility because there is no longer the need for two separated models that must be kept in sync. Fortunately, most of the BPM products on the market catch up with BPMN in some way. However, the definition of technical details is not part of the standard. For instance, the format to express the actual decision behind a gateway is not specified. Decisions and expressions are just textual labels of the gateway and its outgoing sequence flows [1, page 290].

From a business perspective, the use of *business rules* helps to simplify complex decisions and computations. Rules describe business knowledge in a formalized way that can be automated. E.g., to grant a mortgage a rule is required which is checking the conditions. Nevertheless, there is no common understanding how to structure and integrate the several process and rule models.

Without well-defined prescriptive guidelines, it is difficult to reuse models even in the same project. This not only involves technical aspects. It is rather a

R. Dijkman, J. Hofstetter, and J. Koehler (Eds.): BPMN 2011, LNBIP 95, pp. 136–141, 2011.

question of whether the models can be understood when they are exchanged. As an example, business rules can be expressed by all means using BPMN process elements. By doing so, the process becomes overwhelmed with too much details (see figure 1). This is obviously bad design and it is hard to maintain.

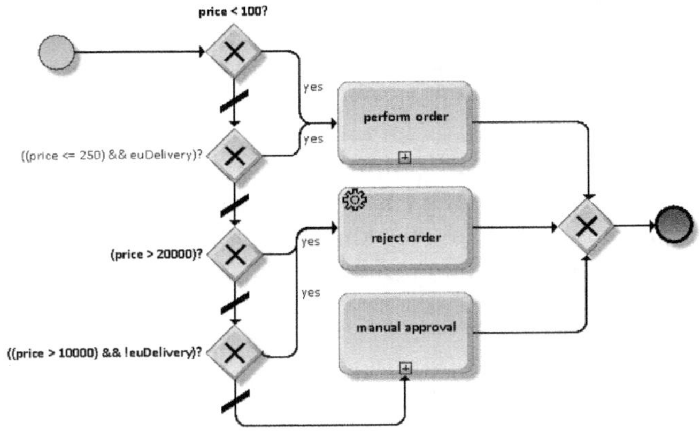

Fig. 1. Business Rule as Cascading Gateways

In summary, the notation for business rules must be specified together with a mechanism for connecting processes. BPMN defines some elements for the association of rules, e.g. business rule activities. But as a matter of fact, specialized notation elements are only rarely applied as shown by a survey with respect to BPMN artefact usage ([2]). Moreover, the consistency between rules and processes must be ensured by an appropriate method.

2 Related Work

The *Semantics of Business Vocabulary and Business Rules* (SBVR) is specified in [3] and deals with the fundamental base of business rules. It contains definitions for rule related terms and a method starting with business processes. The representation is based on the so-called Concept Diagram Graphic Notation that refers to the *RuleSpeak* language [4] as a formal notation. Hereby, the business rule manifesto [5] describes the preferred approach. SBVR regards BRM more or less separated from BPM as it uses processes as input. Another methodology for BRM is defined by the *BRS Proteus Methodology* [6].

The OMG initiated a Request for Proposal called *Decision Model and Notation* (DMN) that standardizes the underlying meta-model as well as an interchange format based on SBVR for the business aspects and *Production Rule Representation* (PRR) [7] for IT related information.

The need for the integration of rules and processes is outlined in [8]. In this context, [9] introduces a framework to identify potential inconsistencies between BPMN and SBVR models and [10] proposes the integration of SBVR, DMN and BPMN 2.0 to get a seamless integration. While it is a technical and conceptual base it is rather theoretically and must first be proved by practical use. In addition, it provides no method for the integrated design of processes and rules.

3 Best Practices

This section contains best practices for BRM and the integration with BPMN that are based on the experience from projects at Capgemini. Hereby, the method for the transformation of business knowledge to executable processes and rules is separated into four phases as shown in figure 2. This phases have been developed empirically by performing customer projects over several years. Ideally, the phases should be finished by some kind of review before continuing to ensure the soundness of the intermediate results.

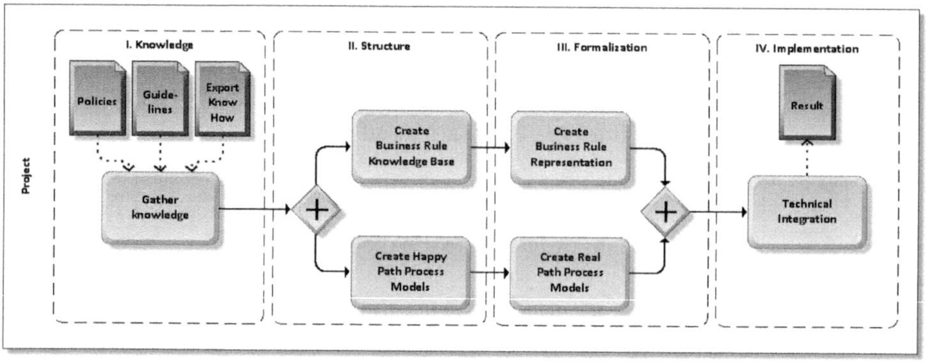

Fig. 2. Best Practices Method

3.1 Gather Knowledge

The first phase is to gather business knowledge concerning project goals and objectives. Typical sources are policies, operational guidelines, and domain experts. Based on this explicit or implicit input, business analysts design high level process landscapes and document business rule summaries.

Since processes and rules share the same data basis the development of an initial underlying data model has proved to be crucial. We distinguish process local data and persisted business data getting modified by service calls and residing in individual enterprise applications. Rules should be stateless and not affect these data. Changes are realized by invoking business services in the process.

Business rules outlined in this phase and refined in subsequently are linked to policies and guidelines to ensure that the automated decision process can be traced back up to the policies. This may be important to justify process decisions later on and helps for easy rule and process adaptations and maintenance.

3.2 Structure Knowledge

The second phase is to organize and structure knowledge. This includes creation of a logical rule model as well as process maps and first process models. However such process models only model the default flow as the ideal business case (aka happy path). The most critical challenge concerning structuring business knowledge is to decide what knowledge should be modelled as processes and what knowledge as rules (*golden section*). It has proven as good practice to design rules whenever the knowledge tends to change often, the computation is more complex, and no user interaction is needed (see [11]).

We recommend to treat business processes and rules as layers, where processes are on top and more corsair while rules are below and more fine grained. This is illustrated for reaction rule sets in figure 3. The same applies for tasks and services as proposed by [12] for the connection of BPM and SOA.

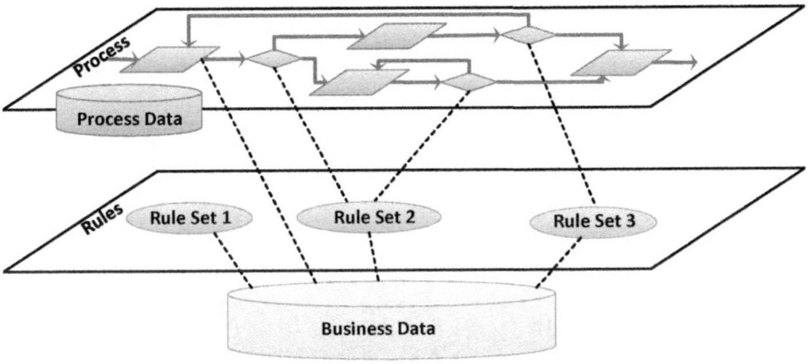

Fig. 3. Interaction between Process and Rule Models

Usually, rules are organized in so called *rule sets*, i.e. groups of rules for a particular business need. As an advantage of such groups, knowledge is structured logically and organizationally. This might be orthogonal to the original rules since one rule may belong to different rule sets as well as rule sets can be reused at different places. Also, complex computations are abstracted because computations within rule sets can be seen as a single steps.

Business rule sets are categorized depending on their usage scenarios. This is helpful for structuring applications, assigning correct responsibilities, and improving understandability. [13] proposes four different types of rule sets.

1. *Integrity rule sets* ensure data consistency. Ideally, they are assertions that must always be satisfied and are therefore checked permanently. It can be modelled in BPMN by using an boundary conditional event and associating an action that gets executed if this integrity rule set is violated. Alternatively, validation rule sets can be part of the data model.
2. *Derivation rule sets* deduce new knowledge from existing one by using inference mechanisms or mathematical calculations. Ideally, they are assigned to the data model. They can also be used in BPMN business rule tasks.

3. *Reaction rule sets* describe the controls of operation and the logistics. In general, the purpose is to decide on the order of the process steps to fulfil a process. In this paper, we want to reduce their scope to decisions. Though not fully compliant with BPMN, some tools allow to associate business rule sets directly with gateways. Otherwise, gateway conditions must be based on the results of preceding business rule actions that make the association more explicit and even allow to specify required input parameters.
4. *Deontic rule sets* connect the organization model to the activities in a process. These are authorization rules or rules about the allocation of human tasks. Usually, these rule sets should be assigned to BPMN process lanes.

The flavour of the visualization itself is not that important. However, in one context (project or IT-landscape) you should decide for one form and then stick with it in order to prevent confusion.

3.3 Formalize Models

During the third phase the logical rule model is formalized into a business rules representation making use of a business vocabulary. There are several methods and standards of notation like SBVR [3]. Concerning processes, initial models are detailed and completed to cover the real life of the business (e.g. including manual proceedings as exception handling if automated processing failed). When supported by the BPM tool, integrated modelling of rules and processes has been very advantageous in our projects.

Furthermore, it is important to choose the right form to express business rules. *Decision tables* are easily understandable notations (see [14]). Business rules are visualized as tables where the conditions (usually attributes) and results are depicted as columns and each rule (conditions and conclusion) is expressed by a row. Besides tables, there are also decision trees and numerous other notations to represent business rules. Hopefully, DMN ([10,15]) will bring along some standardized language or notation for business rules in the future.

3.4 Implement Models

Finally, the rules and processes have to be implemented to be fully executable. This includes integration of processes, rules, external services, and legacy applications as well as adding technical aspects such as transactions or compensations.

From the execution point of view the *business process engine* (BPE) and *business rule engine* (BRE) need to be integrated. If separate products are used, they are mostly loosely coupled, e.g. by invoking business rule sets as web-service. However, integrity and derivation rule sets then have to be actively invoked repetitively where ever needed in the process. On heavy use of these types of rule sets a deeper integration is suggested for reasons of maintenance and performance. From experience, it is better to choose BPM tools that provide both BRE and BPE. Often, they additionally allow deeper model integration of processes and rules. Finally, deontic rule sets can typically only be integrated if supported by the BPE.

4 Conclusion and Further Work

This paper introduced BPM and BRM that are both promising approaches to gain efficiency and flexibility. They should be combined as they complement each other. The provided best practices explain how to realize it properly. They also address general aspects for doing efficient BRM. Furthermore, the integration of according products has been addressed as a critical factor. It should be considered by enterprises when choosing BPM products.

While BPMN is quite established as a standard, its product support still has to be improved. In the area of BRM, standards like SBVR have high attention and also DMN looks promising. However a central standard remains to be seen. As future work it is desired to do more research on how BPMN models can be extended and connected with BRM standards in order to be exchangeable and executable in a more vendor neutral way.

References

1. Object Management Group: Business Process Model and Notation (BPMN) Version 2.0. (2011)
2. zur Muehlen, M., Recker, J.: How Much Language Is Enough? Theoretical and Practical Use of the Business Process Modeling Notation. In: Bellahsène, Z., Léonard, M. (eds.) CAiSE 2008. LNCS, vol. 5074, pp. 465–479. Springer, Heidelberg (2008)
3. Object Management Group: Semantics of Business Vocabulary and Business Rules (SBVR), v1.0 (2008)
4. Business Rule Solutions, LLC: RuleSpeak
5. The Business Rules Group: The Business Rules Manifesto
6. Business Rule Solutions, LLC: The BRS Proteus Methodology
7. Object Management Group: Documents associated with Production Rule Representation (PRR) Version 1.0 (2009)
8. Recker, J., Indulska, M., Rosemann, M., Green, P.: How Good is BPMN Really? Insights from Theory and Practice (2006)
9. Cheng, R., Sadiq, S., Indulska, M.: Framework for business process and rule integration: A case of bpmn and sbvr (June 2011)
10. Linehan, M.H., de Sainte Marie, C.: The Relationship of Decision Model and Notation (DMN) to SBVR and BPMN. Business Rules Journal 12 (June 2011)
11. Muehlen, M.Z., Indulska, M., Kittel, K.: Towards integrated modeling of business processes and business rules (2008)
12. Behara, D.G.K.: BPM and SOA: A Strategic Alliance. BPTrends (May 2006)
13. Wagner, G.: How to design a general rule markup language? In: Proceedings zum Workshop on XML Technologien für das Semantic Web - XSW 2002, GI, pp. 19–37 (2002)
14. Kohavi, R.: The power of decision tables. In: Lavrač, N., Wrobel, S. (eds.) ECML 1995. LNCS, vol. 912, pp. 174–189. Springer, Heidelberg (1995) $10.1007/3-540-59286-5_57$
15. Object Management Group: Decision Model and Notation (2011)

Extending the BPMN Syntax for Requirements Management

Sascha Goldner[1] and Alf Papproth[2]

[1] Cassidian, Landshuter Straße 26, 85716 Unterschleißheim Germany
Sascha.Goldner@cassidian.com
[2] Fraunhofer Application Centre for Logistics System Planning and Information Systems ALI
Konrad-Wachsmann-Allee 1, 03046 Cottbus, Germany
Alf.Papproth@ali.fraunhofer.de

Abstract. Regulations and laws are a very determining factor in every business domain. Therefore it is absolutely necessary to consider these legal constraints already in the early design phase of business processes in order to create process descriptions which are legally valid. The business process modeling notation (BPMN) has become the method of choice when it comes to business process modeling. We extended the syntax by specific artifacts in order to explicitly represent legal constraints directly in the BPMN models. Legal constraints can be considered as necessary requirements for business processes. Therefore it is important to track whether all requirements respectively legal constraints have been represented within the process models. As a consequence we extended our BPMN editor by an export functionality to be able to transfer the legal constraints as requirements into a requirements management tool.

Keywords: BPMN, regulation, legal constraints, requirements management.

1 Introduction

One of the critical infrastructures of modern society is air transport, with airports being both its operational bases and potential targets of terrorist attacks. Past and recent security incidents at international airports show that new and innovative methodologies are needed in order to improve airport security. This task is often just tackled by the implementation of new technology without assessing the effectiveness of the security measures as a whole. Besides security technologies, business processes, business rules and regulations also have to be considered. Especially regulations, i.e. laws, organizational guidelines, etc., are one of the most important and influencing factors in the security domain. They define the overall scope and framework the operational processes can be implemented in. As a consequence, these legal constraints already have to be taken into consideration when designing the business processes, respectively when creating the business process models. Thus, the need arises to explicitly visualize regulations within business process models.

Within our approach we use BPMN for defining the process models. To integrate the regulations into the process models we extended the BPMN syntax by new

R. Dijkman, J. Hofstetter, and J. Koehler (Eds.): BPMN 2011, LNBIP 95, pp. 142–147, 2011.

artifacts that enable us to define different types of legal constraints. Beyond that we also extended the BPMN editor in order to parameterize the new artifacts. These attributes contain for example the complete reference to legal text as well as the text itself. Thereby we are able to indicate for all tasks, subprocesses and processes the relevant legal conditions.

The next goal in our work was to evaluate whether all relevant regulations have been represented within our process models. To achieve this, all regulations are considered as requirements in the sense of requirement engineering. Finally to keep track whether all regulations respectively requirements have been implemented within the process models, we use a COTS requirements tracking tool and all of the advantages that come along with that. The necessary interface between the BPMN editor and the requirements tracking tool has been implemented so that an automatic transfer of the requirements into the tracking tool is possible.

As for the editor we use the web-based BPMN editor ORXY from the Hasso-Plattner-Institute. For the requirements tracking we apply the requirements management component of the Erudine Behavior Engine from Erudine.

2 Visualization of Regulations within BPMN

The ORYX editor offers support for extensions which are integrated via a plug-in mechanism. Two different types of extensions can be applied: a stencil set extension or a functional plug-in. Stencil set extensions allow only an enhancement of the notation whereas the functional plug-ins can be used to extended the overall functionality of the whole editor. In the following we introduce our first plug-in that extends the BPMN syntax by new artifacts in order to illustrate legal constraints within BPMN process models.

2.1 Extending the BPMN Syntax in ORYX

The BPMN elements that are supported by the ORYX editor are described in a so called *stencil set*. In order to extend the graphical notation a stencil set extension has to be implemented. Therefore the following tasks have to be performed.

First, a JSON (JavaScript Object Notation) file has to be created. The file contains a formal specification of the new elements, their properties and the rules that determine how they can be connected to other BPMN elements.

Second, a SVG (Scalable Vector Graphic) file has to be created which contains a description of the graphical representation of each new element.

Third, a PNG (Portable Network Graphics) file is needed as icon for the visual representation of the new element in the editor.

2.2 The Extensions

In our case we extended the BPMN syntax by two new artifacts: *Regulation* and *Regulation Group*.

Regulation. The *Regulation* artifact has the role of documenting business process models with a single law or regulation. This artifact can be linked to following BPMN elements: *abstract task*, *manual task*, *gateway*, *sequence flow*, *message flow*, *start event*, *end event.*

The new artifact Regulation comes with five properties specific to a regulation: LawName, LawText, Article, Paragraph and Organization. The properties offer the possibility to document following information:

- *LawName*: the name of the law that applies;

- *LawText*: by making use of this attribute, the user can directly store the law texts that apply to the BPMN element, respectively the business process.

- *Article*: the article number of the regulation

- *Paragraph*: the paragraph number of the regulation

- *Organization*: the name of the organization that must prove the fulfillment of the law modeled by the regulation object

Regulation Group. The *Regulation Group* artifact can be applied when more than one regulation or law applies and has to be documented, e.g. national and European law. This artifact can be linked to the same BPMN elements which have been stated for the artifact *Regulation*. The *Regulation Group* comes with three properties specific to a group of regulations: *LawNames*, *LawTexts* and *Organizations*.

- *LawNames*: this attribute specifies the names of the relevant laws. Their article and paragraph numbers are already stated in the law names. Different laws are separated by a semicolon.

- *LawTexts*: the specific law texts

- *Organizations*: this attribute specifies the names of the stakeholders responsible for fulfilling the documented laws.

Fig. 1. The shapes of the *Regulation* and *Regulation Group* artifact

In Fig. 2 and Fig. 3 we can see an example how the new artifacts have been placed in the ORYX editor canvas. The property pane is shown on the right side of the screen.

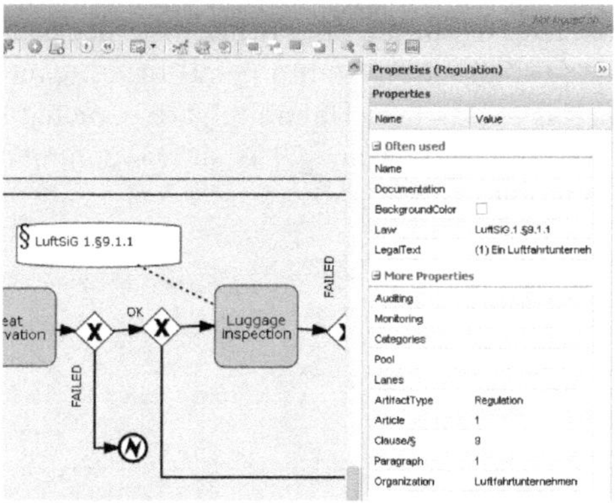

Fig. 2. The *Regulation* artifact within the ORYX editor

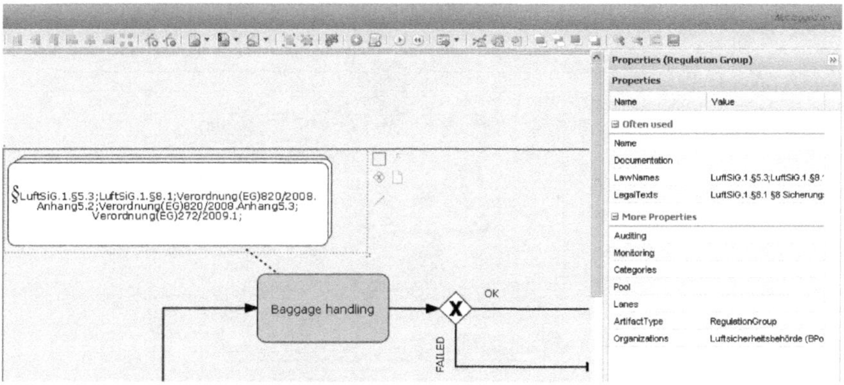

Fig. 3. The *Regulation Group* artifact within the ORYX editor

3 Requirements Export Plug-In

The following section describes the development of a new plug-in for ORYX that supports the export of the defined regulations within a BPMN process model. The regulations are saved to a CSV-file (Comma-Separated Values-file) that can be imported by the requirements manager of the Erudine Behavior Engine (EBE). We use the requirements manager to keep track which legal constraints have already been covered in the business process models and which still have to be done.

The functionality of the ORYX editor is once again extended, this time by a functional plug-in. In order to implement a plug-in two tasks have to be performed. First the plug-in itself has to be developed in JavaScript (JS), and second, the plug-in has to be added in the configuration file of the ORYX editor. Each plug-in has access to an interface allowing communication with the editor. The interface to the editor's core complies with the façade pattern which is a software engineering design pattern. For offering the export functionality for the regulations, we implemented a façade method containing two parameters: a link to the facade interface and configuration parameters. Fig. 4 shows the ORYX editor with a detail of a business process. The regulations that apply to the task "Baggage Handling" are depicted by a *Regulation Group*. Further the Erudine Requirements Manager is shown containing the exported regulations from the process model.

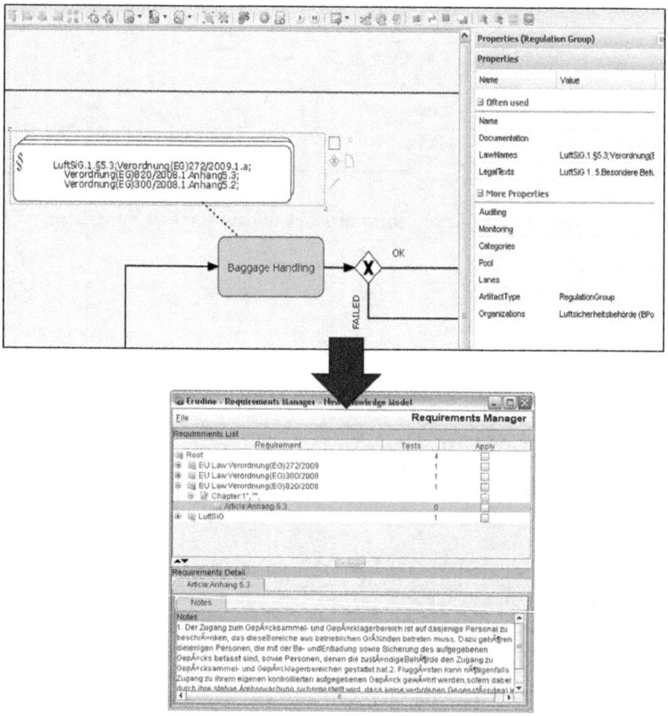

Fig. 4. Transfer of regulations within the ORYX editor into the Erudine Requirements Manager

4 Conclusion

Legal constraints are a main influencing factor in the security domain. Therefore it is absolutely necessary to make these constrains explicit in operational guidelines which include business process models. Therefore we implemented new BPMN artifacts within the ORYX editor to explicitly visualize theses legal constraints. Further, to have an overview of the modeled regulations within the process models, we implemented an export functionality that allows us to keep track of them using a requirements management tool.

Later this year we will release the DIN SPEC 91285 which combines a graphical process description with a formal process description in order to get a holistic process definition.

Acknowledgments. Part of the presented work has been achieved during the project SiVe (Verbesserung der Sicherheit von Verkehrsinfrastructuren) which is co-funded by the German Federal Ministry of Education and Research (BMBF) as part of the Ministry's Hightech Strategy and Security Research Programme.

References

1. The ORYX Project, `http://bpt.hpi.uni-potsdam.de/ORYX/WebHome`
2. Erudine, `http://www.erudine.com/`
3. Freund, J., Rücker, B., Henninger, T.: Praxishandbuch BPMN. Carl Hanser Verlag, München (2010)

Integrating Business Process Models and Business Logic: BPMN and The Decision Model

Jürgen Pitschke

BCS-Dr. Juergen Pitschke, Bautzner Str. 79, 01099 Dresden
jpitschke@enterprise-design.eu

Abstract. Multiple views on an enterprise are needed to model and design business processes systematically. The flow of a process is often the primary model developed. The explicit presentation of the business logic and their use in the business process is another essential artifact.

The article discusses the connection between business process modeling with BPMN and the presentation of business logic with "The Decision Model" framework. The framework includes a visual notation, presentation of rule sets, normal forms, presentation principles and the connection to the process model.

Keywords: BPMN, Decision Model, Business Process, Business Logic, Business Rule, OMG.

1 Why Do We Need an Explicit Presentation for Business Logic?

Business Process Models are central part of an enterprise model. To describe a business process different views are needed – the process flow, communication between process participants, the definition of the concepts used, systems supporting the process and others (see [3]).

The Object Management Group (OMG) published a big number of standards for model presentation. The most popular are "Unified Modeling Language (UML)" and „Business Process Model and Notation (BPMN)". Other standards as "Business Motivation Model (BMM)" are not widely recognized and used. An uncritical use of the standards often ignores that none of the standards is intend to describe all views on an enterprise. We have to decide which standards we want to use for the content needed in our project to be successful. BPMN is for example focused on the presentation of the process flows. Other aspects are not in the focus.

One important aspect is the description of Business Rules and Business Logic used in a Business Process. This was already part of the IDEF0-standard [6]. IDEF0 defined "guidelines" as part of the description of a business activity.

We need an explicit presentation for the Business Logic separated from the process model because both are independent concepts. At the same time Business Logic changes more frequently as the business process. Without an explicit representation of Business Logic reuse and structure for such a model is out of reach. Our models become unstable and not maintainable.

Figure 1 shows a snippet from a bad process model. It contains an embedded decision tree.

R. Dijkman, J. Hofstetter, and J. Koehler (Eds.): BPMN 2011, LNBIP 95, pp. 148–153, 2011.

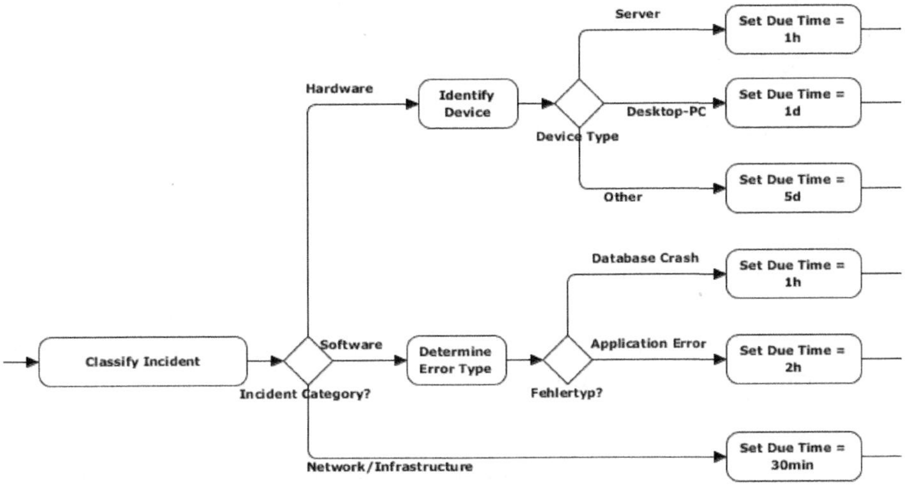

Fig. 1. Snippet of a process model with embedded decision tree

We want to extract the business logic from the process model to make it available for analysis, reuse and maintenance. A significantly reduced process model is the result. The presentation of the logic with a text annotation as shown in figure 2 is not really practicable.

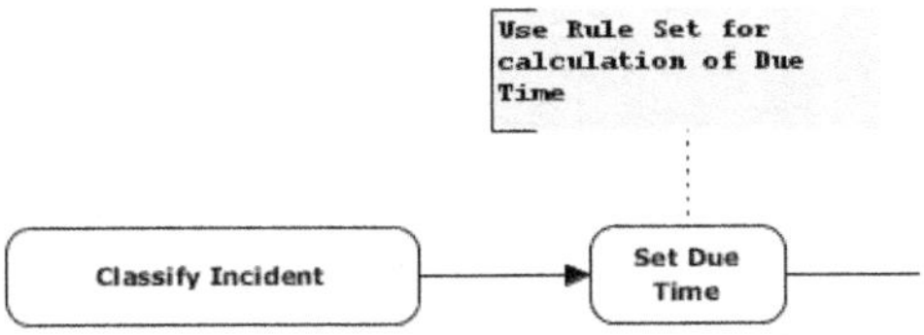

Fig. 2. Reduced process model without the decision tree

2 Modeling Business Logic – Intro to "The Decision Model" Framework

The OMG standard "Semantics of Business Vocabulary and Rules (SBVR)" [5] introduces concepts for the presentation of a business vocabulary and business rules. The standard addresses the presentation of business rules from a business perspective using natural language. In practice the approach has two shortcomings.

SBVR doesn't include any mean to structure large sets of business rules. Managing single rules causes high efforts e.g. in the integration with a business process.

Second: SBVR doesn't address the transformation of business rules into IT systems or Business Rule Engines. This results in high efforts during implementation.

Both issues are addressed by "The Decision Model", which is described in [1]. The Decision Model is not an OMG standard. The procedure to create a standard for a "Decision Model Notation (DMN)" was started by the OMG in March 2011.

2.1 Presentation of Business Logic with "The Decision Model" Framework

What is meant by "Business Logic"? In [1] von Halle and Goldberg define Business Logic as "*... a set of business rules represented as atomic elements of conditions leading to a conclusion*"[1]

The definition contains already all benefits of this approach:

- We don't deal with business rules on a general level. We don't analyze single business rules. We analyze and manage group of operational business rules leading to a defined conclusion.
- This includes a structure of our rule model: Which rules are needed together to make a decision?
- The decision to be made is the link to the business process model. Which activities include decisions and need a refinement in a decision model?

A Business Decision is modeled using an octagon titled with the name of the decision.

Fig. 3. Symbol for a Business Decision

The TDM element "Rule Family" is used to model the set of rules needed for a certain decision.

The name of the rule family should show the name of the fact type of the decision. Our example "Acceptance of Incident" is the name of the rule family. We decide if we accept the incident or not.

The rule family is connected to the Business Decision using the Business Decision Connector (see figure 4).

We need different fact types to come to the conclusion. Fact Types needed for the decision representing a rule family (or a sub decision) themselves are shown above the dashed line in the rule family element. Fact Types shown below the dashed line are not further derived but represent facts we know at runtime. A Decision Model Tree with leaves containing only Fact Types below the line result when creating a complete and normalized decision model.

---

[1] See [1], Page 6.

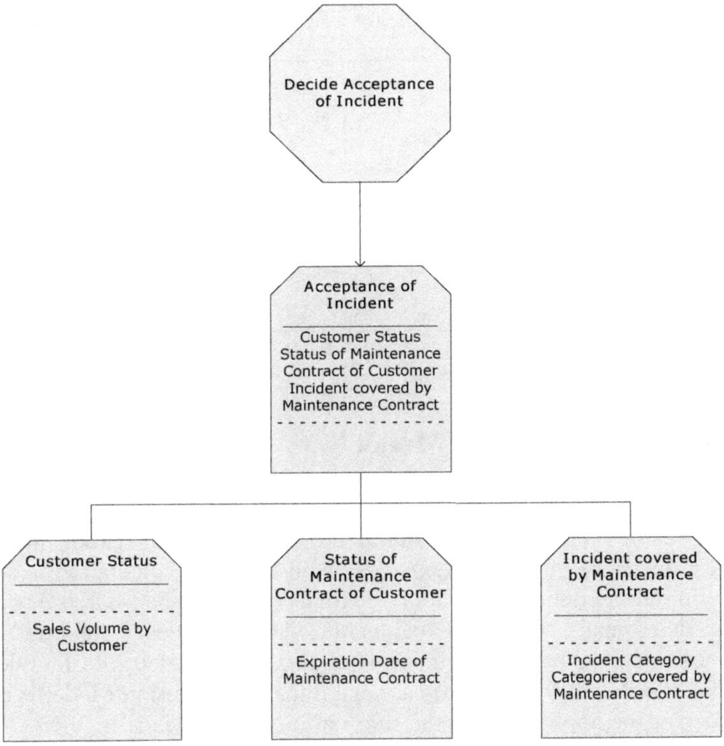

Fig. 4. Example of a Decision Model

Each Rule Family Element owns a "Rule Family Table". This table shows the set of business rules in a two dimensional structure. The columns represent fact types. A single cell represents a fact. One column is the conclusion fact type; the other columns are condition fact types. Each row represents a rule or more precise: The manifestation of condition fact types leading to a conclusion fact. Table 1 shows a rule family table.

The Decision Model is declarative: The order of rows and columns doesn't matter. One column – often the last column – is representing the Conclusion Fact Type.

The same is true for the presentation of the rule families in the Decision Model. The tree doesn't show an order in which the rule families have to be evaluated. Evaluation can be done top-down or bottom-up or even starting in the middle.

The Framework defines not only the presentation of decision models. It also defines normal forms and principles for the construction of rule family tables and decision models. This creates a precision which allows an easy transformation of such models into an IT implementation e.g. using a rule engine. The principles are not in the scope of the OMG standardization but are highly important for the practical use.

The relation to the Business Process Model is obvious. We identify Tasks representing business decisions. Such a task is connected with the corresponding decision model Von Halle/Goldberg suggest the introduction of a new task type "Decision Task" into the BPMN standard.

Table 1. Example for a Rule Family Table

	Condition Fact Types						Conclusion Fact Type	
Rule Pattern	Customer Status		Status of Maintenance Contract of the Customer		Incident covered by the Maintenance Contract		Acceptance of the Incident	
1	Is	Platin					Is	Accepted
1	Is	Gold					Is	Accepted
2	Not in	{Platin; Gold}	Is	Active	Is	Covered	Is	Accepted
3	Not in	{Platin; Gold}	is	Inactive			Is	Not Accepted
4	Not in	{Platin; Gold}			Is	Not covered	Is	Not Accepted

3 Applying "The Decision Model"

The approach can be applied in a pragmatic way. In a first step we analyze the task level of our business process model and identify the "Decision Tasks" meaning tasks containing a decision. In this context a decision can be a calculation, a selection, a check or similar activities. We apply textual analysis and search for "Decision Words" as "determine", "validate", "calculate", "asses", "select", "choose".

In the next step we have to define and analyze the needed rule families. This is usually done top-down. It should be said again that the Decision Model is declarative and no order of the application of the rule families and rules is implied. The normal forms and principles described in [1] ensure that the resulting model is non-redundant, maintainable and reusable.

We show both models explicitly and create the logical connection between Task and related Decision Model as shown in figure 5. This is mainly a tool question. Our modeling tool needs to support logical connections between model elements and other models.

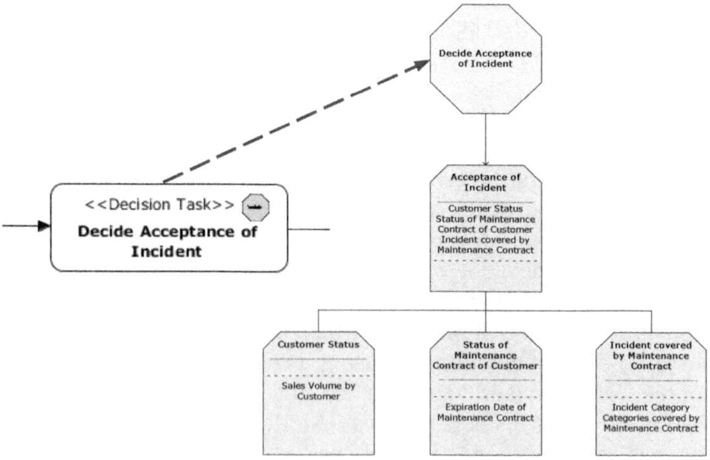

Fig. 5. Logical link between a "Decision Task" and a Decision Model

References

1. von Halle, B., Goldberg, L.: The Decision Model - A Business Logic Framework Linking Business and Technology. Auerbach Publications (2010)
2. Taylor, J., Raden, N.: Smart (Enough) Systems. Pearson Education, Inc., Boston (2007)
3. Pitschke, J.: Unternehmensmodellierung für die Praxis, Band 1: Eine Einführung in die Darstellung von Unternehmensmodellen, 3. Auflage, Book on Demand (2011)
4. BPMN. Business Process Model and Notation (BPMN), Version 2.0, OMG Document Number: formal/2011-01-03. Object Management Group (2011)
5. SBVR. Semantics of Business Vocabulary and Business Rules (SBVR), v1.0, OMG Document Number: formal/2008-01-02. Object Management Group (2008)
6. IDEF0. Integration Definition for Function Modeling (IDEF0). Department of Commerce, National Institute of Standards and Technology, Computer Systems Laboratory (1993)

Building a Business Graph System and Network Integration Model Based on BPMN

Daniel Ritter, Jörg Ackermann, Ankur Bhatt, and Frank Oliver Hoffmann

SAP AG, Technology Development – Process and Network Integration,
Dietmar-Hopp-Allee 16, 69190 Walldorf, Germany
{daniel.ritter,joerg.ackermann,ankur.bhatt,frank.oliver.hoffmann}@sap.com
http://www.sap.com

Abstract. Business Network Management (BNM) provides companies with techniques for managing their trading partner networks by making technical integration, business and social aspects visible within a network view and set them into context to each other. This allows various personas, from the business specialist to the technical integration expert, to monitor, enrich and setup business processes by collaborating on the different contexts. In this paper, we propose a BNM concept, which features inter-connected business and technical perspectives showing the company network. The Business Process Modeling Notation (BPMN) is a well-established standard for describing business process semantics and particularly aims for understandability by technical and business stakeholders. Hence we apply BPMN to BNM, for which we use BPMN as graphical notation on UI and as basis for our Network Integration Model (NIM) by extending a subset of BPMN (mainly conversation diagram) to cover both business and technical integration aspects. We present a novel approach on applying BPMN to our domain and reports on our experiences with it.

Keywords: BPMN 2.0, Business Network, Network centric-BPMN, Network Integration Model.

1 Introduction

Nowadays enterprises are part of value chains consisting of business processes with intra and inter enterprise stakeholders. To remain competetive, enterprises need visibility into their business network and ideally into the relevant parts of partner and customer networks and their processes. However, currently the visibility often ends at the borders of systems or enterprises. Business Network Management (BNM) helps to overcome this situation and allows companies to get insight into their technical, social and business relations. For instance, Fig. 1 shows participants in a sample business network.

Our project evaluates a BNM approach on how to develop a model covering the required entities and perspecitves of a business network. In this paper, we describe the use of BPMN version 2.0 [4] for a Network Integration Model (NIM)

R. Dijkman, J. Hofstetter, and J. Koehler (Eds.): BPMN 2011, LNBIP 95, pp. 154–159, 2011.

and introduce specializations needed for the specific domain. The network approach leads to a multi-relational graph model which challenges BPMN in areas of nodes and edges, semantic links, and management of large amounts of data. NIM covers these areas and proposes new entities relevant for networks.

Section 2 describes the design principles and section 3 explains basic entities for modeling business networks using BPMN 2.0. In section 4 we summarize our experiences with BPMN and section 5 concludes and outlines future work.

2 Design Principles

In our approach, the model for business network serves as visual representation and standardized exchange format for real-world entities like applications and semantically relate the context end-to-end, e.g. from process to system. For that, a human and computer readable notation is required. This notation shall be a well-established standard which covers the requirements for definining entities, their relationships and properties representing the business network. A "one-model" approach shall be followed, to allow views on business and technical aspects, and enable all personas to work with the same model. The semantic model for the business network shall be kept simple without loosing expressiveness.

Alternatives considered were notations like the *Service Component Architecture* (SCA) [5], which focus on the technical communication e.g. within SOA, and business related approaches like supply chains or value networks [7]. However, they miss real-world business and social artifacts like contact person or business partner, thus contradicting the "one-model" requirement.

BPMN is a standard for defining, visualizing and exchanging business procedures within (A2A) and across (B2B) enterprises and is widely used within disciplines related to BNM like BPM. We decided to base NIM on BPMN, since it best meets our requirements. Similar to our domain other authors used and extended BPMN for their domains, as e.g. H. D. Kim [1] for B2B in BPM or V. Torres et al [6] for extensions to BPMN 1.1 in public administration.

3 Network Integration Model

3.1 Basic Business Network Entities

The business network as represented with NIM is defined as subset of BPMN 2.0 by mapping it onto the basic entities of the network. The *Network* itself is represented by a BPMN conversation diagram, as a special type of collaboration diagram, and defines a superset of the computed network and all manual extensions. BPMN *Pools*, referred to as *Participants*, and BPMN *Conversations* within the ConversationDiagram represent the process, document and control flow between business partners, applications and systems. For instance, Fig. 1 shows a NIM representation of an outbound delivery process of an enterprise [2]. NIM differentiates between a business perspective (Fig. 1a) and a (technical) integration perspective (Fig. 1b) to show the same network with different focus and for different personas. The central logistics department (*HQ Logistics*) interacts via application system *HQP* with the distribution centers (*DC Hamburg/ DC Berlin*) that use application system *WMP*. They both work with external transport agencies (*Carrier 1/ Carrier 2*) that communicate via interface standards *FRADOK/ IFTMIN*. Since participants of external carriers are typically not known, they are annotated with the employed interface standards. At the end the finance department (*HQ Finance*) generates an invoice via application system *HQP*. The interaction between business partners, applications and systems is depicted as top-level connections, e.g. between *HQ Logistics* and *DC Hamburg* in Fig. 1 (a), and it can expand to BPMN Conversations and Sub-Conversations, e.g. *OutboundDeliveryProc.* and *GoodMovementProc.* in Fig. 1 (b).

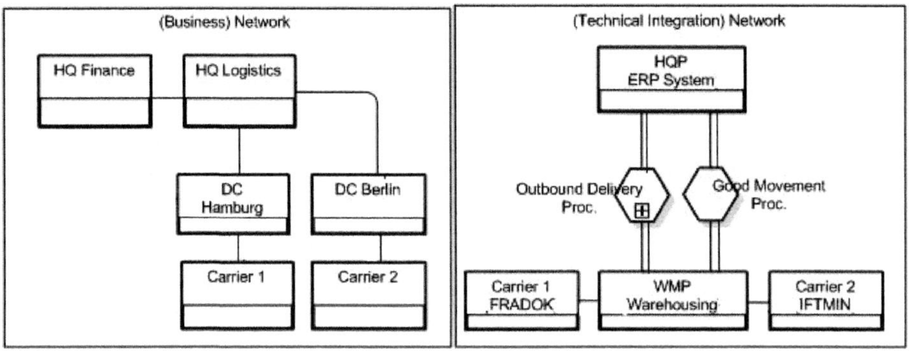

(a) Business Perspective

(b) (Technical) Integration Perspective

Fig. 1. Sample NIM representation of a business network in BPMN 2.0

Nodes and edges are the basic entities of a network. The BPMN *participant* represents a node denoting a real-world entity, which communicates with other participants. A participant has two specializations: *BusinessParticipant* and *CommunicationParticipant*. BusinessParticipants, e.g. *HQ Logistics*, represent organizational units within the enterprise and external business partners while CommunicationParticipants, e.g. *HQP*, have an IT perspective like system landscape, middleware configuration. To relate the two perspectives, a *ParticipantLink* is derived from the BPMN *ParticipantAssociation* (not shown). For example, *HQ Logistics* is related to *HQP* by a ParticipantLink of type "is-implemented-by". ParticipantLinks are not visualized, but are realized implicitly between business and technical network perspectives.

A *Top-Level Connection* is an extension to BPMN to visually represent the interaction/ edges between participants and group their Conversations, Sub-Conversations and MessageFlows. The Conversation links two or more participants and aggregates the *MessageFlows*. The MessageFlow represents the flow of messages between separate participants and is specialized as *BusinessFlow* for business documents and as *CommunicationFlow* for technical messages. Conversation and MessageFlow can be grouped by *SubConversation*. This notion is based on the specification of BPMN 2.0 [4], where B2B is supported by pools, i.e. participants as black box, and message flows, which has also been suggested by M. Owen et al [3].

3.2 Relationship of Basic Business Network Entities

The Network entity is used as entry point for visualizing and operating on the network. BPMN Conversation and SubConversation are the aggregation entities for inter-participant communication while MessageFlow represents a single message exchange (see Figure 1(b)).

A Conversation can be visually expanded to MessageFlows in BPMN 2.0. NIM adds *MediationFlow* as a specialization and proposes a new graphical notation (see figure 2(a)). This flow indicates that middleware capabilities are used while communicating the message. An alternative visualization in flow notation, depicted in figure 2(b), shows the equivalent mediated flow in standard BPMN. For point to point connections without mediation a specialized MessageFlow is used, called *P2PMessageFlow*. In case of asynchronous request/ confirmation

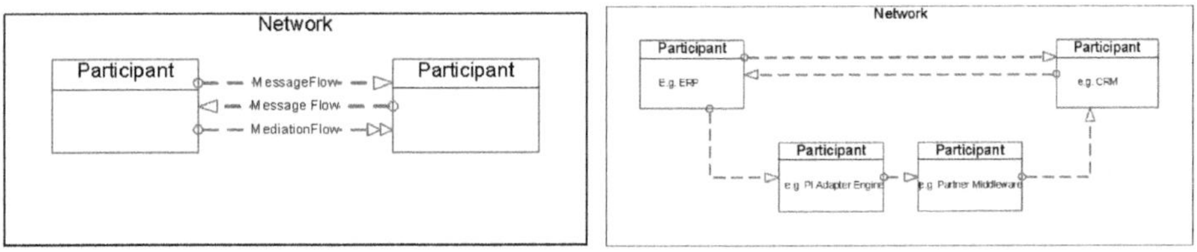

(a) MessageFlow and MediationFlow (b) Alternative notation

Fig. 2. Network with P2PMessageFlow and MediationFlow

communication pattern, two MessageFlows are added, one for each direction, while in synchronous communication only one is used.

The technical entities discussed actually implement business related processing and communication, hence even if the business perspective may differ from the technical landscape, it may follow its structure. For instance, a particular business flow might consist of multiple technical flows of different types. A *BusinessParticipant* defines an organizational entity, receiving and sending messages via *BusinessFlow*. The BusinessParticpant and the BusinessFlow represent the business perspective of the network. For example, the business document *OutboundDeliveryRequest* is sent from *HQ Logistics* to *DC Hamburg* represented by a corresponding business flow. This is mirrored on the (technical) integration perspective by an XML message exchanged between *HQP* and *WMP*. BusinessParticipants are semantically linked to CommunicationParticipants via ParticipantLinks.

BPMN *Messages* are used to transfer data. They can be mapped to synchronous service calls, e.g. in a SOA domain, an event or any kind of asynchronous messages used for A2A/ B2B processes. For that NIM leverages the

BPMN 2.0 service extension point package to describe service interface (structure), operation (method) and endpoint (binding) configuration. This allows an integration of SCA artifacts [5] into NIM. A Participant can be associated to a *ServiceInterface* directly or via *ServiceOperation*, which is linked to the message and describes the action executed on the data. The *ServiceBinding* defines a configuration used for the message exchange.

4 Experiences with BPMN in the Domain of BNM

As outlined in section 2, the decision for BPMN was based on the expectation to benefit from using a widely adopted standard, i.e. faster design of model, lower learning curve, a standardized exchange format, etc. BPMN with BNM extensions allows to link between network integration and business process perspective. Participants can be expanded to show activities and assign them to flows. This combines the domain with BPM, to e.g. start from the business network and drill-in to the activity level.

We adopted new BPMN 2.0 concepts, e.g. conversation diagram, and extended them, since the technical integration perspective is not within the BPMN scope. The proposed extensions contain new model and visual elements. Future work on BPMN may consider re-fining terminology, e.g. naming of conversation vs. sub-conversation, and adding new views. Shortcomings of BPMN for our domain are subsequently discussed.

Customer landscapes and business processes are typically quite large and complex and may contain hundreds or even thousands of participants. A support for structuring such a network is necessary to a) group related participants graphically and show them within a joint boundary (cf. BPMN groups), which allows structuring the network based on organization or geographic location and b) combine multiple participants to a compound participant, where only the compound is visible originally and the included participants are only visible after explicit drill-in. This is useful to show e.g. an external business partner as a compound on top-level and hide information about the included systems. BPMN support for such structuring is limited. For instance, BPMN groups are only specified for flow elements but not participants and a concept of nesting as e.g. for BPMN *Lanes* is missing.

Technical message flows in NIM are characterized by their sending and receiving interfaces and carry technical information like transport protocol, message format, etc. Since that is out of scope in BPMN, we extended BPMN for these aspects with new model entities and visual representation.

When visually expanding a (Sub-)Conversation, the BPMN specification proposes to replace the contained elements. However, in that way the context is lost, which becomes critical in case of many (Sub-)Conversations.

To simplify the network visualization, all flows and conversations between two participants are displayed as one line and details become only available after drill-in. For that, we introduce the new concept of Top-Level Connection. A BPMN conform solution uses a SubConversation, however contradicting its specified semantics.

As encouraged by the BPMN specification, we proposed to use the same notation for business and technical view to bridge the gap between business and technical user. However, using the same shapes for in both views, even when visualized separately, was not accepted in customer design sessions. Therefore we currently experiment with different shapes for business related participants while keeping BPMN notation and shapes otherwise.

5 Discussion and Future Work

In this paper, we presented a novel approach to use BPMN in a network domain, namely the Business Network Management. We showed how a network model can be derived from BPMN and outlined in which areas we see challenges. Future work will be conducted for NIM especially in the areas of grouping, the representation of business data, social aspects and further network extensions.

Acknowledgments. We thank Ivana Trickovic for support on BPMN 2.0, Volker Stiehl for proof reading as well as Gunther Rothermel for sponsorship.

References

1. Kim, H.D.: BPMN-Based Modeling of B2B Business Processes from the Neutral Perspective of UMM/ BPSS. In: IEEE Internaltional Conference on E-Business Engineering, pp. 417–422. IEEE Computer Society, Los Alamitos (2008)
2. Outbound Delivery Processing, `http://help.sap.com/saphelp_crm40/helpdata/en/63/e48939728dd04abac5b86aa66002c2/content.htm`
3. Owen, M., Stuecka, R.: BPMN und die Modellierung von Geschäftsprozessen. Whitepaper, Telelogic (2006)
4. Specification of Business Process Modeling Notation version 2.0 (BPMN 2.0), `http://www.omg.org/spec/BPMN/2.0/PDF`
5. Service Component Architecture (SCA), `http://www.osoa.org/display/Main/Service+Component+Architecture+Home`
6. Torres, V., Giner, P., Bonet, B., Pelechano, V.: Adapting BPMN to Public Administration. In: Mendling, J., Weidlich, M., Weske, M. (eds.) BPMN 2010. LNBIP, vol. 67, pp. 114–120. Springer, Heidelberg (2010)
7. Ritter, D., Bhatt, A.: Modeling Approach for Business Networks with an Integration and Business Perspective. In: De Troyer, O. (ed.) ER 2011 Workshops. LNCS, vol. 6999, pp. 343–344. Springer, Heidelberg (2011)

Requirements Engineering for SOA Services with BPMN 2.0 – From Analysis to Specification

Gregor Scheithauer[1] and Björn Hardegen[2]

[1] OPITZ CONSULTING GmbH,
Weltenburger Str. 4, 81677 Munich
scheithauer@acm.org
[2] MID GmbH, Kressengarten Str. 10, 90402 Nuremberg
b.hardegen@mid.de

Abstract. This paper presents experiences in requirements engineering analysis, service identification, and service specification that were gained during a service development project in a public government organization. These experiences resulted in a method comprising techniques relying on a combination of BPMN 2.0 and UML. This method shows that using a combination of these notations and model generation of IT artifacts leads to fewer documents for different stakeholders, alignment of service specifications to original requirements, and semantic unambiguousness for service specifications.

Keywords: BPMN 2.0, Requirements Engineering, Service Specification.

1 Introduction

Requirements engineering is a mature discipline of the software development process that includes eliciting and analyzing needs and demands from stakeholders, and their transformation into requirements that need to be met by resulting software products. The software development process that targets service-orientation [1] touches requirements engineering in terms of analyzing business processes and business objects, service identification, service specification, and the development of test cases. This holds the following challenges: (1) limiting documentation efforts for different stakeholders (analysis, specification, and implementation), (2) ensuring a business requirements-driven approach (top-down), (3) guaranteeing traceability between business requirements and service specification, and (4) assuring semantic unambiguousness of specification for developers so as to reduce degree of freedom and ambiguity of implementation details.

In order to address these challenges, the method that this paper introduces takes the following approaches. To limit diverse documentation needs, requirements analysis and specification follow a model-based style, that being a combination of UML [2] and BPMN 2.0 [3]. Furthermore, this method targets a stringent top-down refinement of business requirements into service specification to limit unnecessary technical implementations. In order to address semantic unambiguousness for developers, service specifications distinguish between external and internal service behavior (choreography vs. orchestration) as well as generation of IT artifacts from service specification

R. Dijkman, J. Hofstetter, and J. Koehler (Eds.): BPMN 2011, LNBIP 95, pp. 160–165, 2011.

(contract first) [4], e.g. WSDL and XSD. The method was applied in a project with a German public government organization that employs over 120,000 people in over 750 subsidiaries in Germany. 2,000 employees within the IT department are responsible for planning, realization, running and maintaining of software. In line with the organization's IT strategy for 2015, a program was initiated for a company-wide introduction of SOA that touches on technical as well as organizational aspects. The main objectives included a rollout of novel software frameworks for software development, a reduction of single-purpose silo applications and an overall faster and more flexible software provision process. The following sections present the overall method (cf. Fig. 1) that is initially introduced in section 2. Section 3 then goes on to explain how service specification was conducted with BPMN 2.0 [3] and section 4 concludes with some findings of the method's application.

2 Project Method Overview

The method for the requirements analysis for SOA services can be divided into four logical but not necessarily consecutive high level steps. Those steps, which are shown in Fig. 1, are: requirements analysis, service identification, service specification and definition of business driven test cases.

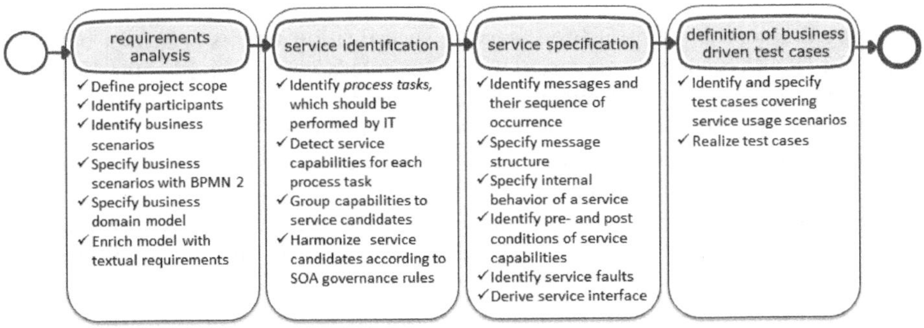

Fig. 1. Project Method Overview

The scope of the project is defined within the requirements analysis using UML use cases [2]. Each use case stands for a business scenario that creates business value. Therefore the internal and external participants or actors have to be identified to describe who has to be involved to achieve an identified business scenario. Subsequently, the business scenario is specified using BPMN 2.0 whereas a use case is represented by a BPMN collaboration and an actor is represented by a BPMN participant. The processes of the different participants communicate with messages. In order to do so, data objects are defined within the processes providing the information to fill the messages. The structures of the data, both internally and process externally used, have to be specified within the requirements analysis. The previously mentioned modeling artifacts of the requirements analysis are a valuable input for the service identification and specification, which are described in detail in the following sections.

In the aforementioned project, service identification targeted at a top-down approach in order to derive coarse-grained SOA services from business requirements. Techniques for service identification include (1) business objectives and key performance indicators, (2) functional domain decomposition, (3) system analysis, and (4) process-orientation [1]. In the project itself, the process-oriented technique was applied as the organization in question already follows a process-driven approach regarding requirements engineering. The process-oriented technique ascribes to identify service candidates on the basis of business processes, objects, and messages. For the business process shown in Fig. 2, capabilities are grouped into three services: *Customer Information Service, Accounting Service, and Notification Service.*

The identified services then need to be specified. This is further described in section 3. Furthermore, it is also important to define business driven test cases for the identified and specified services which are derived from the requirements and have to cover the service usage scenarios. After service realization these test cases can then verify the correct behavior of each service operation. This means that test cases require proper implementation using test frameworks and tools. In the project, the automated test cases are integrated into the build management so that their specified behavior was guaranteed after each deployment of the service.

3 Service Specification

Following the service identification, service specification targets a formal basis for realization. Service specification does not substitute a service architecture. Instead, service specification is aimed towards further-refining business requirements as well as establishing a result document for service implementation.

In terms of the aforesaid project, service specification includes seven steps that were performed using a combination of BPMN and UML. This combination provided an appropriate and common basis for analysis and specification. The starting point of service specification itself is one or more business processes. This is why the notation allowed a top-down approach and perfect traceability between analysis and specification.

The first step ascribes identifying the choreography of a service. The basis for this step is a BPMN collaboration diagram, including a business process along with identified service candidates (cf. Fig 2). For each task that should be performed by IT, messages need to be identified between a task and a service operation. Following this, the message sequence of the choreography needs to be recognized. Different message exchange patterns apply, e.g. Request-Response pattern. Task related business objects may contribute to message identification. Fig. 2 displays identified messages that are exchanged between process tasks and acknowledged services. For example, the process task *determine customer details* exchanges two messages with the service *Customer Information Service*. This step concludes the service choreography.

Two scenarios are possible following the choreography specification. The first scenario is that a service matching the choreography specification is available in organizations' service portfolios. If this is the case, the available service description needs to be imported into the modeling tool and integrated into the BPMN

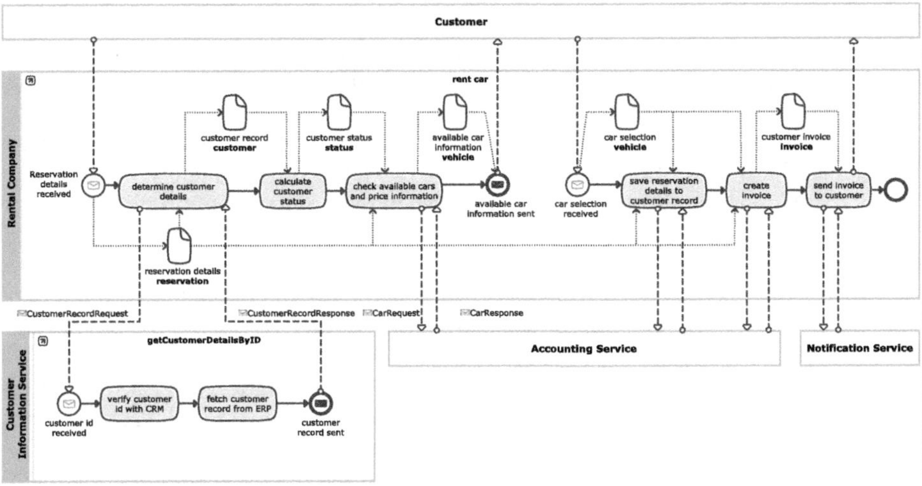

Fig. 2. Example BPMN Collaboration. While the participants Customer and Rental Company represent the business process, the participants Customer Information Service, Accounting Service, and Notification Service denote identified services, along with identified messages.

collaboration diagram. The second scenario is that no matching service exists within the organization. If so, the third step includes structuring identified messages. While business objects were aligned during process analysis and refer to a normalized set of business entities, messages represent a set of attribute bundles with a de-normalized character that are exchanged between participants. As an example, customer ID needs to be provided to determine the customer's information. While it is possible to send an empty instance of the business object *customer record* (except for the customer ID attribute), it is advisable to use a message instead of a business object for reasons of service interface understandability and semantic unambiguousness.

Following the message structure definition step, the external specification is completed. This part of the specification is now the basis for defining the internal service behavior. The behavior depicts a (technical) way of achieving the external specification [4]. This may include an orchestration of other SOA services or an integration of enterprise applications, including CRM or ERP systems. In either case, it is highly recommended to include service architects and those responsible for enterprise applications. The internal specification is a result document that is appropriate for service developers.

In the project, a BPMN process diagram was used in order to depict services' internal behavior. The diagram represented an orchestration of existing SOA services, including a service for accessing information about customers as well as a system for managing tasks. For example, the lower section of Fig. 2 that shows the *Customer Information Service* participant's process *getCustomerDetailsByID* represents an orchestration of two systems for accessing customer records.

Following services' behavior specification, step five continues with describing conditions which need to be valid prior to and after invoking of a service capability. These pre and post-conditions elevate the semantic unambiguousness for service developers as well as potential consumers of a service. While a possible pre-condition for the service capability *getCustomerDetailsByID* could be *Customer with a valid ID must exist*, *customer record provided* could be a valid post-condition.

In addition to message identification and structure definition, step six involves naming possible service faults for each service capability. In the project, faults were distinguished between functional and technical faults. Functional faults refer to possible situations that do not comply with business requirements or are contrary to specified service (external or internal) behavior. Technical faults denote technical situations, e.g. hardware malfunctions or server infrastructure issues. In the project, functional faults were derived from aforementioned pre-conditions. For example, it is possible to reuse the pre-condition *Customer with a valid ID must exit* as the fault *unknown customer*.

The final step of service specification comprises the generation of IT artifacts from a service specification. This step relates to the objective to elevate semantic unambiguousness of the specification. With the *external* service specification including service capabilities, messages and their structure definition, it is possible to generate abstract Web Services Description Language (WSDL) documents along with corresponding XML Schema Definition (XSD) files. While abstract WSDL documents describe web service functionality in terms of their capabilities, XSD files define necessary message and data type formats. With the *internal* service specification, it is possible to generate abstract Business Process Execution Language (BPEL) files for orchestrating web services. Along with the service specification itself, these documents are input for the development process. In the aforementioned project, WSDL and XSD files were generated from the service specification. The generation process relies on the modeling tool as well as OpenArchitecture model-to-text transformation scripts.

4 Conclusion

The previous sections have shown how to use two notations in order to analyze requirements as well as identify and specify SOA services. Both notations merely cover aspects of the requirements analysis for SOA services. That is why both notations were combined in order to utilize the best points from each notation. While BPMN 2.0 focuses on the process and interaction description (dynamic aspects), there are no notation elements defined i.e. for the specification of data structures (static aspects). UML, on the other hand, includes static and dynamic aspects but lacks the comprehensibility of BPMN 2.0 when it comes to the modeling of dynamic aspects. UML offers different options to describe interactions. While the UML activity diagram is appropriate to describe a sequence of steps, sequence diagrams stress the message exchange between participants. The BPMN 2.0 collaboration combines the advantages of activity and sequence diagrams, while maintaining the readability for business departments. The model is a beneficial artifact for communicating what was understood during the requirements analysis phase. This leads to semantic errors or oversights being found and corrected in an early phase of the process; this in turn helped to avoid confusion and extra effort during service development.

An advantage of a model based approach is the possibility of generating documentation based on templates. These templates consist of information only relevant to the respective stakeholders of the project. While the initial configuration of templates may take some time, providing these audience specific documentation during the project is effortless.

Instead of modeling interactions, processes, messages and data structures only for the purpose of documenting development results, it is possible to leverage the model for different aspects of the service development lifecycle by refining the model during the design and specification process. Due to the fact that the specification arises from the requirements model, *traceability* to the original business requirements is ensured. The resulting service specification is characterized by *semantic unambiguousness for developers*, which reduced the degree of freedom and ambiguity of implementation details. One key success factor to accomplish this goal was the contract first approach which allows internal and external service behaviors to be separated. The model driven approach and the usage of UML and BPMN 2.0 go hand in hand with the meta models of both notations. Combined with a proper tool chain, the generation of IT artifacts from the service specification model enforces this contract first approach at the transition from service design to service implementation. For instance, the service interfaces with their defined service operations and message parameters are used in the project to generate a web service description (WSDL) with corresponding message schema definition (XSD) and message structure definition (XSD).

Furthermore, the business driven test cases that are derived from the business requirements and executed after the deployment of new service implementation helped to verify the correct internal service behavior and ensure that the service still *meets the business requirements* of the service consumers. The project's success originates from the previously mentioned aspects. It also demonstrates that a model based approach is also applicable and beneficial to small projects and is not reserved for projects with many project collaborators.

References

[1] Arsanjani, A., Ghosh, S., Allam, A., Abdo, T.: SOMA: A Method for developing Service-oriented Solutions. IBM System Journal 47 (2008)

[2] OMG. Unified Modeling Language, Superstructure Specification (2010)

[3] OMG. Business Process Model and Notation (BPMN), version 2.0 (2011)

[4] Quartel, D.A.C., Steen, M.W.A., Pokraev, S., van Sinderen, M.: COSMO: A conceptual Framework for Service Modelling and Refinement. Information Systems Frontiers 9, 2–3 (2007)

Introducing Entity-Based Concepts to Business Process Modeling

Klaus Sperner, Sonja Meyer, and Carsten Magerkurth

SAP Research Switzerland
Kreuzplatz 20, 8008 Zürich, Switzerland
{klaus.sperner,sonj.meyer,carsten.magerkurth}@sap.com

Abstract. The so-called Internet of Things (IoT) that comprises interconnected physical devices such as sensor networks and its technologies like Radio Frequency Identification (RFID) is increasingly adopted in many industries and thus becomes highly relevant for process modeling and execution. As BPMN 2.0 does not yet consider the idiosyncrasies of real-world entities we suggest new modeling concepts for a physical entity as well as a sensing task and an actuation task to make BPMN IoT-aware.

Keywords: Internet of Things, IoT, Business Process Modeling, BPMN.

1 Introduction

Today, the gap between the sensors and actuators in the Internet of Things and the business systems at the higher layers of the enterprise world is still a reality. A unified reference architecture is therefore a key prerequisite for realizing interoperability within the IoT world and especially for integration with business processes, so that applications can be realized that are both IoT-aware and meet the requirements of enterprise systems. Currently, the IoT domain is being standardized based on a unified IoT domain model [4] that is discussed in the next section. We apply core concepts from the IoT domain model to the Business Process Model and Notation (BPMN) 2.0 [2]. As BPMN focuses on activities and the implicated flow of process steps while the IoT domain model stresses the relationship between entities and other constructs for which well defined processes might or might not exist, a mapping and integration problem between both domains becomes apparent.

In the remainder of this paper we will use the following typographical conventions: Concepts from the IoT domain model are typeset in sans serif, and concepts from the BPMN metamodel are typeset in `constant width`.

2 A Domain Model for the Internet of Things

Based on [1] and [3] a first version of the domain model for the Internet of Things has been developed in [4]. As this model is an extensive conceptual representation

R. Dijkman, J. Hofstetter, and J. Koehler (Eds.): BPMN 2011, LNBIP 95, pp. 166–171, 2011.

of the IoT domain, it serves as a basic fundament for the presented research work. In this section we shortly explain its core concepts, please confer Fig. 6 in [4].

As the term Internet of Things suggests, the *thing* is the most important concept in the domain model; it is called Physical Entity. The main purpose of the domain model is to show, in which way any kind of User can interact with a Physical Entity, so the association interacts with between the User and the Physical Entity is the key concept of the model.

To represent a Physical Entity in the digital world, a Virtual Entity is associated to it. While a Physical Entity exists only once, there can be multiple Virtual Entities representing it. Every combination of a Virtual Entity and its Physical Entity forms one Augmented Entity.

In order to make the Physical Entity accessible from the digital world some hardware, a so-called Device, is attached to the Physical Entity. To distinguish between Devices which observe a Physical Entity and Devices which control a Physical Entity, three subclasses of Device are introduced in the domain model: A Sensor can be attached to a Physical Entity to monitor it, an Actuator can be attached to a Physical Entity to act on it, and a Tag can be attached to a Physical Entity to identify it.

To close the gap between the Device and the digital world, it hosts several software components in its memory, which are called Resources. Depending on the type of the Device, such a Resource has information about the Physical Entity, or it can act on the Physical Entity. Virtual Entities can be associated with Resources via the Device and the Physical Entity.

As the Resources hosted on the Devices are expected to have different interfaces, Services are introduced as an abstraction concept; they access the Resources. These Services provide well-defined interfaces to the Users for invoking them. Since the Virtual Entities are associated with the Resources, they can be associated with the Services, which access these Resources, as well.

Summing up, the interaction of the User with the Physical Entity can be detailed as follows: The User invokes a Service, which accesses a Resource, which is hosted on a Device, which either monitors the Physical Entity or acts on the Physical Entity.

3 Mapping between IoT Concepts and BPMN Concepts

To bring the IoT domain and business process modeling together, we analyse, how the concepts from the domain model can be modeled in BPMN, and if the chosen BPMN concepts are adequate to reflect the specificities of the Internet of Things. Table 1 summarizes the proposed mapping of IoT and BPMN concepts.

A Physical Entity can be modeled as a `TextAnnotation` to an `Activity`. Since the concept of a Physical Entity is not defined in BPMN, we use the `TextAnnotation` as the general BPMN concept for attaching further details to a modeling element. The usage of a `TextAnnotation` for the modeling of a Physical Entity is not sufficient, and leads to multiple problems: As specified in [2] a `TextAnnotation` only provides additional information for the reader of a

Table 1. Mapping of IoT concepts to current BPMN concepts and their sufficiency for modeling of IoT aware processes

IoT concept	BPMN concept	Sufficiency for Modeling
Physical Entity	`TextAnnotation`	not sufficient
Virtual Entity	`DataObject`	sufficient
Augmented Entity	—	not needed in BPMN
Sensor	`Participant`	sufficient
monitoring	`ServiceTask`	not sufficient
Actuator	`Participant`	sufficient
acting	`ServiceTask`	not sufficient
Tag	—	not needed in BPMN
Resource	—	not needed in BPMN
Service	`ServiceTask`	not sufficient
User	`Participant, Event`	sufficient

diagram, but does not affect the flow of the process. Accordingly, the specification of a dedicated Physical Entity in the model would not be obeyed during the execution of the process. Second, a `TextAnnotation` can be attached to only one object in the collaboration diagram, but one Physical Entity could for instance be monitored by multiple Sensors. Third, there is no definition of a lifecycle for a `TextAnnotation`, but a Physical Entity naturally persists between several process executions.

The Virtual Entities relating to the Physical Entities can be modeled as collection `DataObjects` in a BPMN collaboration diagram, because this is the concept for modeling data, which BPMN provides. As the concept of a Virtual Entity is not only specific to the IoT domain, but a general concept in informatics, this approach of modeling is considered to be sufficient, and fully serves our purposes.

As the Augmented Entity in the IoT domain model is only an abstract concept to combine a Virtual Entity and a Physical Entity, there is no corresponding concept in BPMN. Since such an abstract concept would not add any benefit for the practical modeling of business processes, the Augmented Entitiy is not needed in BPMN.

Sensors and Actuators can sufficiently be modeled as `Participants` in a collaboration diagram, because this concept is defined in BPMN to represent a `PartnerEntity`, which executes a process. If multiple instances of Sensors or Actuators are involved, the corresponding pools can be decorated with multi-instance markers.

As a Sensor is described in the domain model to monitor a Physical Entity and an Actuator is said to act on a Physical Entity, these monitoring and actuation associations can be expressed with `ServiceTasks` in a BPMN diagram. In BPMN `Tasks` are the central concept of execution during the process flow, so this modeling is appropriate. The particular `Task` can implicitly be identified as a `Task` for monitoring or actuation through the `Participant` executing it, the Physical Entity, which is represented in the attached `TextAnnotation`, and the name of the `Task`, which states the means of monitoring or actuation. So far it can not be explicitly marked as a specific `Task` for monitoring or actuation.

Even though the concept of attaching Tags to Physical Entities to make them identifiable is one of the most widely adopted applications of Internet of Things technologies, it is a low-level technology, and an introduction to BPMN is not needed. If the process of this identification is of particular interest, the Tag can be considered as a Physical Entity, which is monitored by a Sensor.

The Resources introduced in the domain model are the software components running on the Devices. Since BPMN collaboration diagrams focus on `Participants` executing `Tasks`, introducing the Resource to BPMN is not reasonable.

In the domain model the Services provide a consistent interface for the Resources, which are hosted by Sensors and Actuators. In BPMN these Services can be modeled as `ServiceTasks`, which are executed by the `Participants`, which represent Sensors and Actuators. As described above, the Physical Entities, on which these `ServiceTasks` operate, are referenced in the attached `TextAnnotations`. Although the modeling of the Services via `ServiceTasks` seems appropriate, it is not sufficient: In a collaboration diagram it is impossible to distinguish, if the Service performs a sensing or an actuating interaction with the Physical Entity.

For the User in the domain model, who invokes the Service, the different BPMN concepts for the invocation of `Tasks` can be considered. This could be a `Message` from another `Participant` or an `Event`. As there are many concepts for the invocation of `Tasks` in BPMN, no new concept for the User needs to be introduced.

The result of our analysis is summarized in Table 1: The Physical Entity and the monitoring and actuating Services can not be represented sufficiently in BPMN.

4 New Modeling Concepts

4.1 Modeling of Physical Entities

To facilitate the modeling of Physical Entities we propose a new BPMN element `PhysicalObject`, which is subclassed from `FlowElement` in the BPMN metamodel. In contrast to the `DataObject` the `PhysicalObject` is not subclassed from `ItemAwareElement`, because these are designed to store items, but a Physical Entity is an item itself. Accordingly, the BPMN elements `DataState` and `ItemDefinition` are not needed for the `PhysicalObject`. To enable the modeler to refer to the same Physical Entity in multiple places of a diagram, we introduce a `PhysicalObjectReference` analogous to the `DataObjectReference`.

We propose the illustration of a brick shown in Fig. 1 as stencil for the `PhysicalObject` to make this new concept usable in a BPMN collaboration

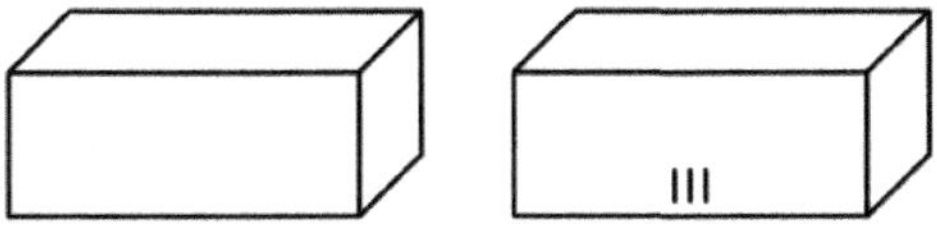

Fig. 1. Stencils for a single `PhysicalObject` (left) and a collection of `PhysicalObjects` (right)

diagram. As it is possible that not only one instance of a PhysicalObject is used in a process, the stencil can be decorated with a multiple instance marker, like it is defined in [2] for DataObjects. The name of the PhysicalObject will be placed above the base line of the stencil.

As PhysicalObjects are obviosly physical, their lifecycle is not limited to the lifecycle of the modeled process; they persist between process instantiations. This differentiates them from DataObjects, which are defined in [2] to not persist between process instantiations, but is similar to DataStores, which are also persistent according to [2].

4.2 Modeling of monitors and acts on Associations

To empower the modeler to express that a Task reflects a monitors or an acts on relationship between the Participant and the Physical Entity represented in the TextAnnotation, we introduce dedicated SensingTasks and ActuatingTasks as new subclasses of the Task class.

Since a Sensor produces data about a Physical Entity by monitoring it, the SensingTask must output this data and provide it for the remainder of the process. Hence, we can derive the following constraint for the SensingTask: The InputOutputSpecification, which is associated with the Activity superclass of the SensingTask, must reference at least one DataOutput, which must also be referenced by at least one OutputSet of the InputOutputSpecification. Because an Actuator needs an actuating value, an analogous constraint applies to the ActuationTask: The InputOutputSpecification associated to the ActuationTask must reference at least one DataInput, which must also be referenced by at least one InputSet.

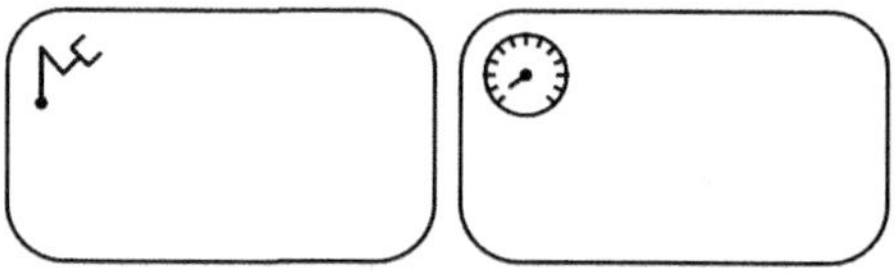

Fig. 2. Stencils for an ActuationTask (left) and a SensingTask (right)

For the new Tasks we propose the icons shown in Fig. 2 to decorate the stencil for the Task with: The ActuationTask is decorated with an illustration of a robot arm and the SensingTask is depicted with a gauge.

4.3 Connecting PhysicalObjects with ActuationTasks and SensingTasks

Analogous to the DataAssociation defined in [2], we define a new abstract class PhysicalAssociation, derived from BaseElement, and two concrete subclasses

ActuationAssociation and SensingAssociation. The former is a directed connection from an ActuationTask to the PhysicalObject, on which the represented Actuator acts on; it can be considered as a *flow of physical interaction*. The latter is directed from a PhysicalObject to a SensingTask; this can be considered as a *flow of physical information* from a Physical Entity to a Sensor.

To depict such associations in a BPMN diagram, we propose to reuse the same stencil as it is defined for a DataAssociation (cf. Fig. 10.65 in [2]).

5 Conclusions and Outlook

With this paper we have demonstrated first concrete steps towards bringing together the Internet of Things and Business Process Management. We have come up with first suggestions for augmentations to the BPMN 2.0 standard to reflect the most important aspects of the IoT domain model.

Our future work will deal with the further elaboration of the concepts presented in this paper including serializations of the new modeling concepts in the BPMN CMOF and the BPMN XML Schema and the serializations of the diagram elements in the BPMNDI XML Schema.

Acknowledgments. The authors would like to thankfully acknowledge the support for this work provided by the European Commission within the FP7 project IoT-A, contract number 257521. In this context we thank Stephan Haller, Alessandro Serbanati, Martin Bauer, Ralf Kernchen, Joachim Walewski, and Alessandro Bassi for their work on the Internet of Things domain model, and all other contributors to the model.

References

1. Haller, S.: The Things in the Internet of Things: Poster at the Internet of Things 2010 (2010), http://iot-a.eu/public/news/resources/TheThingsintheInternetofThings_SH.pdf (accessed June 30, 2011)
2. Object Management Group (OMG), Business Process Model and Notation (BPMN) Version 2.0 (2011), http://www.omg.org/spec/BPMN/2.0/ (accessed June 30, 2011)
3. Serbanati, A., Madaglia, C.M., Ceipidor, U.B.: Building Blocks of the Internet of Things: State of the Art and Beyond. In: Turcu, C. (ed.) RFID/Book 3. InTech, Rijeka (in press, 2011)
4. Walewski, J.W. et al.: Project Deliverable D1.2 - Initial Architectural Reference Model for IoT (2011), http://www.iot-a.eu/public/public-documents/project-deliverables/1/1/D1%202_Initial_architectural_reference_model_for_IoT.pdf/at_download/file (accessed June 30, 2011)

On the Capabilities of BPMN for Workflow Activity Patterns Representation

Lucinéia Heloisa Thom[1,2], Ivanna M. Lazarte[3], Cirano Iochpe[2], Luz-Maria Priego[2], Christine Verdier[2], Omar Chiotti[4], and Pablo David Villarreal[3]

[1] Departamento de Informática, Universidade Federal do Rio Grande do Sul, 15064, 91501-970, Porto Alegre, Brazil
[2] LIG, UMR 5217, SIGMA team, Joseph Fourier University, Grenoble, France
[3] CIDISI, National Technological University Santa Fé Faculty, Lavaisse 610, S3004EWB, Santa Fé, Argentina
[4] INGAR-CONICET, Avellaneda 3657, S3002GJC, Santa Fé, Argentina

Abstract. This paper provides a complete version of the Workflow Activity Patterns (WAP) in the Business Process Modeling Notation (BPMN) as well as an extended evaluation of the capabilities of BPMN and their strengths and weaknesses when being utilizing for representing WAPs. When implementing the activity patterns in existing Business Process Modeling tools, it is fundamental to represent them in BPMN. This representation may facilitate the adoption of the WAPs by BPMN tools as well as the use of the WAPs in process design.

Keywords: Workflow activity patterns, BPMN, process design.

1 Introduction

Process models can be assembled out of a set of recurrent business functions (e.g., task execution request, approval) of which each has a specific semantics. In an earlier work we related such business functions to a set of well-defined workflow activity patterns (WAPs): request for activity execution with/without answer, approval, notification, decision-making, and information request [1]. This pattern set is closer to the vocabulary and abstraction level at which business processes are usually described by domain experts. This fosters pattern reuse when modeling business processes and therefore contributes to more standardized and better comparable business process models. Generally, multiple WAPs can be composed in a process model using workflow patterns like Sequence, AND-Split, AND-Join or XOR-Split [5].

In order to facilitate the adoption of the WAPs by BPMN design tools as well as their use in new approaches it is fundamental to represent them in BPMN. If we have the patterns in BPMN and the tool supports BPEL output from BPMN diagrams, we already have BPEL output implemented for the pattern designed processes.

The remainder of this paper presents the WAPs in BPMN and a discussion on the strengths and weaknesses of BPMN when being utilizing for representing them.

R. Dijkman, J. Hofstetter, and J. Koehler (Eds.): BPMN 2011, LNBIP 95, pp. 172–177, 2011.

2 Representing Workflow Activity Patterns in BPMN

A WAP refers to the description of a recurrent business function as it can be frequently found in business processes [1]. We had developed an empirical study, in which we analyzed more than 200 real-world process models in order to confirm the existence of the seven WAPs [2]. The study showed that the analyzed process models can be designed based on the investigated patterns; i.e., the set of identified WAPs is necessary as well as sufficient to design the 200 process models, at least at a certain level of granularity.

2.1 WAP1: Approval Pattern

An approval shall be done by a single role or by multiple roles either concurrently or iteratively (see Fig. 1).

- **Single approval:** a requestor sends an approval request to exactly one reviewer. This reviewer performs the revision either resulting in approval or rejection.
- **Iterative approval:** based on a list of reviewers (BPMN collection data object) a requestor sends an approval request for the first reviewer from the list. This reviewer performs the approval resulting either in approval or rejection. If approved the next reviewer from the list will receive a request for approval, and so on; if one reviewer rejects, all previous approvals (in case they exist) will be cancelled and the overall approval procedure will be aborted. At the end, a final decision - approval or rejection - is made concerning the object under revision.
- **Concurrent approval:** given a list of reviewers a requestor sends an approval request to all reviewers simultaneously. After all reviewers have performed their approvals the final decision is made. To represent the parallelism we used the collection data object and the multi-instance marker for parallel instances.

2.2 WAP2: Question-Answer

Major design choice regarding the question-answer pattern is whether the question will be send to one or multiple roles and actors, respectively (see Fig. 2).

- **Single-Question-Answer:** Based on a question description an organizational role with expertise in the respective domain is chosen to answer the question. The sender waits until the response arrives and then continues process execution.
- **Multi-Question-Answer:** Based on a question description multiple organizational roles with expertise in the respective domain are chosen to answer the question. The sender waits until all responses arrive and then continues process execution.

2.3 WAP3: Unidirectional Performative

Major design choice is whether the activity execution request shall be sent to one or multiple actors (see Fig. 3).

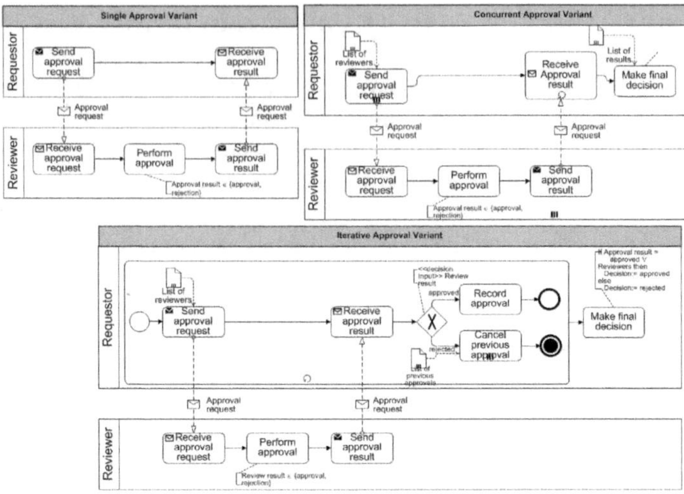

Fig. 1. Approval Pattern Variants

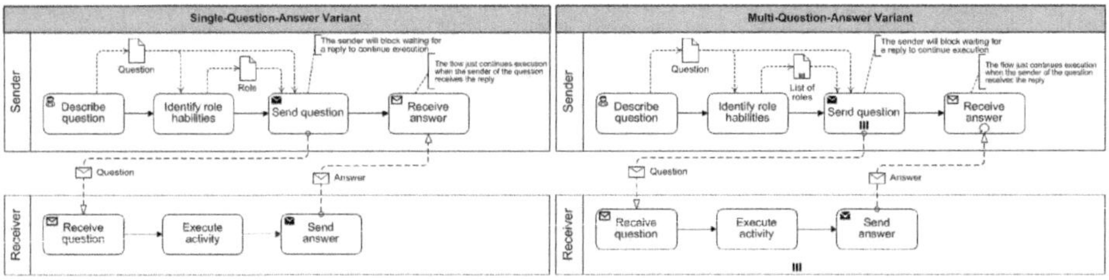

Fig. 2. Question-answer Pattern Variants

- **Single-Request:** A requestor sends an activity execution request to a receiver and continues process execution without waiting for response.
- **Multi-Response:** A requestor sends an activity execution request to multiple receivers simultaneously and continues process execution afterwards, i.e., without waiting for any response.

2.4 WAP4: Bi-Directional Performative

Major design choice is whether the activity execution request is sent to one or multiple actors (see Fig. 4).

- **Single-Request-Response:** A requestor sends an activity execution request to one receiver. He waits with continuation of his part of the process until the receiver notifies him about the performance of the requested activity.
- **Multi-Request-Response:** A sender sends an activity execution request to multiple receivers simultaneously and continues execution only after having received respective notifications from all performers (cf. Fig. 4).

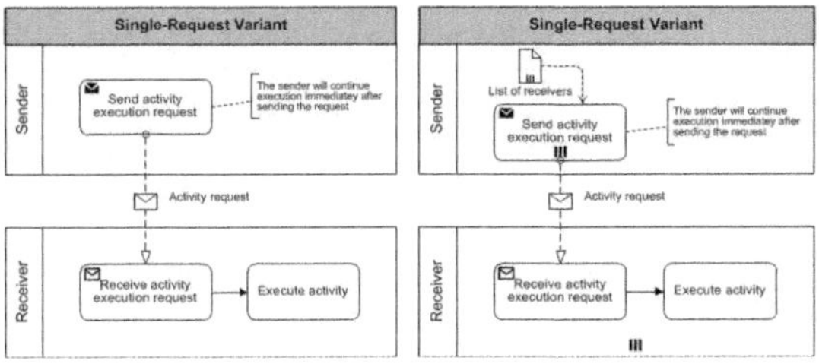

Fig. 3. Unidirectional Performative Pattern Variants

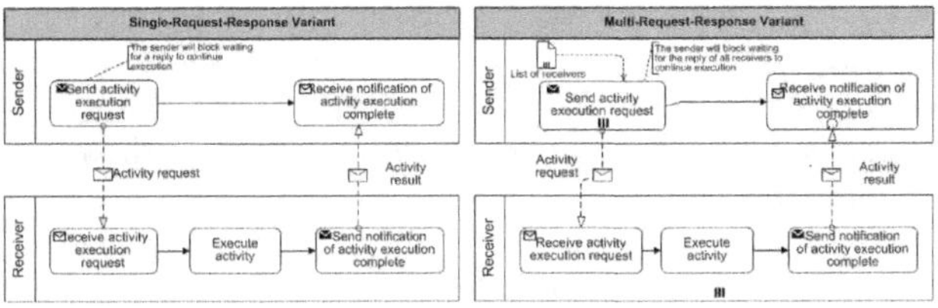

Fig. 4. Bi-directional Performative Pattern Variants

2.5 WAP5: Notification

Major design choice is whether the notification is to be sent to one or multiple actors (see Fig. 5).

- **Single-Notification:** A sender sends a notification to a single receiver.
- **Multi-Notification:** A sender sends a notification to multiple receivers simultaneously.

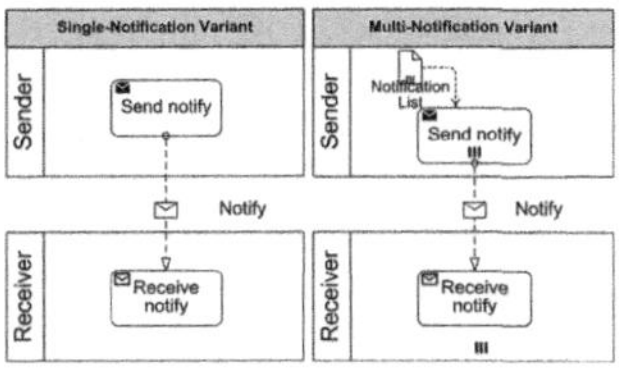

Fig. 5. Notification Pattern Variants

2.6 WAP6: Informative Request

Major design choice is whether the information request is sent to one or multiple actors (see Fig. 6).

- **Single-Information Request:** A sender sends an information request to a receiver and does not continue process execution before having received the requested information.
- **Multi-Information Request:** A sender sends an information request to multiple receivers simultaneously and does not continue process execution before having received responses from all receivers.

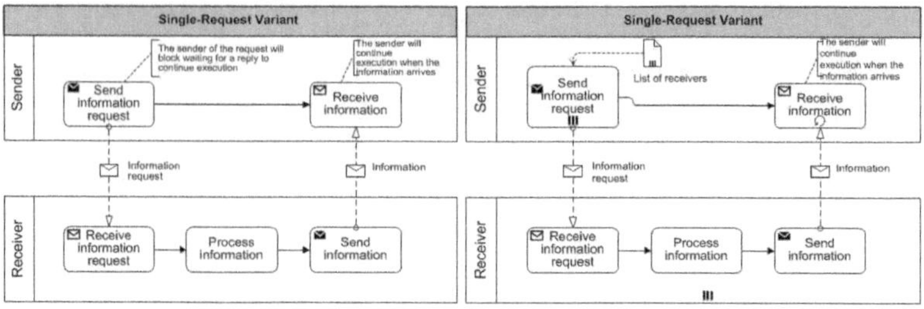

Fig. 6. Informative Pattern Variants

2.7 WAP7: Decision

Major design choice is whether the final decision is based on the results of one single activity or a set of activities.

- **Single-Decision:** Based on the execution result of an activity one or several succeeding branches are executed.
- **Multi-Decision:** An activity execution request is sent to multiple performers. Based on the results of the activities one or several succeeding branches are executed.

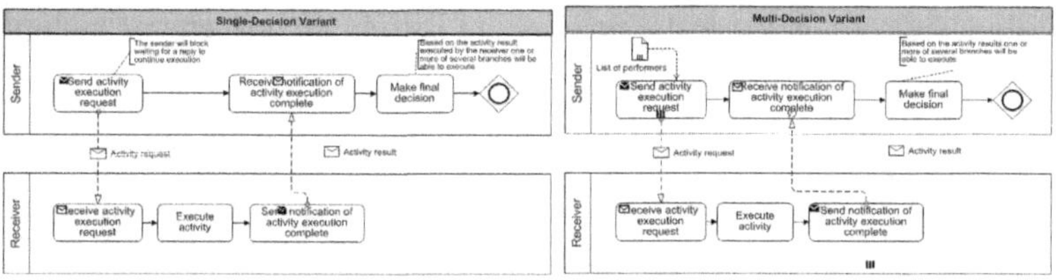

Fig. 7. Decision Pattern Variants

3 Discussion and Conclusions

Basic advantages of the representation of the WAPs in BPMN are: (a) BPMN is becoming a well-known standard notation for business process modeling. When comparing with UML 2.0 some aspects look clearer like the message exchange between process participants. Having the patterns in BPMN makes possible to perform experiments to compare process design with and without the support of WAPs; (b) BPMN showed suitable for modeling most of the WAPs. We observed that some structures (e.g., participants related to a multiple instance activity) can be represented in different ways in BPMN. We believe that not always the proposed WAPs will be directly identified.

We have experienced that the use of WAPs for designing integration business process models brings several advantages: automate and facilitate the design of process models, reduce process modeling time and cost, improve process model quality, and enable the reuse of the process knowledge captured in them to generate the public and private activities [3]. Also, the use of WAPs ensures the interoperability in the message exchange between integration business processes by providing synchronization among the sending and receiving tasks generated in the processes. As drawbacks we can mention that the WAPs do not express how to generate the business document to be sent in each business message.

The WAPs in BPMN are very important for designing process models executed in virtual organizations [4]. The WAPs showed to be very effective for representing single/multi participants either requesting the execution of activities or being notified about executed activities. In addition they help to add more semantics and details for the activities description.

As future work we are going to use the WAPs in BPMN for designing processes from different application domains and organizations. Our goal is to verify how effective the patterns are for process design when comparing with the same design using only BPMN elements.

Acknowledgements. We are very grateful for the SticAmSud and PNPD Program from the Brazilian Coordination for the Improvement of Graduated Students (CAPES).

References

1. Thom, L.H., Reichert, M., Iochpe, C.: Activity patterns in process-aware information systems: basic concepts and empirical evidence. IJBPIM 4(2), 93–110 (2009)
2. Thom, L.H., Reichert, M., Iochpe, C.: On the Support of Workflow Activity Patterns in Process Modeling Tools: Purpose and Requirements. In: 3rd WBPM, Brazil (2009)
3. Lazarte, I.M., Villarreal, P.D., Chiotti, O., Thom, L.H., Iochpe, C.: An MDA-Based Method for Designing Integration Process Models in B2B Collaborations. In: 13 ICEIS, China (2011)
4. Priego-Roche, L.M., Rieu, D., Front, A.: A 360 vision for virtual organizations characterization and modelling: Two intentional level aspects. In: Software Services for e-Business and e-Society, pp. 427–442 (2009)
5. Russell, N., ter Hofstede, A.H.M., van der Aalst, W.M.P., Mulyar, N.: Workflow Control-Flow Patterns: A Revised View. BPM Center Report BPM-06-22, BPMcenter.org (2006)

Author Index

GPSR Compliance

The European Union's (EU) General Product Safety Regulation (GPSR) is a set of rules that requires consumer products to be safe and our obligations to ensure this.

If you have any concerns about our products, you can contact us on ProductSafety@springernature.com

In case Publisher is established outside the EU, the EU authorized representative is:

Springer Nature Customer Service Center GmbH
Europaplatz 3
69115 Heidelberg, Germany

Batch number: 10844619

Printed by Printforce, the Netherlands